CONFRONTING THE CUTS

A SOURCEBOOK FOR WOMEN IN ONTARIO

Edited by
Luciana Ricciutelli
June Larkin
Eimear O'Neill

with
Sandy Birnie
Lorraine Greaves
Karen Charnow Lior
Elsie Nisonen
Emily Scott
Lynne Slotek
Rebecca Sugarman

Inanna Publications and Education Inc.
Toronto, Ontario

The articles printed in this book do not necessarily
reflect the views of the funders, the publishers, the editors,
the members of the Ad Hoc Committee for the publication of the book,
nor the agencies they work for.

Published by:
Inanna Publications and Education Inc.
212 Founders College, York University
4700 Keele Street
North York, Ontario M3J 1P3

Printed and Bound in Canada
by University of Toronto Press, Inc.

Cover Design/Interior Design: Luciana Ricciutelli
Cover Photographs: David Smiley
Front Cover: International Women's Day, Toronto, March 1997
Back Cover: Days of Action, Toronto, October 1997

The support of the Canadian Women's Foundation, Toronto, Canada,
is gratefully acknowledged.

Canadian Cataloguing in Publication Data
Main Entry under title:
Confronting the cuts: A sourcebook for women in Ontario
Includes bibliographical references.
ISBN 0-9681290-1-3

1. Women – Ontario – Social conditions. 2. Women – Canada – Social conditions.
3. Ontario – Social policy. 4. Canada – Social policy. 5. Government spending
policy – Ontario. 6. Government spending policy – Canada. I. Larkin, June, 1952–
II. Ricciutelli, Luciana, 1958– . III. O'Neill, Eimear, 1949– .

HV1448.C32072 1998   362.83'09713   C97-932102-6

Part III
The Impacts on Women in Ontario

Part IV
Responses and Organizational Strategies

Postscript

Our mandate as a publisher has always been to make issues of concern to women accessible to the widest possible audience of women across the country, and internationally. It was in this spirit that Inanna Publications and Education Inc. joined forces with a number of women's organizations based in the province of Ontario to produce a resource tool for women dealing with the impact of the cuts in their daily lives. The idea for this book came out of the Women of Action Day held at Toronto's Metro Hall in January 1996. This gathering of over 500 participants representing over 300 organizations and agencies, was one of the first collective responses from Toronto's women to the provincial cuts in social programs. On that day of action, women from several agencies formed an ad hoc committee, to document the effects of cuts on women and children in Ontario and exemplify local responses.

We began by seeking input from among the people who attended the Day of Action and who were, for the most part, front line service providers. In retrospect, it is not surprising that this book has taken one year longer than expected to bring to fruition. We were seeking responses from those on the front line: those individuals, community agencies, and institutions, pressured to provide service to ever increasing numbers from dramatically reduced resources. There was no time to reorganize themselves, let alone to write about their experiences. It is thanks to the resilience and persistence of the ad hoc committee members, the editorial staff of Inanna Publications, and those women directly affected, that this publication ultimately was able to be completed. Our special thanks to Lynn Raskin and Elizabeth Forestall for their contribution to this project.

The voices in this book come from those struggling at basic levels of subsistence and from those working in social policy reform, human services, and popular organizing. The articles reflect what is happening to our most vulnerable citizens, and in particular to women and children, as a result of dramatic spending cuts to social programs locally in Ontario, nationally across Canada, and, in many countries globally.

In the table of contents the contributors to this book describe many levels of response to the current fiscal crisis. Armine Yalnizian's critique of social policy reform and Sunera Thobani's examination of immigration policies explore the implications of the cuts at the policy level. Others address the impact of the cuts on specific communities, like those discussed in Emily Scott's article on social assistance recipients in Thunder Bay. A number of articles evaluate current strategies developed in response to the cuts, like Valerie Tarasuk's study of the effectiveness of community kitchens, while several present detailed analyses like Olena Hankivsky's article on the costs of violence against women to Canadian society and Anne O'Connell's report on the Parkdale community audit project. The Ontario Association of Interval and Transition Houses' report on the economic, social, and legal implications of the cuts for battered women and their children, Kim Anderson's article on the First Nations communities, and other writers weave together the effects of the cuts in many areas.

This book captures the current impact of the cuts on women and their families in Ontario, exposes some of the myths that surround fiscal policy development, and provides and overview of the range of responses. It is perhaps too soon to present a comprehensive overview of some of the new and innovative strategies that women and community groups are developing to deal with the cuts. This book is an attempt to help women understand the current economic climate, and to explore solutions and ways of coping with some of the changes that are presented as inevitable and indisputably long-term. It is important to make connections about what is happening locally and globally, examine the immediate and longterm effects of the cuts on social welfare, critique the strategies and techniques that are being developed, and ultimately, be aware that the process is ongoing, and the search for viable solutions is only just beginning.

In order to facilitate the use of this resource in popular and adult education, in women's studies and social policy classes, as well as in community discussion, the articles have been divided into four sections. Section one presents the global, federal, and provincial context for the cuts; section two documents what has been cut to date in specific areas such as health, education, and income support; section three demonstrates the impact on individuals and communities; and finally, section four provides some examples and guidelines for emergent response strategies.

It is hoped that some of the material presented here will seed further community action. The Ad Hoc Committee for the publication of this book is committed to placing any profits from the sale of the book in trust for a second volume addressing issues that the community defines as an important follow-up.

CONFRONTING THE CUTS
A SOURCEBOOK FOR WOMEN IN ONTARIO

From Global Economies to Local Cuts
Globalization and Structural Change in Our Own Backyard

by Eimear O'Neill

As a feminist psychotherapist, community activist, and educator in women's studies, I have spoken with many women—women on subsistence living, middle-class professional women, front-line workers, educators, writers in social policy, and those involved in popular organizing—about the effects of the cuts over last two years. Their message is consistent. Far from saving money at the level of government, cuts to social programs appear costly in terms of any form of sustainable economics, as well as in terms of their harmful impact on the daily lives of vulnerable members of our society, particularly women and children. Secondly, cuts in social spending undermine basic human rights to shelter, food, health care, education, healthy environment, and protection from violence, exploitation, and discrimination. Thirdly, in Canada, the reduced transfer of funds from federal to provincial levels, with federal standards for care no longer attached, and the subsequent downloading of responsibility for care from provincial to municipal levels, means that social services like education, health care, shelter, and income support are increasingly being paid for by the individual rather than by corporate taxation. Lastly, the movement towards the amalgamation of services means less access to government locally and tighter control of funds from the top down, resulting in a shift from a universal basic minimum standard of community care to a "charity" model, where a non-representative few decide who is deserving of common funds and who should be "cut-off" in the name of "less government."

This article examines local spending cuts in the global context. In fact, an exploration of the broader context in which the cuts are taking place not only highlights the profound complexity of the problem but also the urgent need for long-term responses.

Global Context

The program of cuts in spending to social services, health, and education being followed by municipal, provincial, and federal governments across Canada and North Americia, is one continuous with a worldwide restructuring of wealth, resources, and growing consumerism that began with the emergence of capitalism during the Industrial Revolution, and has gained rapid momentum since the fall of the Soviet Block opened new markets (Clarke). The agenda being followed is that of elite transnational corporations, with compelling influence on national and local governments around the world. Given that 50 of the top 100 economies in the world today are transnational enterprises rather than nation states, it is not surprising that they control huge resources and political power. Their influence on world governments is wielded through interlocking formal corporate and government institutions such as the World Bank, the International Monetary Fund, and the World Trade Organization. In Canada, the Business Council on National Issues is made up of 160 corporations (including the five largest banks) and leading corporations in each of the main sectors of the country's economy. Yet, the globalization of economies/cultures and the depletion of natural resources led by western consumerism fails to meet even basic human needs (O'Sullivan).

What is even more disturbing, is that recently established free trade agreements like the North American Free Trade Agreement (NAFTA) and the General Agreement of Trades and Tariffs (GATT) effactually guarantee these transnational corporations rights and freedoms that can supercede those of local taxpayers secured by the legislation of their elected national and provincial governments (Barlow and Campbell). By the time this book is in print, Canada may well have been successful in getting other nations to sign the Multilateral Agreement to Investment (MAI), designed to protect the investments of those same corporations. MAI will allow multinational corporations to move money freely with no committment to the local people and lands from whom they profit; indeed, this treaty will allow such corporations access to our domestic courts to challenge any legislation such as labour laws, copyright protection, environmental regulations, or Canadian content rules, that could be seen as contrary to the interests of foreign investment. In fact, the MAI will even allow multinational corporations to sue nation states for compensation if local policies protective of human rights reduce their profits (Clarke and Barlow).

In this new global economy Canada, like other nation states, is competing for transnational investment by surrendering some of the sovereign powers and social policies required to protect the social, economic, and environmental living conditions of their own peoples. Canada is doing well in that competition; so well, that in the *1997 Global Competitiveness Report* published by the World Economic Forum, Canada had risen up to fourth place from eighth the previous year. Canada's major weaknesses, chides the report, are a tax system that does not encourage competitiveness, unions with too much power, inadequate research and development spending by business, social policies that discourage people from seeking work, and an inability by companies to convert academic ideas into products. As Tony Clarke points out:

> Since the ... government's tax reforms of the 1980s, corporate tax revenues have dropped from approximately 15 percent to as low as five percent of overall federal revenues, the lowest rate amongst G-7 countries. More than 80,000 profitable corporations in Canada end up paying no income taxes at all due to numerous tax loopholes and write-offs. (78)

To make their countries investor-friendly, governments locally, nationally, and globally appear to be abdicating responsibility for their role in ensuring that the basic rights of its citizens in terms of employment, housing, education, health care, environmental protection, and social equality are met. Canada, until recently, has had an enviable record as a country that not only peacekeeps globally, but is recognized by the United Nations as the best place in the world to live. Yet in 1997, the UN had to also point out Canada's extremely poor record for child poverty and youth unemployment, second only to the poor record of the U.S. amongst industrialized nations. According to Statistics Canada, 15 per cent of our country's children live in poverty (Statistics Canada 1997a]. In Toronto, 36 per cent of children aged ten and under live inpoverty... with increasing numbers, more than 71 per cent in the first six months from June 1995, having to use food banks (United Way).

To assume that business rather than government is more qualified, ethical, or effective in providing the sorts of services which maintain the quality of our local community living is absurd. Yet this is the assumption that lies behind the national and provincial moves towards privatizing health care, education, public utilities, and waste management. Profit, not commitment to the care of local communities, is the agenda of business and transnational corporations.

The 1995 United Nations Progress of Nations Report points out that in 1960, the top 20 percent of the world's richest individuals had an income 30 times higher than the bottom 20 per cent. By the 1990s, the top 20 per cent earned 60 times more than the bottom 20 per cent. Over that same time period, only 15 countries benefitted from globalization. Instead, in 40 per cent of countries around the world standards of living have dropped since '60s. With the opening up of free trade, the livelihoods of small farmers—80 per cent of the population in developing countries—are threatened by the influx of cheap subsidized imported foods from industrialized nations (Kohr). In industrialized nations, the global workplace bids down wages and benefits as well as the number and quality of jobs available. As Susan George indicates, multinational corporations are not in the business of job creation, employing less than one per cent globally. Even a country like Chile, touted as an example of economic success, has a local poverty level of 30 per cent, despite a 1500 percent growth in its economy, with 90 percent of its exports coming from its own natural resources (Larrain).

Globalizing profits and prices only works economically for everyone if incomes are also globalized. Furthermore, globalization wrecks havoc environmentally, contributing significantly to global warming, the systemic eradication of biodiversity, and the increase in world pollution (Mander and Goldsmith). It is not sustainable and it does not improve the quality of life for most of this planet's peoples.

Deficitism

We are told that we are cutting social programs and restructuring government delivery of services to deal with crises around "the deficit" and "the debt." What is happening in Ontario, and across Canada, is what the World Bank calls "structural adjustment." This term is used more commonly in media reports of so-called third world countries where debt is paid by ravaging social programs with no expectation of maintaining human rights. In Ontario, what is being attacked is a rich network of social programs that include livable wage support, accessible child care, quality education, programs of violence prevention and employment equity, universal health care and affordable shelter, all of which have cushioned us from the effects of globalization felt earlier by New Zealand, Britain, and the United States. This cushioning network that made Canada the best place in the world to live, is being slashed, and the responsibility for maintaining its vestiges is being downloaded onto local municipalities. One example of this is Ontario's 21.6 per cent cut in welfare payments, combined with more stringent qualification rules, fingerprinting of recipients, snitch lines for welfare fraud, and the downloading of 80 per cent of responsibility for subsidized housing onto local municipalities. Although social spending, of which welfare is a small part, constitutes less than six per cent of provincial debt (Clarke), the provincial government is prepared to spend $31 million on fingerprinting systems to save $9 million in assumed welfare fraud (Mallan). No matter how much might be saved, it seems pointless to spend millions more trying to catch people possibly committing welfare fraud while ignoring corporate actions that are removing millions more dollars from our financial and environmental resources. At the federal level, Statistics Canada suggested in 1990 that the country's debt-cutting strategy would be much more effective if it focussed on the two main causes of Canada's rising debt between 1973 and 1989, i.e. the 50 per cent rise caused by tax breaks to wealthy individuals and profitable corporations, and the 44 per cent increase caused by the excessively high interest rates (Clark). Clearly the cuts are not about saving money and reducing the debt. They are about restructuring where our tax dollars are being spent, and this is being done rapidly and with minimal community consultation.

Structural Adjustment and Women

The fact that this fabric of social protection, funded by our tax dollars and developed over 30 years of social activism, can be so swiftly dismantled in such a short period of time demonstrates the urgent need for public consciousness-raising, immediate response, and new thinking about the effects of the cuts within communities. The section of the 1995 UN report focusing on women's services globally clearly indicates that Canada and the U.S. are unique amongst industrialized nations in their rapid downsizing of such services at a time when others are responding with increased awareness for their need. Globalization of economies and the structural adjustment that accompanies this affects women's work and well-being in ways very different from the affect on men's.

As Mira Shiva, community health activist, indicates the commodification, medicalization, and pharmacolization of health at the hands of transnational corporations has led to further erosion of rights to basic healthy conditions—unpolluted water, clean air, shelter—while increasing poverty and its associated diseases. Eighty per cent of India's previously publicly-funded heath care system is now privatized, and this is the second largest cause of rural indebtedness. Its harshest effects are felt by women, particularly as public health and preventative care is no longer covered by the system. Currently 85 per cent of India's pregnant women are anaemic and the women there, like those in many othere developing nations, eat last and least. Even women's knowledge of traditional healing, such as the use of anti-bacterial herbs in daily food preparation, is being patented and controlled for profit while vitamins—which were unnecessary with the traditional diet—are heavily marketed.

In many developing countries, women are viewed as passive recipients of development rather than active participants. What is more, increasing technology and agribusiness methods of farming have displaced women from their traditional productive functions, further reducing the income, status, and power they had in traditional gender relationships. Furthermore, as New Zealander Marilyn Waring points out, women's work in daily nurturing and care of community members, including current and future workers, has never been considered part of any country's economy.

Even in so-called developed countries like Canada, there is ample evidence of inequitable recompense for that small part of women's work counted in gross national productivity combined with continued promotion of motherhood and childbearing as women's role. Statistics Canada reports a slightly diminishing gap with women earning about 70 per cent for work comparable to men's (Statistics Canada 1997b) More recent figures revealing slightly less of a gap occur, however, only because the average price being paid for men's labour has dropped since 1995, despite the astronomical rise in earnings for those men in the top ten per cent (Monsebraaten). Other Statistics Canada analyses of welfare data and employment patterns from the 1995 census support the view that women on public subsidy like mother's allowance come off welfare as soon as jobs and child care are available and accessible (Monsebraaten). Of course, when jobs and child care are not available, they are trapped.

The fact is with the advent of debt crises since the 1980s, women have increasingly been relied upon to fill the gaps in services cut by governments. What we have heard repeatedly in Ontario, is that the "the community" must take on greater responsibility for child care and early childhood education, for managing nutritious food on limited budgets, for coping with the mentally ill, the elderly, the differently-able, and those discharged early from hospital care. For "the community" read "women." What structural adjustment does is shift the responsibility for services from the paid to the unpaid economy, through the use of women's unpaid time.

Local Context

In Ontario, millions have been cut from education, general health care, environmental protection, legal aid, and social services. Huge legislative changes have been brought in too rapidly in terms of their ramifications on the face of local democracy, access to resources, and restructuring the control of public funds from locally elected community representatives to top down provincially appointed "commissioners," for their effects to be fully seen. While many of us agree that we have been spending beyond our means and in ineffective ways, it is the methods, the speed, the lack of consultation, and the question of who pays for the cuts that are at issue here.

Women's services were first hit. The network of anti-violence services were next. Shelters, rape crisis and sexual assault centres, and help lines were told that any services that could be deemed "education," "prevention," or "advocacy" would be cut. After that, announcements came almost daily, of cuts to welfare, to hospitals, to agencies dealing with the poor, to legal aid, and more recently a staggering $700 million to be taken from our children's education (Jenish). The most vulnerable are bearing the brunt of the costs at the same time as the six largest banks announce unheard of profits of $7.4 billion in one year ("Big Six Profit Soars to $7.4 billion").

The shelters are overcrowded, the homeless and impoverished beg on the main streets, the numbers of women and children killed trying to leave violent men are mounting, hospital beds are at a premium as more and more nurses are let go and hospitals close. Universal pension, health and education programs are being dropped as private companies spring up for profit. Fear is evident in those who still hold jobs and despair is growing in those who continue to seek work in a daily shrinking job market. The changes are presented by transnationally controlled media as inevitable, unavoidable. There is surprisingly little public outrage when the recently re-elected federal government states that issues like child poverty and chronic youth unemployment will be dealt with only *after* the deficit, already shrunk below all predictions.

Responses

In other places where this restructuring has been going on for some time, in Britain and New Zealand for example, there are not only critical analyses of the cuts in local social services that are creating economic apartheid between the rich and the poor, but there is organized opposition and lobbying for viable alternatives (Douthwaite).

In Ontario, Days of Action protests by various unions, town hall meetings and strong No! responses to referendums on the forced amalgamation of municipalities, did not draw the tremendous public response that the province-wide teachers' strike against Bill 160 effected. Bill 160, otherwise known as the Education Quality Improvement Act, gives the provincial government unprecedented control of Ontario's $14-billion education system, stripping locally elected school boards of their authority, and giving appointed cabinet ministers exclusive control over schools' taxation and budget, class size, teachers' time, length of school year and, indeed, curriculum content. Even the judge who ruled against the government's attempt to legislate the teachers back to work commented that "Bill 160's provisions are so broad and sweeping that they may be open to challenge under the Charter of Rights and Freedoms" (Jenish).

In November 1997, one meeting of the International Forum on Globalization drew 85 delegates from all over the world to Ontario to discuss the issues and participate in a "Teach-in on Globalization" that packed Toronto's Convocation Hall with 5,000 educators and activists. This meeting was held in Canada because this country is considered key to the worldwide movement to reverse the course of the global economy towards a revitalized democracy, more local self-sufficiency, and ecological health. It is our government that is seen as capable of affecting the global financial casino that enables transnational billions to be shifted in seconds with devastating effects on local economies and no cost to speculators. And it is our government that is still seen as publicly supporting universal systems of health care, income support, and education despite the increasing downloading of responsibility for costs and standards.

The issue of protecting human rights is central to dealing with the effects of "globalization." However, by framing the problem as the failure of governments to protect human rights and sustainable economies of their own citizens under pressure for investment-friendly environments, it is clear the strategies and proposed solutions must be broader and more long-term. The problem is not only local and national; it is worldwide. What many have suggested (see Barlow *et al.*) are a revitalized politics and committed activism:

1) A need for a new citizens' politics based on reassertion of fundamental human rights and of the rights of the earth itself;

2) A set of legal protections that are effective at the level of the local community, protections which will hold corporations responsible for their actions making corporate flight a punishable offence. At the local level, the community's right to welfare and protection should have priority over corporate decisions;

3) Development of a strong civic culture through education, media, political, and corporate literacy;

4) The encouragememt of local economic development that is independent of the global market casino and the manipulations of rapid money transfers;

5) An awareness that health care and welfare is not one of managed care and limited budgets; rather it is of basic care and the responsible use of public funds decided democratically;

6) The seemingly pre-emptive need for profit must be questioned. As communities we must remind ourselves that there is a whole cycle of human needs that must be addressed including the need for community;

7) Increased corporate responsibility for local sustainability through taxation of international investment; a multi-lateral agreement to fairer taxation of the wealthy and corporations globally; collection of unpaid/deferred taxes from high earning CEO's and corporations to restore and sustain universal health, income support, and education; and the tying of government subsidies for profit-making organisations to their responsibilities for local effects.

Education and consciousness-raising is the beginning.

Eimear O'Neill is a psychotherapist and community educator who publishes, teaches, and trains in anti-violence work and short-term psychotherapy.

References

Barlow, Maude, and Bruce Campbell. *Take Back the Nation.* Toronto: Key Porter Books, 1993.

Barlow, Maude, Tony Clarke, Susan George, Martin Kohr, and Mira Shiva. Panel. "Teach-in on Globalization." University of Toronto Convocation Hall, 7 November 1997.

"Big Six Profit Soars to $7.4 billion." *Globe and Mail* 5 December 1997: B1.

Clarke, Tony, and Maude Barlow. MAI *and the Threat to Canadian Sovereignty.* Toronto: Stoddart Publishing, 1997.

Clarke, Tony. *Silent Coup:Confronting the Big Business Takeover of Canada.* Ottawa: Canadian Centre for Policy Alternatives and James Lorimer, 1997.

Douthwaite, Richard. *Short Circuits: Strengthening Local Economics for Security in an Unstable World.* Dublin: The Lilliput Press, 1996.

Jennish, D'Arcy. "The Battle for Ontario's Schools." *Maclean's Magazine* 17 November 1997: 23.

Kohr, Martin. "Teach-in on Globalization." University of Toronto Convocation Hall, 7 November 1997.

Larrain, Sara. "Teach-in on Globalizsation" University of Toronto Convocation Hall, 7 November 1997.

Mallan, Carolyn. "Sweeping Welfare Reforms Introduced: Legislation Outlines Stricter Rules." *The Toronto Star* 13 June 1997: A1.

Mander, Jerry, and Edward Goldsmith. *The Case Against the Global Economy.* San Francisco: Sierra Club, 1996.

Monsebraaten, Laurie. "Baby Bommer Women Climb Pay Ladder, Study Finds." *The Toronto Star* 23 July 1997: A3.

O'Sullivan, Edmund. *The Dream Drives the Action: Visioning Education for the 21st Century.* London: Zed Books, in press.

1997 Global Competitiveness Report. World Economic Forum.

Shiva, Mira. "Teach-in on Globalization." University of Toronto Convocation Hall, 7 November 1997.

Statistics Canada. "Social Transfers, Changing Family Structure, and Low Income Among Children." Catalogue no. 11F0019MPE95082. Ottawa: 1997a.

Statistics Canada. Catalogue no. 11F0019MPE94068. Ottawa: 1977b.

United Way. "Metro Toronto: A Community at Risk." Toronto: United Way, 1997.

United Nations. *Progress of Nations: The Nations of the World Ranked According to Their Achievements in Child Health, Nutrition, Education, Water and Sanitation, and Progress for Women.* New York: United Nations Children's Fund (UNICEF), 1995.

Waring, Marilyn. "The Invisibility of Women's Work: The Economics of Local and Global 'Bullshit.'" *Canadian Woman Studies* 17.2 (1997): 31–39.

What's The Debt and the Deficit?

Excerpted from "'Doesn't Anyone Want to Question What's Going on Here?' Understanding Deficit Mania: An Illustrated Guide" by Tony Biddle. Reprinted courtesy of Tony Biddle, Perfect World Productions.

Conserving a Caring Society
Social Solidarity in Canada

from Inter Pares

As governments in Canada cut back and scale down, the voluntary sector is being cited as the solution to respond to increasing economic dislocation, poverty, and social alienation. Those who promote a reduction in the role of government argue that charitable organizations can pick up the threads of our unravelling social safety net and compensate for the diminishing responsibility of government for health, education, housing, local economic development, and environmental protection. It is difficult not to see this as a regressive vision of governance and social solidarity. It is a vision that is eroding the historic social contract between Canadians and their government, reducing it to a mere service agreement—one that diminishes the essential universality and equity of social programs that should be financed through the tax system, while at the same time undermining the authentic role, integrity, and values of voluntary sector efforts.

Voluntary action expresses and builds community throughout Canada. People participating in voluntary action at the local level make a significant difference in their communities. They provide mutual support among citizens. They improve relations among diverse groups within communities. They create support for local economic development and the wise use of resources. As Canadians we discover what is best in ourselves through our participation as citizens in community action for justice, cultural development, education, or recreation.

However, Canada's national social programs are also an essential expression of our values as citizens and as communities. These programs were won through decades of struggle, as citizens organized to make their elected governments express through economic and social policy the aspirations of Canadians for a caring society—a society of fairness and equal opportunity for all.

Around the world we witness the ingenuity of women and men working together to transform situations of great deprivation and suffering. We have learned that the best community development affirms the dignity of human beings and leads to a shared awareness of the power of people working together for the collective good. At the same time, such voluntary efforts also expose the limits of local action, and the importance of democratic systems of government to provide essential services and support the civic action of people at the local level. This is as true in Canada as it is elsewhere. When elected officials attempt to transfer responsibility for the common welfare of citizens from government to the voluntary sector, the essential democratic element of that responsibility, won over decades, is destroyed. The responsibility that our governments are abdicating cannot be taken up by the diverse expression of voluntarism at the community level. Although the best and most effective organizations in the country will continue to do what they can in cities and towns across the country, they will never have the mandate, nor the resources, to ensure equity and opportunity for all citizens. Nor should they be expected to.

As social spending cuts increase, needs intensify and greater demands are placed on the voluntary sector to fill the gap. But this gap is not a hole to be plugged. It is a fabric to be mended and rewoven, using the complementary strengths of the public, private, and voluntary sectors. Without this consolidated effort, the social and economic consequences will be far worse than the fiscal dilemmas we face today, and a grim and tragic legacy for the next generation of Canadians.

This article has been reprinted with permission from Inter Pares (January 1997).

The Dismantling of a Nation
Public Perceptions of Debt, Deficit, and Social Policy

by Armine Yalnizyan

These are critical times for Canadian social policy. For those who work in the field, there is much rethinking to do. What are our choices at a moment in history and in the presence of a culture that, for whatever reason, is changing a direction characteristic of Canadian social policy making since the Second World War? Instead of building on the strengths of social programs, since the late 1970s, we have been slowly eroding advances made in the 1940s, 1950s, and 1960s. What can be done about these changes?

Perhaps we need to remind ourselves that social policy is not just concerned with income support programs: with welfare, unemployment insurance, and pensions. Matters of health, education, and housing are also the focus for social policy making. Social policies affect the quality of life of all Canadians, the equitable distribution of opportunities and social integration: for example, how we relate to First Nations and Aboriginal people, how we welcome new immigrants and refugees, how it is that we live together. Social policy making is about direct services: home-making services for the elderly, foster care, adoption services. Social policies provide pharmaceuticals, dental care, and vision services for the poor and disabled. Social policies influence programs for integrating people with disabilities into our communities.

These concerns all involve decisions about public versus private provision. They raise questions about jurisdiction. Who is responsible for what? And while many of these are matters of provincial, and even local, jurisdiction, as the history of social policy making reveals, federal policies shape this country. Equalization payments are one means by which we have achieved a measure of equality among very different regions of the country. We have, in our modern history, been committed to a measure of equality: the transfer of resources to "have-not" provinces so that they can provide programs and services we believe should be common to all Canadian citizens. Therefore, how we see and understand social issues and the social and fiscal policies that address them is of considerable political significance.

What is Fiscal Policy?

In recent years, for too many people, fiscal policy has become synonymous with policies that address debt and deficits. But fiscal policy is far more than a matter of budgetary shortfalls. It is about taxation. It is about how we use and redistribute wealth in our society. How do we establish social insurance programs? What are the levels and rates of contribution? What are the conditions for accessing these programs? How are unemployment insurance and pension benefits to be paid out?

In sharp contrast to the fiscal policies that have guided us since the Second World War, we are diminishing social spending at a time when social need has increased. This contrasts with the Keynesian logic of spending in hard times when the need for social assistance is high, and compensating for these through budgetary surpluses during economically better times. Are there other, more innovative ways of addressing the problem of need? In what ways are block funds preferable to cost-shared programs? What would this country look like without equalization payments and the redistribution of resources from the wealthier provinces to the poorer ones?

The Relationship Between Fiscal and Social Policy

It is obvious that the relationship between fiscal and social policy depends on a culture's mood—and this mood is a product of the ways in which policy matters are articulated, seen, and subsequently, discussed. We can talk about *social* imperatives. Our language can convey that there are some things we believe *must* be provided to Canadians by right of citizenship and in recognition of human need. The starting point, in other words, is people and ideas about who we are and what people require in order to live fulfilling lives and to participate in Canadian society. Technical matters follow. What are the limits on our resources, and what are the mechanisms for meeting human needs?

On the other hand, our language can convey a message about *fiscal* imperatives. In other words, we can start our discussion of social policy with attention to debt and deficit, and use the rhetoric of fiscal responsibility to shape our discussion of public provision. This, in fact, is how we are now speaking about social policy reforms. No longer is the discussion centred on profligate spending and the collapse of the social safety net—with the idea that reform could make the system work better. Rather, the rhetoric is focussed on cutting the federal deficit by cutting social spending.

What logically follows is the assumption that social spending has been responsible for our debt and deficits. Yet social spending is *not* responsible for the federal debt or deficit. As numerous studies have shown, our problem has been one of revenue generation, commencing in the 1970s with the introduction of an increased number of tax shelters and a shift from corporate to personal income and other forms of taxation as sources of revenue.

There are other implications of taking this approach to dealing with social policy development. It removes those of us concerned about social policy making from the policy discussion table. The debates over social policy now take place in the Ministry of Finance. One ethic has come to dominate discussion: an overriding concern for balancing the budget, not by addressing revenues, but through cutting public spending—especially on social programs.

What Canadians are facing is dramatic social change: a movement away from the provisions of the welfare state that, in many ways, have defined our national character. This suggests that we need to ask ourselves tough questions. What are the merits of the welfare state? Is our support for the principles and concepts of welfare synonymous with our support for the actual level of services and benefits that are offered?

Some Aspects of the Status Quo

Traditional ways of delivering services have not necessarily helped people. Since its inception, there have been serious criticisms of the Canada Assistance Plan (CAP): about administrative deficiencies, about the fact that it hasn't done enough for the working poor, that welfare is a program where a person with more than a token amount of earned income can lose a dollar of benefits for every dollar of earnings. Poorer provinces have complained that the 50–50 cost-sharing formula of CAP put them at a disadvantage; that provinces with greater tax revenues could spend more on programs and thus capture more federal monies.

Before we get swept away by the emphasis on cutting the deficit and reducing the national debt, perhaps we should take another look at how well Canada's liberal welfare state has worked. Its contribution to the well-being of immigrants, the elderly, the unemployed, and poor has been significant. It has contributed to cities that are quite liveable by any international standards. It is a system that mitigates against regional differences and addresses what would otherwise be internal migration driven by economic desperation. We need only look south of the border to see the tangible results of an approach to welfare significantly different from the provisions we have developed. In 1994, the United Nations Development Program ranked Canada, in terms of quality of life, the most desirable place in the world to live. The evidence that the social safety net we have created has played a significant role in managing the gap between rich and poor in Canada is overwhelming. The welfare provisions we have put in place since the Second World War explain, in great measure, the quality of life that Canadians enjoy.

Canadian support for existing programs is considerable. Surveys of public opinion, taken immediately before the 1995 federal budget, indicated a wide range of support for Canadian social programs. A poll published in *Maclean's* magazine in 1995 shows that Canadians identify their country with the social programs that have distinguished us from our neighbour to the south. We see ourselves as less violent, more caring and generous in our attitude toward those who are poor, disabled or, for whatever reason, not as privileged as many Canadians.

This is why current attempts to cut federal spending by making major changes to Canadian social programs warrant a closer look. The reform of social programs has implications beyond cutting the deficit and redefining social policy. There are major implications in these initiatives for who we are as a country. The role of the federal government in sustaining nationhood is being eroded. Details from the federal budget of February 1995, which introduced new and significant changes to Canadian social programs, are illustrative.

The budget proposed reducing the federal deficit by $29 billion over a period of three years. In the budget papers, the resulting impact was referred to as the biggest series of changes to the Canadian economy since post-war mobilization. Of the $29 billion in deficit reduction measures, $25 billion comes from reduced expenditures. Half of this comes from the social policy envelope. The single biggest contributor to these savings is the $7 billion eliminated from the Canada Health and Social Transfer Program (CHST), the new block fund that transfers monies from the federal government to the provinces for health, post-secondary education, and social assistance. By 1997, federal contributions to the provinces will have dropped 40 per cent from the time the current federal government took office in 1993. There can be little doubt that the federal capacity to enforce national standards for those programs that Canadians identify as defining our national character has been considerably reduced.

The Canada Health and Social Transfer Program

The CHST, which, as of April 1, 1996, replaced CAP and the *Canada Health Act,* is being sold on the merit of giving the provinces greater flexibility and fiscal responsibility in the administration of welfare. But with the capacity to set welfare rates, which have varied greatly from province to province, provincial governments have always had considerable flexibility in the delivery of social assistance. Under the CHST, the provinces now have the capacity to divert funds from social assistance into other programs, to introduce workfare. This newly injected discretion will leave behind a country characterized by considerable social difference in the way provinces and regions exercise responsibility for the poor, unemployed, disabled, the elderly, and others. What does this say about our national character and how we will come to relate to one another?

The evidence that national standards are under attack is everywhere. This is an era that lauds provincial flexibility and local decision-making. Whether necessitated by significantly reduced federal funding or increased decentralist clamouring for autonomy and self-determination, it is getting more difficult to agree on what we might consider common essentials worth fighting to preserve.

The government of Alberta has repeatedly challenged the Canada Health Act in using public resources to establish a two-tier health system. In British Columbia the provincial government defied the only remaining standard for financing social assistance after the death of the Canada Assistance Plan by denying emergency financial assistance to those who had not lived in B.C. for more than three months. Though it has since dropped this condition, it was the province's prerogative—not Ottawa's pressure to make it conform to this weakest "national standard"—that led to the position it adopted and the decision to reverse that position. With reduced financing, Ottawa simply did not have enough clout to enforce this standard. In Ontario the lack of standards under the Canada Health and Social Transfer has permitted the imposition of "workfare" (where people who do not agree to work at jobs found by the government—paid at welfare rates and not minimum wage—get cut off assistance). The process of downloading social services to the municipal level in Ontario will further create a checkerboard of public provisions across that province. The administration of the downloading process, both with respect to the lack of common standards for outcomes and lack of centralized reporting structures, may well mean that we won't even be able to assess how different we are becoming in the different parts of the province, let alone the nation.

Who Pays for Canada?

Canadian taxation policies have also affected public perceptions and attitudes. We are constantly reminded of the mutual responsibilities between private citizens and the state, leading some to wonder what happened to the corporate citizen, the backbone of capitalism, and the generator of our economic well-being. Corporate tax revenues have been constantly declining in the post-war period as a proportion of total federal revenues. This is happening in Canada as elsewhere in the industrialized world. The National Accounts show that in 1955 corporate taxes provided 25 per cent of all federal revenues. This fell to 17 per cent in 1975 and was only 7 per cent of all federal revenue by 1992. The resulting revenue gap has been filled by increasing direct taxes on individual private citizens. Finance Department figures (from its Economic and Fiscal Reference Tables of September 1994) show that these revenues have *risen 70 per cent* since 1980 (adjusted for inflation). The same tables reveal that direct corporate taxes have *fallen by 36 per cent* since 1980 (again, accounting for inflation).

Not surprisingly these changes have engendered a so-called "tax revolt." Identified with right-wing politics, this agenda is more about cutting back the size of the welfare state than seeking tax justice. True, the rhetoric is focussed on Canadians paying too much tax. And it is inarguable that most Canadians have been paying more and getting less, a frustrating situation when day-to-day economic security is on the decline for a growing segment of the working population. But the "tax revolt" is also reflective of other frustrations. It is, in part, about the lack of transparency in how government operates. One of the most profound challenges posed by the tax revolt is to reconnect the issues of taxation with what that money buys, not just in terms of the range of public provision. A second challenge is to transform the logic of tax justice to mean not just less taxes for all, but less taxes for some (the middle classes and lower) and more taxes for others (corporations and higher-earning Canadians), thereby redressing some of the imbalances that have been recently created in the system of paying for Canada.

The Canada Health and Social Transfer, rather than making public sector spending in the fields of health, education, and welfare more transparent, moves the responsibility for unpalatable decisions from the federal government to the provinces. Provincial and even municipal governments become the necessary targets of public concern over how welfare dollars are spent and programs administered. The CHST effectively shields the federal government from being at centre stage. Having unilaterally reduced allocations with no public input, the federal government now "cedes" responsibility, accountability, and flexibility to the provinces for making the dirty decisions as to what shall be cut.

The Great Divide: Intergenerational Conflict

Public perceptions are also affected by generational considerations. What used to be called the generation gap now intersects—even collides—with issues of class. On the one hand, there is a generation of older Canadians who helped create, support, and have benefitted considerably from the welfare state. The Depression and the war were both collective experiences; one of great deprivation and the other that made it necessary for Canadians to work together. This is a generation with historical experiences relevant to the creation of the Canadian welfare state. As the population ages, this consciousness is increasingly being lost from our social and political landscapes.

But there are also important material, not just cultural, differences between this older generation and a generation born in the 1960s, 1970s, and even the 1980s. Hours of work are illustrative. In the 1960s, one person averaged 42 hours per week to produce a modest income for a family with two children. In 1991, a generation later, it took 74 hours of work to generate that same amount of income. In the post-war period, unemployment affected older workers more than the young. Youth unemployment and underemployment are, today, among our most serious social problems.

In the post-war period, interest rates were generally low and stable. Mortgage money and other programs were available to house a generation of young people and families growing up after the war. The period of the 1970s to the 1990s has seen housing prices soar and interest rates rise and fall irregularly. Following the Second World War, the government offered generous training allowances to young returning veterans. In the late 1960s, the state spent considerable sums on post-secondary institutions for a generation that has benefitted considerably from academic and vocational training. What awaits a generation now entering its twenties is in stark contrast. Tuition fees for students have increased and are still increasing dramatically. Rents and mortgage payments represent an increasing proportion of the average personal or family income.

Responsibility for maintaining the public sector has fallen on personal income taxation. It is possible that in the immediate future a younger generation that is having considerable difficulty finding stable and adequate employment will be saddled with severe levels of taxation to support many programs that benefit an older, generally privileged generation.

In our current exercise of so-called policy reform, it is no coincidence that reforms to pensions appear to be the last major social policy arena that the current government is willing to address. The political fallout from making major changes to either of these will likely be considerable. The generation that has benefitted from measures created as part of the welfare state in the several decades following the Second World War will likely defend the two policy measures from which it will continue to derive considerable advantage. Meanwhile, social assistance and support for post-secondary education—those programs from which a primarily younger generation derives benefit—are expendable. Unemployment insurance, for a generation facing unstable employment prospects, is extremely important. Why should this generation continue to have any commitment to the welfare state?

Yet many Canadians born in the 1960s, 1970s, and 1980s should be concerned about the fate of their own health care and economic security if Medicare and old age security programs are eliminated. Medicare benefits all generations of Canadians, not only older people. Many young Canadians should realize that they will not be in a position to accumulate substantial savings in the form of RRSPs and private pension plans. Public pension plans will be key to avoiding poverty among the elderly.

Some Canadians are also concerned about facing the heavy burden of having to support elderly relatives and having to meet their health care expenses. Older generations without personal financial resources will have to be supported collectively through the public sector, privately by relatives and charitable institutions, or be abandoned.

In one way or another, all generations have to face the implications of relinquishing a collective commitment to some version of the welfare state.

Conclusion

What binds us together as a nation? It is obvious that social policies and programs have played a significant role, not only in defining who we are, but in establishing relationships among us, both generationally and regionally. The current discourse on social programs, the focus on debt and deficit as the starting point for discussion and debate about the future of these programs is a recipe for social—and then economic—disaster. A country that is regionally and socially divided cannot, for very long, continue to function as a social and economic unit that has, historically, been an international example of how disparate peoples and regions can work and live together.

The original version of this article was based on a speech presented by the author at the Seventh Conference on Canadian Social Welfare Policy entitled "Remaking Social Policy," held in June 1995 in Vancouver, B.C.

This article has been excerpted and revised from a longer version, co-written with Frank James Tester, and published in Critical Choices, Turbulent Times: A Companion Reader on Canadian Social Policy Reform, *edited by Frank Tester, Chris McNiven, Robert Case (The School of Social Work, University of British Columbia, 1996). Reprinted with permission.*

Armine Yalnizyan is the program director at the Social Planning Council of Metropolitan Toronto. She is the author of several publications on the restructuring job market and the transformation of social security. She is past chair of the Employment and Economy Committee of the National Action Committee on the Status of Women, and served on the federal advisory group on issues of working time and the distribution of work, reporting to Minister Lloyd Axworthy in 1994. She is currently working with a variety of local groups documenting social change at the community level, monitoring the fallout from the withdrawal and restructuring of the welfare state.

Racism, Women's Equality, and Social Policy Reform

by Sunera Thobani

Current social policy reforms and discussions about the Canadian economy have contributed to racism and a growing spirit of meanness among Canadians. These attitudes have been directed particularly at immigrants. In 1994, when the Social Security Review was announced, a review of immigration policy was announced separately, but at the same time, as if the two had nothing to do with each other. The immigration policy review gave voice to the charge that immigrants and refugees come to this country only because of generous welfare programs. The implication is that this is why those of us who were, or who are, recent immigrants to Canada lie and scheme our way into the country! And once we're here, the claim is made that all we do is drain the welfare system. The rhetoric continues: immigrants should not have rights to social services in this country.

It is obvious that we need to be aware of important links among different areas of government policy making. Immigration policy and social policy reforms are not separate concerns. It is evident that immigration policy is evaluated by many Canadians in relation to its implications for Canadian social policies and programs. The attitudes expressed are often blatantly racist. Immigrants are often portrayed as a drain on the Canadian economy and on social programs. The truth, however, is quite the opposite. Research has shown that after ten or more years in the country, immigrants have incomes greater than the average Canadian and contribute more in taxes than they receive in social services. In 1990, the dependence of immigrant women on social assistance was six per cent—the same as for Canadian-born women.

Therefore, in addressing so-called policy reforms, those of us involved in non-governmental organizations and movements concerned about social justice issues must make these links, and not become divided in our efforts. The analysis we develop must include all of us.

Consider, for example, the idea of a sponsorship bond, advanced in a 1995 publication of the C. D. Howe Institute, *Diminishing Returns: The Economics of Canada's Recent Immigration Policy*, and also an idea that the Department of Immigration has been discussing for some time with the provinces. The C. D. Howe Institute, far from being a neutral or public policy think-tank, clearly represents conventional business interests in the country. The book has suggested that a five-year bond of between $20,000 and $25,000 should be posted by a sponsor to cover costs should the sponsored immigrant wind up on social assistance within the five-year period after her or his arrival. Which family in Canada today, apart from the very wealthy, can provide a guarantee to the government that their relatives will not use social services in this country—that they will not have to use income assistance—given the economy of today? Yet immigrant families are being asked to make this guarantee.

Other significant changes to immigration policy are also underway. In fact, what we already have is a head tax—a $975 "right-of-landing" charge introduced by the federal government in its February 1995 budget. This charge is levied in addition to the $500 processing fee already in place. No one needs to be reminded of the history of such taxes in this country: the Chinese head tax of $500 imposed on male Chinese labourers arriving in Canada between 1885 and 1923, and the blatant discrimination directed at the immigration of Chinese women. No one presumably needs to be reminded of the role such discriminatory taxes played in furthering racism in this society, and effectively barring immigrants from certain countries from entering Canada.

These taxes and increased charges for other immigration services, introduced in 1995, simply add to the burden of debt borne by many immigrants and refugees. These taxes and charges can represent years of salary or savings for an immigrant coming from a poor Third World country. For somebody coming from Britain, from France, from the United States, or from other countries of Europe with a high per capita income, the charges might be less than a month's salary.

Other recent changes to immigration policy include awarding additional points in the assessment process for post-secondary education and for fluency in English and French. Given the limited access of girls and women to post-secondary education in many Third World countries, it is clear that there is a blatant gender bias in our policies. Sponsors will now need more income to sponsor a relative. Previously a family of four needed an income of $34,000 to sponsor a relative. Effective March 1996, this figure rose to $41,000—at the same time as family incomes for all Canadians are declining due to economic circumstances. Such policies are clearly discriminatory.

These policies also have racial implications. Many of the world's poorest countries, with low average incomes and limited access to education, are home to people of colour. At the same time, people of colour are vulnerable to increasing discrimination in the workplace, given the attacks on equity legislation I noted previously.

Consequently, the impact of recent policy changes will be to keep many immigrants of colour out of the country; to keep out low-income immigrants, to keep out working-class immigrants. It will be the wealthy and privileged who will be able to gain access to landed immigrant status in this country. By way of illustration, the government of British Columbia recently announced a policy of allowing rich immigrants into the province in return for a $350,000 investment in the province.

We have to recognize that current reforms to government policies in many different areas encourage the worst aspects of Canadian society: racism, hatred, and victim-blaming behaviour directed at immigrants, refugees, the poor, single mothers on social assistance, and others.

What this bashing of immigrants and the poor does is effectively direct the attention of Canadians away from the government's failed economic and social policies. The course of policy reviews currently under way and the claims of many right-wing politicians divert our attention away from the real causes of economic and social problems: failed policies such as the North American Free Trade Agreement (NAFTA), and tax policies that benefit corporations and the wealthy at the expense of ordinary Canadians.

Canadians are supposed to blame the person next door who needs income assistance, or the immigrants who live down the road. We are supposed to believe that they only come here to rip off the welfare system. These are the feelings, these are the sentiments, these are the prejudices that are being fostered in Canada today. The worst damage that can be done to any society is to change the values of people so that inequalities become not only acceptable, but are enthusiastically supported.

The Attack on Women's Rights

If we look at women's rights, it is easy to make the case that they are being eroded and that women's inequalities are being increased as a result of current federal and provincial changes to economic and social policies. But it is perhaps more important to acknowledge that current economic and social policies inherently create the inequality of women. The phenomenon of women's poverty in this society is an inherent feature of the economic and social policies being followed by our governments. In other words, tinkering with what we already have will do little to advance the status and rights of women in Canada.

Employment equity is under attack, and not only in Ontario where progressive legislation has been repealed by the provincial government. It is true that employment equity legislation and affirmative action policies have benefited some women more than others. But who suffers particular hardship when employment equity and affirmative action programs are undermined? The target right now is people with disabilities. The target right now is Aboriginal people. The target is people of colour. As a society, we are at a crossroads. There are two groups of questions facing us. The first asks: What kind of society are we? What are our values? What are the rights and entitlements that we are going to ensure for everybody in this country? The second group of questions has to do with how we work to achieve certain rights and entitlements. What kinds of movements are we? What kinds of organizations are we? What issues are priorities? How do we make our organizations more inclusive so that they really do represent the interests of all the constituents with whom we claim to be working?

There is an important observation to be made with respect to the status of progressive groups in this country at a time of government cutbacks and policy changes. One aspect of the spirit of meanness I noted earlier—fostered by the "blame-the-victim" behaviour that accompanies current policy reforms—is the backlash against progressive movements and groups. The attacks currently being directed at the women's movement are very serious. These come at exactly the time when the women's movement is growing, becoming more inclusive and broadly-based and, consequently, becoming stronger.

The analysis being developed within the women's movement is clearly a threat to the idea that responsibility for our current social and economic problems rests with individuals. The strength of the women's movement has always been to take women's inequality from out of the personal and private sphere of the family—to cut across the boundaries of the public and the private—and to look at the systemic structural nature of women's inequality. We have formed organizations and a movement on the basis of that understanding. When women come together, when we form our organizations, when we build our movements, our understanding is that we are changing structures. We are working to change the world.

One line of attack directed at the women's movement is to portray it as a movement of women who only want to wallow in their status as victims. The claim has been made that the only message we have of any importance is that women are victims. To take this even further, the claim has been made that women's groups are actually benefiting from this portrayal of women as victims, and that this image is being deliberately manipulated to create as much dramatic effect as possible.

This is an attack on the ability of the women's movement to mobilize. Many women, understandably, do not want to be associated with a movement that portrays women only as victims. They do not experience their lives this way, even where they have been victimized by racism, sexism, or other forms of discrimination. We are being deliberately misrepresented, and this does affect the willingness of some women to join the women's movement. The truth is that women's organizations are based on the knowledge that when we, as women, join women's organizations, it is an act of empowerment. We believe that, just as the women's movement has done in the past, we will make changes that will affect the status of all women. This is hardly consistent with playing the role of victim.

Government cutbacks are another form of attack which have affected our ability to mobilize. One tactic intended to undermine our credibility and public image is to focus on organizations that get government funding and to make headlines out of how much the executive coordinator earns. The headlines in the papers shout out: "Do you know that this organization pays this kind of money to its staff?" The implication is that we are using taxpayers' money and that nothing valuable is being done with it other than to promote "special interests."

Defining the women's movement as a special interest is a peculiar—and perverse—form of logic. If working for women's equality is a special interest, then what is the national interest? Patriarchy? Sexism? Is that how we define the national interest?

Let me give you an example of the kind of work that women's organizations do. In my term as president of the National Action Committee on the Status of Women (NAC), I met with the federal Minister of Finance, on at least five separate occasions. Each time, myself and others put forward policies we wanted the government to commit to, such as a national child care program. We asked important questions: "How was the government going to deal with changes to unemployment insurance?" and "How were these changes going to affect women?" We asked him whether his department does a gender analysis of the budget, the most important policy-making instrument in the hands of the government. Did his department know how budgetary decisions affect women and women's equality? And he said "No," he does not do that; his department does not do that.

This is unacceptable. Women are 52 per cent of the population of this country, and all of us are affected one way or another by government policy.

Consequently, it is organizations like NAC who must do the gender impact analysis of government budgets and programs. It is we who must lobby for progressive change. That is part of the work that women's organizations do, as well as organizing to bring political pressure to bear on government so that they take our initiatives seriously. The women's movement is the only place where this kind of thinking and this kind of work is being done. Any democratic government that is committed to the political partici-pation of women and the representation of women in policy making has a responsibility to be funding that kind of work—especially when the government remains incapable of doing it.

Becoming More Inclusive

More young women are getting active and are joining women's groups in very large numbers. The reasons, I believe, are obvious. Women live in a society and have grown up in a country which has had a strong, active women's movement for at least the past 20 years. Consequently, young women have been brought up thinking that women have equality in this country. But young women are increasingly discovering that they do not have equality. Young women are the ones who are having the hardest time finding full-time employment. Young women continue to experience violent sexual assault. The majority of sexual assaults take place on women before the age of 16. Facing these realities is an incredibly radicalizing experience, and this is what is happening with young women in this country.

One of the most important challenges facing the women's movement is to find new ways of working with young women and of passing on the experience we gained in the women's movement. We must also change our analyses. Young people today are facing a changed reality. The analyses that we used ten or fifteen years ago do not speak to their reality. We must bridge the generation gaps between us and find ways of working together.

Within the women's movement today, we are building spaces where women from different historical experiences and from different racial backgrounds are coming together and struggling with new ways of building unity and alliances directed at a common goal. For this, we are being marginalized. For example, the claim is being made that now NAC only speaks for immigrant and refugee women. But in 1993, our priority was the federal election. Last year, our priority campaign was social policy. Are these issues that only affect immigrant and refugee women? Yet the claim that NAC is primarily concerned with immigrant and refugee women is commonly found in the media. Such claims are part of attempts to marginalize NAC at a time when the organization is gaining strength, becoming more inclusive, and building something new in this society.

Conclusion

We need to build strong coalitions: these will sustain us in the long run. It is through sharing our ideas, interests, and insights that we can build a clear analysis of what is currently happening to Canadian society. Working together also gives us the strength to stop the "meanness"—the poor bashing, racism, sexism, and homophobia that is developing in Canada as we struggle to deal with changing global circumstances.

The original version of this article was published in Critical Choices, Turbulent Times: A Companion Reader on Canadian Social Policy Reform (*School of Social Work, University of British Columbia, 1996). Reprinted with permission.*

Sunera Thobani is past president of the National Action Committee on the Status of Women (NAC). She is currently the Ruth Wynn Woodward Endowed Professor in Women's Studies at Simon Fraser University in British Columbia.

The Mean-Spirited Nineties

I have a lady friend who is 81 years old. She had been using Wheel-Trans for the last three or four years. She has had two strokes and has a heart problem. A while ago, she had to go with others who were in wheelchairs and had walkers and canes, to get re-assessed to see if she was still eligible for Wheel-Trans. My friend was turned down. They told her that she could just walk to a bus. One 65-year-old lady told them she was blind in one eye. They said "Well, you can see out of the other." So far, only about 300 have been accepted. Hundreds of people may not be using Wheel-Trans anymore. Who is going to be next?

—Carolyn J. Day is a senior-activist who suffered a severe head injury when she was hit by a drunk driver in 1984. She lives in Toronto.

Locked In, Left Out
Impacts of the Budget Cuts on Abused Women and Their Children

by the Ontario Association of Interval and Transition Houses (OAITH)

Violence against women is a complex form of oppression. It touches every aspect of life for women and their children. Government cuts to women's shelters, while they highlight the impact of social program reduction on abused women, are only one part of a web of cuts to the supports women need to escape danger. To be free, survivors of violence—both women and child witnesses—literally need a safety net of programs and policies protecting their right to safety and equality.

Cuts to Direct Services for Abused Women and their Children

> *These cuts of the government have affected my family profoundly. I seem to be caught in a crack, as I hear so many others are. My abusive and controlling ex-husband has the ultimate control over us now.*
>
> —Dorothy, a survivor.

The first blow to abused women was the cut to services that directly work with survivors and their children—those services that, historically, have been the strongest advocates against violence. These services have supported countless numbers of survivors, often being credited with saving their lives. Women's grassroots services have educated the community, changed the policies and practices of systems, and provided the expertise needed to effectively pursue an end to violence against women. All of these services have been imperilled, where they haven't already been eliminated entirely.

Emergency women's shelters: On October 1, 1995, emergency shelters that provide front line crisis intervention to women experiencing violence had a 2.5 per cent provincial funding cut; and in April 1996 another cut of 2.5 per cent. Shelters have been chronically underfunded since their inception almost 20 years ago. A five per cent overall cut, therefore, has had dramatic consequences on services that shelters are able to provide. Furthermore, cuts to women's shelters must be examined in the context of provinvical government requirements that services fundraise 20 per cent of their costs for basic core services.

Second stage women's shelters: On December 31, 1995, the government eliminated all provincial funding for programs in second stage shelters for abused women and their children. Services reduced or eliminated included counselling for women and children, advocacy, language interpretation, and other programs. Second stages provide temporary housing for three months to a year. They are used by women who have been unable to secure permanent housing, have multiple barriers to escaping abuse, or need additional support. Since women in second stage shelters have decided to separate permanently from abusive partners, they may be particularly vulnerable. Survivors in second stage shelters use the service during the first few months after leaving an abusive relationship, a time when women are often stalked, harassed, assaulted, and murdered by former partners.

Crisis lines: Cuts were made to provincial funding of 24-hour crisis intervention phone lines in Ontario, including The Assaulted Women's Helpline in Toronto and SOS Femmes, the only crisis phone line assisting Francophone women in distress. These crisis intervention lines are front line services, and are often the first contact with assistance for women fleeing from violence.

Community counselling: The five per cent overall cut to community programs included cuts to those counselling programs specifically addressing violence. Largely delivered by family and children's service agencies in Ontario, these programs provide individual and group support for both women and child witnesses experiencing violence.

Child protection: Children's Aid Societies had budget reductions as a result of provincial cuts. These services provide supports to children experiencing violence, including support to child survivors of incest.

Culturally specific services: First Nations and Aboriginal social service programs were also reduced. Community counselling groups for specific racial and cultural communities as well as services specifically for Francophone women also received severe cuts. Many of these services gave direct counselling and advocacy support to abused women and their children on addressing issues of violence.

Community advocacy: Services providing housing and legal advocacy were cut along with other front line agencies. Agencies such as housing help centres, free legal clinics and so on, have been used frequently by abused women attempting to find safe, affordable housing, or to explore their legal rights. Provincial cuts also affected provision of necessities such as food and clothing for abused women starting anew.

Cuts to Other Essential Supports for Abused Women

It is important that the public and all partners in the justice system understand the implications cuts to legal aid will have on the administration of justice in Ontario.

—Susan Elliott, Head of the Law Society of Upper Canada, in "Changes to Ontario's Legal Aid Plan, a Guide for Legal Aid Lawyers."

Most critical among the supports survivors use to leave an abusive situation are those programs and supports women and children need to provide basic needs (such as food and shelter), address legal issues, become financially independent, and ensure the health and safety of themselves and their children. All women leaving an abusive relationship, whether or not they use, or have access to direct shelter and counselling services, will find fewer supports as a result of funding cuts.

Legal Aid: In October 1995, the Ontario Legal Aid Plan, managed by the Law Society of Upper Canada, was cut by $153 million. In response, the Law Society made drastic changes to both the eligibility criteria for legal aid and to the fees Ontario lawyers may charge for providing legal services to clients receiving legal aid assistance. The eligibility changes included making "spouse or child at risk" a priority for assistance, but the definition of "at risk" has still not been determined, other than to restrict it to physical injury. (Subsequently, the Plan included "very serious psychological harm" as part of its first priority definition.) Guidelines for assistance in family law matters, already underfunded by the Plan, cut the hours lawyers can bill for divorce, child custody and access, support, and property settlements dramatically, sometimes by half.

Other changes affecting abused women included the introduction of fees for applications to the Plan, a lower limit on certificates issued per year, restrictions on legal aid recipients changing lawyers, and restrictions on eligibility for immigration and landlord/tenant matters. A program offering one free two-hour legal consultation for abused women, initiated in conjunction with the Ontario Women's Directorate, has also been limited.

Criminal and family courts: Reductions in the number of court officials and prosecutors has resulted in chief judges in Ontario predicting "chaos" for criminal court proceedings (Tyler). For abused women, who must testify as "victim witnesses" in assault trials, the chaos caused by cuts will only increase the pressures of a justice system chronically unresponsive to their needs.

Social Assistance: On October 1, 1995, welfare recipients received a 21.6 per cent cut to their monthly assistance cheque from the provincial government. These cuts drove recipients further below the poverty line (Monsebraaten). On a monthly basis, a sole support parent with one child currently receives a *maximum* of $511 for rent, and $446 for food, clothing, transportation, and other basic necessities.

Housing: Along with social assistance shelter allowances, housing subsidies to tenants whose rent exceeds social assistance guidelines were cut by 21.6 per cent. In some cases, social assistance recipients were threatened with termination of benefits unless they moved into less expensive housing (Morrison). Funding for creating new co-operative housing has been frozen, and the government is strictly adhering to full market/rent geared to income ratios within co-op housing.

Child care: Changes to child care delivery and subsidies for low-income women in Ontario have reduced crucial support for women escaping violence. In August 1996, the government released the results of a child care "review" suggesting 15,000 new child care spaces could be created by a number of changes to child care delivery, including recommending lower wages for staff, subsidies for space in unlicensed, unregulated child care arrangements, increases in child to staff ratios, and decreases in government inspections. But according to the Ontario Coalition for Better Child Care, subsidies for child care spaces have already been reduced by 9,000 and most municipalities in Ontario are not accepting any new applicants for subsidized daycare (McCuaig).

Language interpretation services: Cuts were made to interpretation services for women whose first language is not English or French. The cultural interpreter service for multilingual access to social assistance was eliminated, cutting off this important option for abused women needing to seek financial assistance to leave abuse situations.

Services for people with disabilities: Abused women with disabilities will encounter increased barriers to escaping danger or using what services remain for addressing violence. For example, funding for Wheel-Trans, public transit for persons with disabilities in Toronto, was reduced, and eligibility for use of the service restricted by a new definition of "disability." Persons that are approved to access this service must now pay a user fee when applying for registration. Doctors' forms that confirmed eligibility for the pay-per-use service are no longer acceptable as "proof" that the service is needed.

Cuts that Compound

Women's lives are not defined only by abuse they suffer at the hands of intimate partners. Nor can their experiences of violence be narrowly defined within their personal relationships. Destroying services in the following areas further prevents women and their children from gaining freedom from all forms of violence against women.

Anti-racism and anti-discrimination work: Severe cuts and changes have been made to programs and policies that specifically work to end racism, create or ensure the rights of First Nations and Aboriginal Peoples, and assist persons with disabilities. This area includes anti-racism education, advocacy, and legal protection for disenfranchised communities (Ontario Social Safety Network 4).

Education and training: Women have seen large increases in their tuition fees for post-secondary education and cuts to training programs as a result of provincial budget reductions of 20 per cent. Further cuts and increases are expected in these areas. Women who are recipients of welfare are no longer able to attend school (Toughill), thus post-secondary education is a prerogative only for those who are financially well-off.

Pay equity: The provincial government has frozen funding to support pay equity implementation guidelines required of women's workplaces in the broader public sector. Pay equity by "proxy comparator," the method used to bring equity to over 80,000 women working in poorly paid workplaces, such as women's shelters, has been eliminated. The current government favours a voluntary pay equity policy which requires women to launch—and win—a public complaint against their employer before equity is assured.

Employment equity: Also eliminated was the provincial employment equity legislation that ensured protection for women, people of colour, First Nations and Aboriginal Peoples, and people with disabilities, in hiring and promotion practices. To replace employment equity in Ontario, the provincial government has proposed an Equal Opportunity Plan which would again put the onus on victims of discrimination to challenge unfair practices in a public complaints process.

Impacts

In our August 1996 survey of OAITH members, we asked shelters to report the impact of the cuts on women's decisions about remaining with, or returning to abusive partners. Our results clearly show that a significant number of women in Ontario are now making decisions to remain in, or return to abusive situations based primarily on barriers created by budget and service cuts. Moreover, more than half of the shelters answering our survey say women are now forced to use the shelter more as a temporary respite from violence, rather than as an avenue of escape.

Social assistance: One hundred per cent of shelters responding to our surveys reported that the cuts to social assistance had a severe impact on survivors. Shelters continued to report that as women struggle to survive on General Welfare Assistance and Family Benefits (GWA/FBA), they are being forced to make choices between food and rent or clothing and prescription medication and so on. More women are coming to the shelter with large debts as a result of desperate struggles against poverty. Women who still have credit cards are using them to the limit to provide basic essentials for their children. Some women, even after struggling for years to win custody of their children, have returned children to abusive partners who have money to feed and shelter them.

Abused women, many of whom have been prevented by violence from receiving training or education, have been cut off welfare as a result of the provincial government decision to deny assistance to students. Staying in school has become very difficult, often impossible, for survivors with children. This has been devastating to women who have planned to improve their future by recreating their lives.

Women are waiting longer before receiving their benefits after applying for GWA/FBA and many of the procedures now instituted in social assistance offices, such as home visits and checks on adults living in the same residence, demean women and make them feel blamed for leaving the violence. Shelters reported that women are having child and spousal support payments deducted from their GWA/FBA allowance, even though they are not actually receiving the court-ordered support payments from their ex-partner.

Welfare workers tell survivors to find part-time or casual work to supplement their assistance, but with a slight increase in income, they may no longer qualify for General Welfare or Family Benefits (GWA/FBA). Women who are receiving Unemployment Insurance from the federal government also struggle because they cannot obtain a drug card, moving allowance, or other minor supports from the General Welfare system.

Elimination or reduction of these additional supports under GWA or FBA have also affected the supports to abused women starting over with nothing. Before cutbacks, women were eligible for community "start-up" funds to purchase beds and other very basic furniture and supplies. Shelters report these funds have decreased, or become inaccessible, depending on the discretion of the social assistance caseworker. Transportation costs, dental coverage, and repairs have all been eliminated or reduced for women. Ontario Drug Benefit user fees on prescriptions for GWA/FBA recipients mean that women unable to afford the user fees go without proper health care or use the personal needs supplement for other basic needs to pay for the increase in costs.

> *It is becoming increasingly more difficult for women to even retain a lawyer as the tariff set out by Legal Aid really restricts hours of service on any issue. A women in our program spoke with 25 firms before she found someone to take her on a [legal aid] certificate.*
> —Second stage shelter worker, southern Ontario, October 1996.

Legal Aid: Since cuts to the Ontario Legal Aid Plan came into effect, many abused women have been denied legal aid or legal representation for family law matters in Ontario. Again, 100 per cent of shelters responding to us reported women having problems either with accessing legal aid itself, or with finding a lawyer who would accept a legal aid certificate. This, in spite of Legal Aid Plan eligibility guidelines designating "spouse or child at risk" (Law Society of Upper Canada) as a priority for assistance.

It would appear that in the absence of any clear definition of abuse, other than it *must* be physical, local Legal Aid Plan offices are using their discretion on deciding which abused women are "deserving." One shelter survey respondent reported: "Legal aid is only issued with physical abuse, *and* police involvement *and* if a woman is only requesting custody and support, *and* is not a property owner (even jointly). Therefore, most women don't qualify." Other local Legal Aid offices have given similarly incorrect information; for example, that legal aid is available only if the father has actually threatened to abduct the children, or only if the abused is *convicted* of assault. One woman was told, wrongly, that there is no legal aid for family law matters.

Some shelters find that lawyers who still take some legal aid cases will not take *family* law cases, arguing that restrictions in hours for family law legal aid certificates will not allow them to recover costs for time and expenses involved in representing abused women. Also, as a result of Legal Aid Plan time restrictions for family law, shelters report that some women have been abandoned by lawyers in the middle of court cases because the maximum time allowed by Legal Aid expired. In such cases, women must either represent themselves or rely on appointed Duty Counsel who go unprepared into complex cases. Some judges have shown little tolerance for these circumstances, and women fear their lack of understanding may negatively influence cases.

To generate revenue for a cash-strapped legal aid fund, the Ontario Legal Aid Plan has introduced user fees. Women who qualify for social assistance are exempt from these fees, but there are many low-income survivors outside the social assistance system who now must pay a $25 application fee to *apply* for a legal aid certificate. Women whose applications are rejected must pay user fees to appeal Legal Aid Plan decisions. All of this delays and hinders their chance to escape violence. Shelters report longer delays in processing applications and issuing certificates (one shelter reports the wait at a minimum of six weeks). In some areas, women are being asked to apply to legal aid before making an appointment under the two-hour free consultation policy in order to establish that they are "deserving" of free assistance. Even if women are able to secure a certificate and a lawyer, the reduced amounts of time that lawyers are paid for family law cases often means abused women must assist the lawyer with paperwork involved in the case. Some women have even been told that they must personally serve legal papers *on their abuser*, or pay for a private process server because the lawyer cannot afford the expense and court-based process service for family law has been eliminated. Clearly, such a practice puts abused women in *grave* danger and puts pressure on them to stop legal proceedings.

> *The government is putting out that shelters are still open and this is true, but all supports have been cut or eliminated, making it impossible for us to provide referrals for women to get on with their lives. This means women are staying [at the shelter] much longer and, therefore, we are serving fewer women.*
> —Shelter director, Metro Toronto, September 1996.

Housing: Abused women may still apply for priority status for subsidized units, but many of the shelters noted there is an increased pressure on women to prove they "really are abused" and that their safety is at risk. Other new criteria reported for priority status included: a requirement by one office that women apply within three months of assault; loss of priority status for women who move into an area close to the abuser; and a requirement for co-signers to obtain public housing.

Shelters also reported that waiting lists for subsidized housing were too long to be of any assistance and there were no units becoming available, perhaps as a result of resident reluctance to move in an insecure economy. Other women have been told that there is no longer any rent geared to income (RGI) units available. Due to cutbacks in the funding of co-operative housing, market rent units are replacing the RGI housing in areas when these units become available. Since market rents are not affordable for low-income women, most abused women in shelters cannot consider them. The government's decision not to build new co-operative housing is problematic to abused women, since there are no new options for finding the safe, low-income housing they need.

The "Human Cost"

For abused women, the emotional costs of the cutbacks are terrible: depression, despair, and hopelessness. Survivors live with the increased fear and stress that comes from the inability to act on positive change in their lives. Even if they successfully leave an abuser's control, they find other forces directing their destiny. Many remain powerless and afraid, with few options for building a new life. As a result of extreme emotional demands placed on abused women, overall personal health decreases and illness increases (Day).

Clearly, women in violent relationships face a "no-win" situation. With little support or assistance to return to a life free from violence, women are locked in with abusers who endanger the lives of themselves and their children. When they try to get away, they discover they cannot financially support themselves and their children. Lack of safe, affordable child care or child care subsidy, prevents many women from seeking what few jobs exist.

Women who are trapped with, or forced to return to an abuser will certainly be subjected to further abuse. Already, far too many women die because they lack options and support for escape. Shelters have already noted increases in the number of women talking about suicide, in the level of fear of death from the abuser, and in the amount of time women need before they feel strong enough to try to escape permanently.

The Impacts of Cuts on Children

Miraculously, my sister-in-law sent me some money in the mail. The boys came home from school to find me cooking a big supper. They were so happy! One of them said, "Mom, we were just talking about how hungry we were and how great it would be if we came home to find you making mashed potatoes and gravy and meat!" I suddenly felt so sad and worthless.

—Phyllis, a survivor.

By far, the most devastating effect of the cuts for violence survivors is the impact on their children. Testimonies by women about the impact of government cuts show how heartbreaking the effects of poverty, created by the cuts, can be on women and children's daily lives. When women speak about the future for their children, they see only lost hopes and tragic consequences.

When women are trapped in violent homes, their children are trapped with them. The effects of witnessing violence, coupled with the impacts of severe poverty, suggest a bleak, insecure future for children. Often, children are used by abusive fathers to control and coerce women, at the expense of the children. Often, they are sexually and physically abused by those same men. Children living with an abuser learn the value of power and control over others—a value that has been devastating to themselves and their mothers. Often, they learn that they are worthless. To consign children to continuing violent experiences consigns them to a high risk of bringing the violence into their adult lives.

Legal Aid Plan changes and cutbacks may play a critical part in entrenching the difficulty abused women have always had in protecting their children from abuse. Women who have sought to win custody from an abuser, may more and more lose custody to abusive fathers because they cannot afford legal representation, child assessments, and so on. Children may, therefore, be more often forced to live with, or spend increasing amounts of time with, abusive fathers.

Cumulative Effects

All of the cuts together create an environment that, in effect, revictimizes abused women and reinforces, or rewards, male violence. With little help, support, or assistance, abused women are left to fend for themselves and their children. With the knowledge that the women they abuse have no where to turn, abusers can and do increase their control and power over women with little or no consequences.

For women attempting to escape violence, erosion of already inadequate supports has a devastating effect. The "bottom line" is more than an exercise in fiscal "efficiencies." It is the blocking of escape routes abused women and women's advocates have struggled to open for over 20 years. We are moving back to a time when survivors had "no place to go." Violence will continue unchallenged, unless we take action to move forward again.

This article has been excerpted with permission from the Ontario Association of Interval and Transition Houses. OAITH is a network of women's shelters and other services which lobbies provincially and federally for change to end violence against abused women and their children. Copies of "Locked In, Left Out" are available for $10.00 each from OAITH, 2 Carlton Street, Suite 1404, Toronto, Ontario, M5B 1J3. Tel: (416) 977-6619. Fax: (416) 977-1227. Email: oaith@web.net.

References

Day, T. *The Health Related Costs of Violence Against Women in Canada: The Tip of the Iceberg.* London: Centre for Research on Violence Against Women and Children, 1995.

Law Society of Upper Canada. "Changes to the Ontario Legal Aid Plan: A Guide for Legal Aid Lawyers." Toronto: Law Society of Upper Canada.

McCuaig, Kerry. Ontario Coalition for Better Child Care. Personal communication. 8 Oct. 1996.

Monsebraaten, Laurie. "Welfare's Boogeyman." *Toronto Star* 12 Aug. 1995: C1, 4.

Morrison, Ian. "Welfare Rate Cuts Anniversary Report." Toronto: Steering Committee on Social Assistance, Ontario Social Safety Network, Oct. 1996.

OAITH. "Survey of Membership" Toronto: OAITH, Aug. 1996.

Ontario Social Safety Network. *Social Safety News* 11 (Nov. 1995).

Toughill, Kelly. "University Students to be Cut Off Welfare." *Toronto Star* 12 April 1996: A14.

Tyler, Tracey. "Cuts Mean Justice Chaos Top Judges Warn." *Toronto Star* 31 Jan. 1996.

This image has been reprinted with permission courtesy of The Toronto Star Syndicate.

What is the Public Interest in Child Care?

by Martha Friendly

At the time that Canada's main social programs—health care, unemployment insurance, pensions, and social welfare—were emerging, child care had not yet come onto the public agenda. Child care only became a national issue in the 1980s, with numerous task forces and committees recommending a national policy to shape the emergence of high quality child care/early childhood development programs under provincial authority across Canada. However, by the time the proportion of mothers of young children in the labour force exceeded a majority, and the benefits of early childhood development programs began to be understood, fiscal and political considerations were unfavourable to the introduction of a new, potentially expensive social program. Canada's fiscal and political discourse in the 1990s is closely connected to a key unresolved question that underlies the debate about child care/early childhood development services: should they be regarded, and treated, as a public service or as a private responsibility?

Child Care/Early Childhood Development Services in Canada

As of 1997, Canada still had no coherent strategy to ensure that child care/early childhood development services are available to meet contemporary needs. Indeed, after an optimistic phase in the 1980s, the child care situation has been deteriorating throughout the 1990s from both public policy and service delivery perspectives (Doherty, Friendly, and Oloman).

This article defines child care/early childhood development services as care and development for children from birth to age 12 outside the immediate family and outside regular schooling; this definition includes children with mothers who are in as well as those who are not in the labour force. Most young children in Canada who require care while one or both parents are at work are in private or unregulated arrangements with an in-home caregiver (a "nanny" or "sitter") or an unregulated family daycare provider. These private arrangements are not, strictly speaking, "services"; though some undoubtedly provide adequate care, they are not assumed to be developmental programs.

A key objective of child care/early childhood programs is to promote healthy child development as well as to provide care in the parents' absence. Today each province and territory has a tangle of child care/early childhood development services that concentrate on different populations and have somewhat different purposes. In addition, a variety of demand subsidies are extended to selected parents to allow them to purchase "care." Some programs are targeted to high-risk or poor children, and some are heavily reliant on user fees. In almost all regions, services are either unavailable, have restrictive eligibility requirements, or are not appropriate from a scheduling perspective to even begin to meet the full range of community needs. For example, although public kindergarten is available to almost all five-year-olds, it is usually part-time, so the needs of a working parent for care cannot always be met.

Regulated child care is the only service that is explicitly organized to care for children whose parents are in the paid labour force. It is too costly for modest or middle-income families, not widely available, and sometimes of a standard of quality that is less than adequate. The role of government in regulated child care is generally limited either to correcting the imperfections of the market by regulating services or to funding them for the needy.

For Whom is Child Care a Benefit?

A discussion paper prepared for the federal government's Social Security Review in 1994 identified child care as central to three themes: working/employment, learning, and security. It characterized child care as "lying at the heart ..." of the three areas, a "critical support for employment ... but more than an employment measure ..." and as a way to "provide children with a good environment in which to grow and learn." This provides a paradigm for examining why and how child care/early childhood development is at the centre of many contemporary agendas.

The paper depicts child care as a unique human service with multiple goals and interconnected purposes. If a system of child care/early childhood development is well designed, it has the capacity to meet a range of needs simultaneously. High quality child care/early childhood development has social value: as a strategy to enhance all children's healthy development; as a support to families regardless of their labour force status; and as part of a comprehensive approach to alleviating poverty and furthering women's equality. It is important to note that many of these goals cannot be met unless the child care provided is high quality enough to foster healthy child development.

The benefits of high quality child care arise from two propositions. From these follow a range of subsidiary short-term and long-term benefits to children, to their families, to women who are mothers and to society at large.

Proposition One: *High quality child care/early childhood development programs promote the healthy development, safety, and well-being of children regardless of parental work status.*

This statement is supported by a body of child development research and by the literature on compensatory education. The research shows that if a preschool child care/early childhood development service is of high quality, it provides intellectual and social enhancement that persists into elementary school, establishing a foundation for later success; poor quality child care is demonstrated to have negative impacts. These findings pertain regardless of social class.

Disadvantaged children, who are less likely to succeed in schooling and more likely to become involved in delinquent activities later on, benefit from child care/early childhood programs. American studies of programs like Head Start, show that, for this population, early childhood programs enriched with supports such as parent education, health and nutrition, and social services, can ameliorate the effects of disadvantage.

Healthy development in the early years provides a solid foundation for life-long good health and the underpinning not only for later school success, but for the formation of a competent, civil citizenry. Child care supports parents both as workers and in their parenting roles, so children can benefit from reduction of poverty, reduced family stress, and competent parenting. Healthy social development of individuals and communities fosters prevention of crime, and inclusive early childhood services strengthen appreciation for diversity and promotes equity among classes, levels of ability, racial and ethnic groups, and generations, strengthening social solidarity.

Proposition Two: *Access to reliable child care allows parents, especially mothers, to participate in the labour force, training, or education.*

In the past few decades, women have joined the paid labour force in large numbers so that about 65 per cent of women with children under age six now work outside the home. Without the availability of affordable, reliable child care, women (single parents or those in two-parent families) may be compelled to remain out of the labour force, to work at poorly-paid part-time employment, or not to take advancement; some are forced into dependence on public assistance and poverty. If child care is accessible, low-income parents on social assistance can become self-reliant by participating in employment, training, and education, and contribute to the economic life of the community.

Reliable child care also helps enhance the work effectiveness of working parents across the economic spectrum by diminishing tensions between work and family responsibilities. Finally, inclusive child care/early childhood development services enhance social solidarity and community cohesion through participation in shared experiences by uniting families of all social strata and cultural origins in common activities related to the well-being of their children, and by demonstrating that cooperation among racial groups and social classes is possible and valued.

Child Care in Context: the Ecological Perspective

Child care/early childhood development exists within a set of links that connect the child and the child care program with the family, the community, and the social/political environment. In this way, public policy is both influenced by the social/political factors that shape its development, and also influences how child care develops and is delivered. This perspective emphasizes that child care both has a context and is part of a context. Therefore, it should be conceptualized in a holistic way to develop an effective strategy for dealing with the pieces.

This suggests that it is not effective to try to address child care in a limited manner for targeted sectors of the population—like "the welfare mom," the "high risk child," "Aboriginal children on reserve," "Aboriginal children off-reserve," "affluent families who want early childhood education for their child," "employability," or "a business expense." Targeting almost always means that segments of the population are not served, goals and needs that do not fit the targets go unmet, and public funds are used poorly.

An Essential Public Service or a Private Responsibility?

Many of the benefits of high quality child care/early childhood development services accrue to the community or larger society; they are, in part at least, collective benefits. If self-reliant families, a healthy, proficient citizenry, and cohesive, compassionate communities are desirable features of a society, and high quality child care contributes to their formation and maintenance, then the larger society gains. Thus, if provision of these services is in the public interest, it is appropriate to treat public expenditures for child care as a public investment, not merely as a public cost, and to create public policy to do it effectively.

With the exception of part-day kindergarten under the aegis of education ministries, Canadian child care/early childhood development programs have never been a public service. In the past two decades, many other industrialized nations—notably those of the European Union—have established coordinated systems of early childhood services that provide both "care" for working parents and "early education" to promote healthy child development for all children. This, however, has not been the case in Canada.

Whether services for child care/early childhood development are considered private commodities or a public good is fundamental to the design of public policy and service delivery. The current tools of child care/early childhood development provision in Canada are appropriate to a privatized market model, not to a public service approach. Considerable public funds are dedicated to demand subsidies so parents can purchase care in the market, and developmental programs (except part-day kindergarten) are targeted to the needy. Regulated child care is primarily privately initiated, operated by private non-profit and for-profit operators, and largely funded privately through parent fees.

In contrast, systems of child care/early childhood development programs providing both "care" and "development" in a unified delivery model have been created in most of the nations of western Europe (with the exception of the United Kingdom). These are predominately publicly initiated and publicly operated, and funding is delivered directly to service providers through established budget processes. Parents pay some fees, but because public funding is not solely for the needy, fees are affordable, representing only a portion of the actual costs; this means that modest income, middle-class, and affluent children all participate. Though a variety of models of service are usually available in a single community (like family daycare and centres), they comprise a coordinated system, supported by relatively coherent public policy and public funds. There is some child care that is privately initiated and operated (by voluntary or parent groups), some demand subsidies, and some parent fees. However, the idea that responsibility for the care and development of young children should be shared or supported by governments because the well-being of children is in the public interest is extremely well entrenched in these countries.

In the Public Interest

Canada has not made a choice about whether child care/early childhood develop-ment should be a public service or a private responsibility. Although there is clearly a strong public interest in high quality child care, failure to make this choice means that the existing market model is maintained by default. Without a deliberate public policy approach, there is no way to address the fragmentation, gaps, inefficiencies, and inequities of the current situation.

While the increase in labour force participation of mothers of young children has levelled off in the past year or two, the need for improvement of high quality child care/early childhood development services has not abated. Indeed, new initiatives suggest that child care/early childhood development services may be expected to play a bigger role. The statements of the National Forum on Health and Health Canada's national health goals for children propose that a comprehensive approach to non-parental care and healthy child development for all young children should be a key part of a population health approach to health strategy. The National Crime Prevention Council identifies services to promote healthy development as part of a conception of preventing crime at the community level. Federal/provincial governments have expec-tations that an integrated child benefit targeted at the working poor will constitute an attack on Canada's burgeoning child poverty. It is obvious, however, that an impedi-ment to the workforce and training participation of low-income parents is the absence of affordable, reliable child care. Failure to address this impediment may mean that poor families and children remain poor in spite of the integrated child benefit, and, that Canada's poor children will remain disadvantaged—now and in the future.

Research carried out by the Canadian Policy Research Network (CPRN) describes core Canadian values that include self-reliance, compassion leading to collective responsi-bility, and investment in children as the future generation while maintaining the role of parents as primary. These values are all consistent with a well-designed system of early childhood development services. At the same time, the fragmented, incoherent, market-driven arrangements now associated with child care/early childhood development reflect what CPRN describes as Canadians' concerns about social policy: concerns about waste and inefficiency, a desire for equality and fairness, and a belief that social programs would work better if they were integrated (Peters).

Though the world is moving rapidly towards the twenty-first century, Canada's arrangements for child care/early childhood development combine nineteenth-century ideas that family matters are a private responsibility with 1960s American approaches to correcting the private child care market through targeting. Although public opinion polling by Insight Canada Research in 1993 and 1996 shows that two-thirds of Canadians support the idea of a national child care program, public policy has not caught up with either public opinion or the public interest. When Canadian child care eventually enters the modern age, not only will the private interests of Canada's children and families be met, but the public interest will be served as well.

A version of this article was originally published in Policy Options *(January-February 1997).*

Martha Friendly is the coordinator of the Childcare Resource and Research Unit, and adjunct professor at the Centre for Urban and Community Studies, University of Toronto.

References

Doherty, G., M. Friendly, and M. Oloman. *Women's Support, Women's Work: Child Care in an Era of Deficit Reduction, Devolution, Down-sizing, and De-regulation.* Ottawa: Status of Women Canada, in press.

Government of Canada. *Improving Social Security in Canada: A Discussion Paper.* Ottawa: Minister of Supply and Services Canada, 1994.

Health Canada. *Turning Points: Canadians from Coast to Coast Set a New Course for Healthy Child and Youth Development.* Ottawa: Health Canada, Childhood and Youth Division, Family and Child Health Unit, 1995.

Insight Canada Research. *National Child Care Survey, August 1996.* Toronto: Insight Canada Research, 1996.

National Forum on Health. *Canada Health Action: Building on the Legacy, Volumes I and II.* Ottawa: Minister of Public Works and Government Services, 1997.

National Crime Prevention Council. *Preventing Crime by Investing in Families: An Integrated Approach to Promote Positive Outcomes in Children.* Ottawa: National Crime Prevention Council Canada, 1996.

Peters, Suzanne. *Exploring Canadian Values: Foundations for Well-Being.* Ottawa: Canadian Policy Research Networks, 1995.

The Attack on Motherwork in Ontario

by Brigitte Kitchen with Rosemarie Popham

The speed and brutality with which the provincial government has set out to redefine the role of government as provider of services to the public and protector of the rights of citizens since its election in June 1995 has been by no means gender neutral. While the drastic spending cuts have disrupted the lives of all economically vulnerable, it is women, particularly as mothers, and their children who have had to bear the brunt of the provincial government's agenda of reducing the public sector. The social consensus that legitimated a strong and vital infrastructure of social programs and services, symbolizing the sense of community and caring that defined civil life in Ontario, has been torn apart. From the government's ideological position these programs and services are deemed to have produced a decline in self-reliance and the erosion of family ties. This decline is seen as having spawned an unhealthy abdication in responsibility for dependent family members and encouraged a passive dependency on government programs and services. Consequently the government's restructuring and dismantling of the social sector funded from tax dollars is aimed not only at solving the budget deficit by the turn of the century but also at changing the face of caring as we have come to know it in the last 50 years.

The physical and emotional care for dependent family and community members is to be reprivatized. As "motherwork" (to borrow the term used by Jessie Bernard to describe this kind of unpaid work in families and as volunteers in communities) it will be the primary responsibility of women. The fewer publicly provided social programs and services are made available, the more motherwork women will have to provide. In this paper, because of limitations of space, we focus on the loss of employment opportunities, the changing face of motherwork (we prefer this term to the gender neutral term of caring), and the diminished support from social programs and services that profoundly affect the lives of mothers as a result of the reframing of social policy in Ontario. As workers/employees and as mothers, women's life situations are particularly influenced by governmental policy decisions in these three areas. The central premise of our paper is that Ontario today is a province where the prevalent norms and values governing economic and political life are undergoing profound changes that are particularly hurting mothers. In this distressing climate, it is increasingly difficult for women as mothers to balance the conflicting demands of their different status roles.

Loss of Employment Opportunities

The impact of the dismantling of public infrastructure of social programs and services for women has been so far reaching and is potentially so damaging that it can be seen as a war against women. Women as mothers, because of their continued primary responsibility for dependent children undoubtedly are major consumers of social programs and services but they are also the major service providers as employees in that sector. In Canada, as elsewhere in the western industrialized world, women's massive entrance in the labour market in the last 40 years would not have been possible without the expansion of the public services, particularly in hospitals, education, social services, homes for the aged, nurseries, and others. As a result, women became dependent on the state as a major employer either directly or indirectly in the voluntary social services sector funded with public money. The Ontario government's turn around in policy direction is curtailing women's employment opportunities in the public sector. Its agenda is a clear attempt to turn back the sociological clock of the advancements women have made in the labour market and in the support for their motherwork in the home through the provision of public services. As public sector employees, consumers, and clients mothers suffer more from the dismantling of public services than women without childrearing responsibility or men, whether they are parents or not. Government policy plays a significant role in shaping the quality of mothers' and children's lives as the labour force participation of mothers depends to a large extent on the scope and adequacy of support services by the state.

The emergence of the neo-liberal/conservative agenda in the mid-1980s marked a turning-point in the circumstances of women carrying out their motherwork. It brought with it major layoffs because of economic restructuring, the segmentation of the labour market into fewer secure, high-paying, "good" jobs and into an increasing number of non-standard, unstable, low-paid jobs. The government's deregulation of hiring, employment, and dismissal standards has contributed to the increase in non-standard, contracting out work, the areas of employment where mostly women are concentrated. The polarization of earnings has been among the most significant economic developments of the past two decades (Picot and Myles). For mothers in low-income couple families it has meant that they had to join the labour market for the family to make ends meet. Most families raising children need two income earners to support a family. In 1973, most of these families could live on the earnings of one person working 40 hours a week (Kitchen *et al.*). Today this is the case for only 27 per cent of families. Statistics Canada reports on family income for decades have shown that women are playing an ever growing role in keeping families out of poverty. In 60 per cent of Canada's 6.8 million married and common-law couples both partners are employed. Lacking a second income and not receiving adequate child support from the father of their children, sole support mothers are not able to earn enough to provide for themselves and their children. Their poverty rate stood at 60 per cent in 1995 (Campaign 2000). The earnings differential between women and men which had been narrowing slowly and unevenly is again widening. The Ontario government has increased the labour market vulnerability of mothers in section J of Bill 26 by abolishing employment equity, anti-harassment procedures, and pay equity regulations that had controlled discriminatory employment practices in the province. It considers these measures as interfering with the ability of private investors to engage in profitable business enterprises in the province.

The conditions under which mothers are holding jobs are not the only things that have deteriorated considerably. The government plans to reduce the number of civil servants by 13 per cent (Jenish) and its diminished funding of the voluntary sector are seriously undermining the employment opportunities of mothers. The growth of public sector jobs had particularly benefitted well-educated women qualifying for better paid positions, mostly in the semi-professions such as nursing and social work. The disappearance of these jobs is reversing the economic progress made over the years by mothers who had been able to balance their job and family responsibilities with the support of public services. The government's drastic spending cuts which are behind the job losses in the province (Crane) are contributing to the poverty among many mothers with dependent children. Their earnings or the receipt of public income supports had enabled mothers to achieve a degree of unprecedented economic independence from men. This will no longer be the case. Even as union members, mothers run into difficulties keeping their jobs. As unionized public servants and employees in voluntary social agencies as well as in the education and health care system are facing major layoffs, their union's "dumping system" based on seniority will particularly disadvantage mothers. Many of them, because of their childraising responsibilities, have had only an uneven or intermittent attachment to the job market. As the last hired, they will be the first to receive pink slips.

Social Assistance

For the unemployed, unable to find jobs, social assistance is the program of last resort in their struggle for survival. Social assistance benefits have been cut by 21.6 per cent for all recipients. They were considered to exceed necessary comfort levels. Low welfare rates were expected to motivate mothers to find paying jobs. With a provincial unemployment rate of 8.6 per cent and the high concentration of women in part-time, low-paying service jobs such an expectation is unrealistic. The poverty line for a family of three is $1,833 a month in a mid-sized city (Campaign 2000). A mother with two children receives now a maximum of $1,239 a month on assistance (Statistics and Analysis Unit, Social Assistance Program Branch). Her quality of life and that of her children has been reduced to struggling to get by with $5.91 per person per day. If she worked 40 hours a week at the minimum wage of $6.85 an hour her monthly gross pay would be $1,096. The difference between earnings and social assistance levels is referred to by economists as the fairness differential favouring social assistance recipients. While earnings are based on the market price of individual productivity, social assistance levels are based on family size. This difference does not allow for a strict comparison between the minimum wage and social assistance. Because of the cuts mothers may have to face the difficult choice to either pay their rent or feed their children. Many have to rely on food banks, the use of which has increased by 36 per cent in the Greater Toronto Area since October 1995 when the social assistance cuts were first introduced. Statistics from the Daily Bread Food Bank reveal the extent of despair for mothers of whom 16 per cent reported that their children go without food at least once a week. Children make up 46 per cent of food bank users; 10 per cent of them are of pre-school age ("Thanksgiving in These Tough Times"). Apart from damages to their health caused by the poor diet on the present assistance rates, eviction applications in Metropolitan Toronto have increased by 40 per cent since July 1996 ("Thanksgiving in These Tough Times"). More mothers and children are at risk of being homeless and being separated from each other. Simcoe County Children's Aid Society in Barrie reported a couple on social assistance who had put one of their young children up for adoption because they could no longer afford to care for them (Jenish). Sole support mothers who had financed their community college or university education while on assistance have been declared ineligible for assistance. They are now required to finance their education through student loans and grants. The re-introduction of the "spouse-in-the-house rule" in October 1995 for women who had been living with a man for less than three years, the time period required under the Family Law Act to establish a support obligation, provides further evidence for the stigmatization and harassment of mothers on social assistance. More humilation lies ahead for them. While mothers with dependent children have been spared so far from having to participate in the eleven workfare pilot projects that are currently being testing in the province, the government's intentions seem to be to exempt only mothers with a pre-school child.

Family Responsibility and Support Enforcement Act

The Ontario government is at least indirectly involved in defining and setting standards of parenting which it enforces with penalties and remedies for their breach. Through the Child and Family Services Act it protects children from their parents. Its levels of social assistance and its bungled reorganization of the Family Support Plan, renamed as of October 2, 1996, the Family Responsibility and Support Enforcement Act, reveal, however, its lack of commitment to their material well-being particularly in mother-led households. The 78,000 sole support mothers who had begun to rely on assured payments of court ordered child support from the non-custodial parent of their children through the Family Support Program can no longer do so. The provincial government dismissed the mandatory program of deducting child support from the paycheques of non-custodial parents as having created an unnecessary and overburdened bureaucracy. Offices in eight cities have been closed, staff cut by two-thirds, and a "one-stop shopping" all-purpose office, the Family Responsibility Office, has been opened in Downsview. During this time of transition no enforcements are carried out and investigations why cheques from non-custodial parents registered with the plan have not come in are not taking place. Worse, payments that have been made and handed over for processing to the Royal Bank have not been mailed out to the mothers who need them to cover their families' consumption costs. Mothers have not had their social assistance benefits supplemented by the amount of the cheques that have not arrived. They were told at welfare offices to keep on phoning or writing to the skeleton staff of the Family Support Plan. The Ministry of the Attorney General minimizes the chaos and hardship created for the most vulnerable families in the province by claiming that in transitionary period when the program is largely handed over to the private sector, "people will have to be patient" (Gadd). The government's rationale for the overhaul of the 1992 Family Support Plan is that it did not meet the needs of mothers and children. Close to $1 billion of child support payments are outstanding as 77 per cent of the cases registered with the Plan are not in full compliance, i.e. payments are in delay or incomplete. A desperate situation for mothers only made worse by the mismanagement of the overhaul.

Child Care

To be in the workforce, mothers require child care, one of the fastest growing components of service demands and family spending in Canada, which has increased from $37 million to $2.8 billion (Jackson). It can cost up to $1,200 a month to have a pre-school child cared for in a licensed daycare centre by qualified staff. The costs are unaffordable for many low-paid couples and particularly sole support mothers who earn on average $11,000 less than fathers living in a spousal relationship. These parents require subsidized daycare. The Ontario government proposes in a recently published report on the restructuring of child care services to provide more spaces for pre-school children by lowering the quality of the care available and by cutting the special wage grant in non-profit daycare centres to the average wage grant in commercial centres. The funding formula for the new child care places is to take from one group of lowly paid mothers to pay for the subsidies needed by another group of poorly paid mothers, pitting them against each other. Lowly paid child care workers with average earnings of $19,000 a year, 98 per cent of them women, will see their wages cut by $4,500 if the government follows through with its new version of pay equity by taking the low private sector pay scale as the norm for the entire child care system. Government savings coming from the pockets of this group of women are then to be used to create 8,000 new daycare spaces and fund 12,000 new child care subsidies for working poor mothers. In addition to their lowered pay, the ratio of one daycare worker for up to eight children between the ages of two and a half and three years and eight months is to be increased to nine children. Daycare workers in their private homes will be allowed to add two school age children in the morning and afternoon to the up to five pre-school children they may already care for (Toughill). These women are expected to work more for less pay. Further cost savings are to come from increasing the period of time over which centres are licensed and reducing the number of times they have to be inspected. The government maintains that these changes will not jeopardize the quality of child care in the province. According to the Minister of Community and Social Services, Janet Ecker, the changes are "well within the standards in Canada and well within the research standards of what is quality" (Toughill A24). Parents and daycare advocates disagree. They understand that child care is not just a support for mothers in the workforce but also an important factor in the intellectual, emotional, and social development of children. The restructuring of the child care system is for them a lowering of its quality causing parents unnecessary concern about the safety and developmental opportunities provided for their children.

Less Support for Motherwork

For decades, Ontarians have been well served by good schools, medical services, and community-based social services. Motherwork relies to a large extent on a strong network of community services which have helped women to develop personal and parental competencies. Health care services and health promotion programs, public libraries, recreation programs for both mothers and children, and counselling and support services for mothers and children living or escaping from abusive family situations are vital services that support women in their everyday motherwork. It is at the community level that the pain caused by the provincial government's social spending cuts is felt most deeply. Because provincial transfers to the municipalities are to be cut by 47 per cent, municipal governments have started to charge for library cards, for the use of skating rinks and swimming pools, and have increased the fees for recreation programs in parks and community centres even further. These user fees impose an additional burden on the already strained incomes of mothers in low and modest income families—those with incomes of $30,000 and less—and makes motherwork all the more difficult by forcing women to deny or limit their children's educational and recreational opportunities which the children of better-off families take for granted.

Concern about the effects of provincial spending cuts on the quality of life prompted a community survey of community service agencies receiving minimal funding as well as those with multimillion dollar budgets across Metropolitan Toronto (Social Planning Council of Metropolitan Toronto). It found that in 1995, 162 community service and 20 child care programs had to be cancelled because of loss of funding. An additional 106 programs were reported as likely to be eliminated in 1996 while another 301 programs were under review for cancellation. Programs for mothers and children, and other traditionally vulnerable groups such as seniors, persons with disabilities, and ethno-cultural groups were most severely affected by the cancellation of these programs. A similar survey in the City of York administered to the users of community services from 29 participating agencies in the months of February and March 1996 revealed that 78 per cent of respondents felt they had been hurt by government cutbacks in general and 34 per cent reported specifically how the cuts in community services had affected them (York Agency Crisis Cutback Committee). "Reduction in social services increase feelings of isolation and alienation.... These feelings are intensified when the individual is an immigrant and speaks little or no English," noted the report.

Support for low-income mothers experiencing a family or work-related crisis is declining. Loss of funding meant that Family Services Association needed to introduce a fee for counselling low-income families. In the past, the agency had been able to provide counselling through a Purchase of Service for Counselling Program. There were many benefits of this program to mothers including refugees arriving from countries at war. The program provided support to troubled parents experiencing stress from adjusting to life in Canada, unemployment, suffering from depression, or lacking adequate parenting skills, before a more intrusive and expensive intervention from a child welfare agency, a mental health centre, or correctional services was required.

The limited amount of funding for domestic violence programs continues to seriously undermine community efforts to support abused women and to offer programs for male batterers voluntarily seeking support to change their behaviour. Communities have been further weakened in providing effective, systematic responses to wife assault by the lack of funding for consistent monitoring and coordination of services. This function is provided by Metro Women Abuse Council (MWAC) made up of a Metro-wide group of agencies. It facilitated a joint approach by ensuring consistency among agencies working for the elimination of male violence against women and children. The agencies cannot, however, coordinate their efforts without financial costs and they find themselves hard pressed to do so from their existing funds (Family Service Association). A particularly effective program that has been cancelled was Children Living in Violent Environments (CLIVE). This was an interagency coordinated program providing group support for mothers and their children to deal with the traumatic impact of wife assault. Funding cuts meant that the participating agencies were unable to maintain their level of support and provide a coordinating function. Attempts to secure funding from private sources including corporations and foundations failed.

What Can Mothers Do?

To bring the dismantling of social programs and services to a halt, mothers need a voice in the restructuring of social programs if they are not to seriously jeopardize the advance made in their status as employees/workers and consumers of social programs/ services. We have argued in this paper, that women as mothers have more to lose than men from the impoverishment of public provisions as long as the responsibility for privately and publicly organized motherwork remains gender specific. Women share a common interest in opposing the gendered division of labour which defines their social role as paid and unpaid providers of motherwork. There are many social policy measures that the Ontario government could introduce to improve the social status and economic security of women as mothers. Two such programs are a Child Benefit, approved for further development at the June 21, 1996, First Minister's Conference, and an Advanced Income Support System proposed by Status of Women Canada, a federal government agency assigned to the Minister responsible for the status of women more than a decade ago and supported by various women's groups. Depending on their goals and design, these two programs could go a long way to protect women with or without a partner to a certain extent from the economic vulnerability of motherhood.

A New National Child Benefit

The February 1997 federal budget committed $600 million in additional spending to the working income supplement component of the present child benefit to be introduced in two stages, July 1, 1997, and July 1, 1998. By basing the calculaton of benefits on a per-child rather than a per-family basis the budget has laid the foundation for the possible consolidation of income support for children into a single national program, jointly managed by both orders of government.

A national child benefit is significant in a number of ways for both parents but more so for mothers because of the prevalent role women play in caring for children as was pointed out earlier. It recognizes the costs of raising children, which childless individuals and families do not have, and that society should share these costs with parents. The National Council of Welfare found that the presence of children had a strong effect on women's full-time employment at an adequate level of earnings. The lack of affordable, high-quality child care spaces often forces women with limited earning capacities to live on social assistance. Their earnings are not enough to cover their costs of employment. A national integrated child tax benefit would remove the fairness differential between social assistance and minimum wage levels. It would be paid to all parents whether they are in the workforce or not, the amount of the benefit depending on their earnings. At the same time, it would remove children and parents who can find employment from "welfare" and its social stigma. It remains, however, a questionable contention whether children in families where the parent(s) are unable to find work have been removed from social assistance.

National child benefits and old age pensions have been built into European income support systems as a system of social exchange through a social contract between generations. Child benefits are designed to provide a stable income floor for families with children in the interest of the healthy development of children. As a social wage outside the market, they are intended to offer parents and their children a degree of protection against the vagaries of market forces. In Canada, income supports for children have been greatly misunderstood. Parenthood is widely considered a private choice and responsibility and the typical stereotype of a welfare recipient a mother and her children "milking the system." Parents not eligible for the child benefit could be given a tax credit of perhaps $600 per child to remove this stigma and ensure the acceptance of public support for children as standard social policy.

Benefit levels would have to be adequate to both prevent and reduce family poverty. It should be based on the actual costs of raising children and should certainly enhance the minimal amount of support currently granted for children on provincial social assistance. At the same time, if the federal government is to take over the financial support of children with parents remaining a provincial responsibility, the provinces have to be prevented from lowering the amounts of benefits for parents. To prevent the provinces from lowering their financial support of social assistance parent families, the different levels of government have committed themselves to develop a re-investment framework for freed-up provincial/territorial welfare funds to be redirected to other social support programs such as pharmacare or dental care targetted at children in low-income families. The new national child benefit will not make families worse off than they are now.

Advanced Income Maintenance System

Existing provincial approaches of setting amounts of child support and the enforcement of their payment from the non-custodial parents have failed to meet the income needs of the majority of mothers who find that upon separation or divorce they have to be the major financial provider as well as caregivers for their children. Support payments, however inadequate, make a significant difference on the material circumstances of mothers and children after family break up. In 1986 the National Council of Welfare found that 58 per cent of divorced and separated mothers receiving child support were living in poverty. Even with modest amounts of support, sole support mothers remained on social assistance for shorter times than mothers who received no financial support from the father of their children. The irregularity and unreliability with which non-custodial fathers fulfill their child support obligations makes it difficult for mothers to budget and contributes to their financial problems. If the expected cheques from the children's father does not arrive in time, a mother may not be able to pay their consumption costs.

Increasing professional and public awareness of the difficult financial circumstances of mothers and children led to interest in the idea of an advanced income maintenance system consisting of three components: a child support guideline for the courts (the federal government recently introduced such guidelines); routine withholding of income; and an assured or guaranteed child support payment. This last component could be considered a form of a guaranteed, minimum income for children of family break up. Where the court orders fall short of the guaranteed minimum, or the non-custodial parent defaults on the support obligations, the advance income maintenance system would make up the difference in the first case, and advance the payment to the family in the latter case. In either case mothers would no longer have to worry that their child support payments would not arrive on time or be less than they expected. The most significant change of an advanced income maintenance system would be that the payments of the custodial benefits would no longer be deducted dollar by dollar from social assistance benefits as it is the case now nor could it be considered taxable income for the custodial parent. It is in fact a reimbursement of some of the costs of raising a child borne by the custodial parent which the non-custodial parent has to share according to Family Law policies in all provinces. In his absence or inability to pay, the costs are covered by the public guarantee of a social minimum for children. All maintenance orders would be enforced by automatic income deductions at source against non-custodial parents with court ordered payment obligations in the same way as contributions for the Canada Pension Plan and Employment Insurance are currently deducted at source.

An advanced income maintenance system has been operated successfully in Sweden for decades. In Canada, governments have hesitated to introduce such a scheme because it shifts the responsibility for dependent children away from individual parents onto the public domain. An advanced income maintenance system would remove the direct obligation of non-custodial parents, in the majority of situations, fathers, to their children. The fathers' compulsory deductions from their paycheques would be a recompensation of government costs (Smart).

Support Services for Motherwork

To halt any further dismantling of the infrastructure of community services, upon whose availability much of the quality of life for mothers and children has come to depend requires concerted action on a number of levels. The impact of the cutback of services will have to be carefully documented. Awareness about the damage the cuts are inflicting can be used as tools for community education and mobilization and encourage the formation of a resistance movement. The fight against the cutbacks could be instrumental in helping isolated mothers to come out and join others to bring about policy changes. Against the reality of the importance of social programs/services for mothers, it is perplexing that many of them seem to have bought into the neo-liberal credo of the inevitability of social spending cuts. In order to free themselves of their status as the second sex, to borrow Simone de Beauvoir's term, mothers have to take steps to politically affirm the legitimacy of social programs and community services. If these are gender sensitive and recognize the requirements of children they truly serve the interests of mothers. Women's recognition that their political interests and concerns as mothers are different from those of men should prompt the development of mothers' resistance against any further social spending cuts. Mothers have to demand that their concerns for the well-being of their families and the developmental opportunities of their children override the political agenda of governments wishing to trade-off public services for tax cuts. It is not a question whether mothers can challenge the neo-liberal political agenda of the government of Ontario. They certainly have the political clout in numbers, but will they have the political will to exercise it? Motherwork has been given a new dimension with the need for political engagement and action.

Brigitte Kitchen teaches social policy at the School of Social Work, Atkinson College, York University. She is also a co-chair of the Child Poverty Action Group, an advocacy group committed to the eradication of child poverty and the economic protection of their parents.

Rosemarie Popham is the director of Social Action at the Family Service Association and national co-ordinator of Campaign 2000, a national coalition of 57 partner organizations committed to ensure that Canada's parliamentarians honour the unanimous House of Commons resolution to end child poverty in Canada by the year 2000.

References

Bernard, Jessie. *The Future of Motherhood.* New York: Penguin Books, 1974.

Campaign 2000. *Report Card 1995. Child Poverty in Canada.* Toronto: Family Services Association, 1995.

Crane, David. "We've Paid Unnecessary Price for Inflation War." *Toronto Star* 20 Aug. 1996: B2.

Family Services Association. "Brief to the Standing Committee on Social Development of the Ontario Legislature." Toronto. June 1996.

Gadd, Jane. "Ministry Closings Cause Chaos." *Globe and Mail* 12 Sept. 1996: A1.

Jackson, Chris. "Measuring and Valuing Households' Unpaid Work." *Canadian Social Trends* 42 (August 1996): 25–29.

Jenish, D'Arcy. "Dropping the Axe in Tory Ontario." *Maclean's* 22 Apr. 1996: 18.

Kitchen, Brigitte, Andrew Mitchell, Peter Clutterbuck, and Marvyn Novick. *Unequal Futures: The Legacy of Child Poverty in Canada.* Toronto: Child Poverty Action Group and Social Planning Council of Metropolitan Toronto, 1991.

National Council of Welfare. *Women and Poverty*. Ottawa: National Council of Welfare, 1990.

Picot, Garnet, and John Myles. "Children in Low-Income Families." *Canadian Social Trends* 42 (August 1996): 15–17.

Smart, Carol. *The Ties That Bind: Law, Marriage, and the Reproduction of Patriarchal Relations*. London: Routledge, 1984.

Social Planning Council of Metropolitan Toronto, Metro Community Services, City of Toronto, Planning and Development. *1995 Community Agency Survey*. Toronto. May 1996.

Statistics and Analysis Unit, Social Assistance Program Branch. *Social Assistance and Pension Rate Table*. Toronto: Ministry of Community and Social Services, 1996.

Toughill, Kerry. "$4,500 Pay Cut Urged for Daycare Workers. *Toronto Star* 6 Sept. 1996: A1, A24.

"Thanksgiving in These Tough Times." Editorial. *Toronto Star* 14 Oct. 1996: A20.

York Agency Crisis Cutback Committee. *Report on Community Well-Being. Bulletin No. 1*. City of York: Sept. 1996.

Some Quotes from Teen Mothers

"Last week I went two days without food (I had some food for the kids) until I got my cheque. They want me to get a job, but I can't afford to send out resumes or take the bus to deliver them as well there is the cost of photocopying."

"The kids lose out in the end. We can survive but the kids see their parents stressed or depressed. They have to deal with not getting new clothes or they get made fun of."

"We keep hearing threats of more things being taken away, like 'snow suit allowance,' or, we'll have to pay $2 prescription fees. That $2 buys two cans of juice, or two loaves of bread, or bus fare."

"If I don't get a job soon, my daycare is taken away but I need daycare in the fall for my continuing education. If I lose my daycare it will be years before I get it again."

"The child tax benefit is supposed to go to the child—for clothing, etc.—but it has to go for food. That's not fair."

"I'm never going to get out of debt" (she owes $200).

These quotes were provided anonymously by teen mothers participating in the YWCA of Metropolitan Toronto's Teen Mothers Program.

Ten Deficit Myths

by Duncan Cameron and Ed Finn

Myth No. 1

The overriding objective of government policy must be to eliminate the deficit. *Seen in the light of the need to create jobs and promote income growth, deficits can have positive and constructive effects. They can reduce unemployment and provide needed income for many Canadians. Reducing the deficit through government spending cuts and fighting inflation through high interest rates tends to weaken the economy and thus increase the deficit and the debt. Further spending cuts only make things worse as they reduce the capacity to repay accumulated deficits.*

Myth No. 2

Governments waste money and go into debt funding programs that are either unnecessary or should be privatized. *Even when a government is forced to borrow and go into debt to maintain essential services, this should be considered as much a wise investment as the borrowing by a company to modernize its plant and equipment. The services and programs the government provides best are the ones that people need the most. The rich can afford exclusive schools, private hospitals, security guards, and other privatized services. For the vast majority of Canadians, the best way to have equal access to these and other essential services is to pay taxes to governments, not prices to corporations.*

Myth No. 3

The federal government shouldn't run high deficits any more than the average Canadian should keep running up his or her credit card spending. *The fact is that taxes exceed government program spending. The government is taking in more tax revenue than it is spending. The real issue is: what spending should governments do? When unemployment is high, and incomes are stagnant or falling, government spending increases for programs and services provide a welcome boost to the economy.*

Myth No. 4

As a result of massive government overspending in the past, we can no longer afford such generous social programs. *A Statistics Canada study found that government spending, far from being the main cause of Canada's accumulated national debt since the mid-1970s, was responsible for only six per cent of it. In February 1995, the Dominion Bond Rating Service released a study which attributed the vast majority of the federal debt—93 per cent of it since 1984—to compounding hight interest rates. It is these sustained high interest rates "which are driving the deficit today."*

Myth No. 5

Without drastic cuts in government spending to reduce the deficit, we risk hitting the debt wall, like New Zealand did, and then we'll have even worse cutbacks inflicted on us. *New Zealand's "debt crisis" was deliberately manufactured to deregulate the financial markets, cut business taxes, and slash public services. The free-market reforms imposed on New Zealanders have been a social and economic disaster for all its people except for a privileged minority. They have been described by the New Zealand Council of Trade Unions as "a huge confidence trick perpetrated on the people of New Zealand (designed) to redistribute income from the middle and lower income groups to those at the top." The same intent is behind the similar deficit reduction hysteria that has been whipped up in Canada.*

Myth No. 6

The deficit causes recessions, high interest rates, and high unemployment. *The truth is the exact opposite: the deficit is caused by recessions, high unemployment, and high interest rates. It was the Bank of Canada's high-interest-rate monetarist policy that caused the recessions in both the early 1990s and 1980s, and the recessions which in turn caused the ensuing government deficits. The deficit is no more the cause of our economic illness than sneezing and coughing are the cause of colds.*

Myth No. 7

The deficit can't be reduced by lowering interest rates. *In fact, there is no other way of stopping the debt and the deficit spiral except through reducing interest rates and increasing economic growth. In 1975 the Bank of Canada held over 20 per cent of all federal debt. Today, it holds merely seven per cent of the outstanding debt. The unwillingness of the Bank to finance government is a principal reason why Canada has such a high deficit. Instead of borrowing at virtually no cost from the Bank of Canada, the government is borrowing at the full market rate of interest from financial institutions which are making whopping profits from these transactions. So long as the Bank of Canada tightens credit every time it believes inflation to be a threat, job insecurity, unemployment, stagnating incomes, and rising debts and deficits are going to remain the ugly symptoms of Canadian economic life.*

Myth No. 8

The deficit can't be reduced by raising taxes because the tax burden in Canada is already too high. *Wealthy individuals and profitable companies are not paying their fair share of taxes. If they were, the federal government's deficit could be completely wiped out. Over 98,000 Canadians with annual incomes over $100,000 take advantage of tax loopholes so that they don't have to pay one cent in income tax. The proportion of federal tax revenue collected from corporations dropped by nearly 200 per cent between 1961 and 1994—from 20 per cent to just 7.2 per cent. There is plenty of room for our federal government to reduce its deficit by raising taxes on those who are now grossly undertaxed.*

Myth No. 9

Canada's foreign debt limits our options and puts us at the mercy of foreign money lenders. *While it is true that an average of 26 per cent of the federal debt has been held by foreigners, virtually none of it is in foreign currency. Foreign holdings of Canadian debt are in Canadian dollars. Never before have world financial institutions showed such a keen desire to hold securities denominated in Canadian dollars. The principle reason for so much foreign purchases of Canadian debt has been high Canadian interest rates. Foreign purchases of Canadian debt had the effect of driving up the value of the Canadian dollar, giving foreigners a dividend in the form of more Canadian dollars for their purchases. But the higher Canadian dollar and the high interest rates did enormous damage to the Canadian economy. The Bank of Canada was enriching foreigners by impoverishing most Canadians.*

Myth No. 10

The deficit can only be reduced by cutting government spending, not by creating more jobs, and bringing down unemployment. *A high rate of unemployment deprives all Canadian governments of more than $47 billion a year in foregone taxes and higher social assistance spending. The Bank of Canda, having decided that full employment would be inflationary and thus reduce the value of bondholders' wealth, has chosen to keep unemployment at or near a double-digit level. Some countries have succeeded in keeping their unemployment rates at or below five per cent—a level Canada has not seen for more than 20 years. Pro-jobs nations did not hesitate to intervene in monetary policy, using government leverage to resist market forces and keep interest rates low. They invested in job training and retraining, employee mobility, public works projects, and regional development. In short, they put the interests of the working people ahead of the interests of the wealthy and the powerful. What is fraudulent about the current calls for government spending cuts is that they will eventually make the deficit worse, not better, and increase the debt, not lower it. A government can choose policies that keep both unemployment and deficits low, or it can choose policies that keep unemployment and deficits high. For all but a privileged minority of citizens, Canadian governments have made the wrong choice.*

Excerpted from 10 Deficit Myths: The Truth About Government Debts and Why They Don't Justify Cutbacks *(Ottawa: CCPA, 1996). Reprinted with permission.* To obtain a copy contact the Canadian Centre for Policy Alternatives (CCPA), 251 Laurier Avenue West, Ste. 804, Ottawa, ON K1P 5J6. Tel: (613) 563-1341. Fax: (613) 233-1458.

Duncan Cameron is president of the CCPA and editor of the Canadian Forum Magazine. *He formerly served as a finance officer with the federal Department of Finance. Ed Finn is a tesearch fellow at the CCPA and editor of the CCPA* Monitor. *He was* The Toronto Star's *labour columnist for 14 years and also served a three-year term on the board of directors of the Bank of Canada.*

The Declining Commitment to Equity in Education

by Patricia McAdie

The language of education reform is very interesting these days. We are hearing about "equity," "choice," and indeed "reform" in ways that do not really address the issues of real equity, real choice, or positive reform. The corporate world has taken the language and reworked it to mask the real agenda. I believe that the real agenda will weaken equity, limit choice, and provide positive education reform only for the elite.

The road to equity has been a long one, with many twists and turns along the way. In Canada, the depression of the 1930s followed by the Second World War had a very profound impact on the psyche of the whole nation. The social safety net began to be woven, based on principles of social equality, full employment, national standards, and democratic participation. While not perfect, the programs and principles of this time went a long way to ensuring an equitable base. In education, this generally meant a more inclusive approach, moving from an equity of opportunity approach to equality of results to our current thinking on equity.

Almost as soon as the basic safety net had been woven, its slow dismantling began. I don't want to dwell too much on the historical aspects of our struggles for equity. There are many sources for a more complete analysis (see for example Barlow and Campbell). What I do want to focus on are the current trends in education reform and how they impact on equity. While I will concentrate mostly on the effects on students, I also will note some of the effects on women and women teachers. How women are valued in our society has a very real impact on girls and young women. This effect should not be ignored.

The funding of education, governance issues, and accountability are three areas that have very serious implications for our pursuit of equity. Reforms in all of these areas are going in the direction of providing a less equitable education for our children.

There are two major justifications offered for the need to pursue the various education reforms. The first is that we can no longer afford to have the kind of programs that we once could. The other is that "the system is broken" and is in serious need of an overhaul. These are not always distinct reasons. Indeed, in some provinces they have been combined in unique ways. In Ontario, for example, it has been suggested that the system is broken and the way to fix it is to make further cuts in funding. While most rational, thinking people question the logic of such a statement, those pursuing this approach, build up "evidence" along the way for their attack on teachers and the public education system in general.

Let's look at the issue of funding in more detail. Per pupil spending for elementary and secondary education has fallen in every jurisdiction in Canada over the last few years (CTF). The usual justification for such cuts, sometimes very dramatic cuts, has been that the debts and deficits of our provincial and federal governments are out of control. It is often stated that we simply can no longer afford to fund our social programs, including education, to the same level as in the past.

Public opinion polls have indicated that there is still much support for funding education; most people polled do not favour funding cuts to education to pay down the debt. Nevertheless, the Ontario government cited a study by "experts" from the Ontario Institute for Studies in Education (OISE) (Lawton *et al.*) which stated that per pupil spending in Ontario was much higher than anywhere else in Canada, and that teachers' salaries are largely to blame. The study blatantly ignored some of the reasons for higher education spending in Ontario. For example, Ontario had policies for mandatory junior kindergarten (JK), smaller class sizes in Grades 1 and 2, and a concerted effort to integrate special education students into the regular education system. Recently, in Ontario, we have seen the end to mandatory JK, and funding cuts so deep that resultant program cuts are staggering:

•25 public boards have eliminated their JK program; another 20 have gone to providing JK for full days every other day. Sixty per cent of our public school boards have made decisions about JK to accommodate budget restraint rather than based on pedagogical considerations.

•68 per cent of our boards have made cuts to their special education programs.

•27 per cent have made cuts to their music programs.

•41 per cent have made cuts to the library programs.

What does this mean for our pursuit of equity? It should be very clear that funding cuts are not neutral. In Jim Laxer's recent book, *In Search of a New Left,* he states:

Cost cutting, of course, is no socially neutral phenomenon. It establishes a very clear hierarchy of winners and losers. It is based on a precise notion about what is essential and what is secondary in contemporary society. (22)

The program cuts outlined have a very different impact on girls and less privileged children. Early education programs are very important for ensuring an equitable education for everyone, securing the ability of children from all backgrounds to benefit from early intervention. They ensure that no one slips through the cracks. The loss of programs such as music, art, and library will be felt more by children in poor families. I can still provide music classes for my son, but not everyone in his class will have this benefit. And we have all seen how the distribution of resources is skewed towards boys when money and programs are tight. I was quite struck by a quote from one of the *A Cappella* papers: "They took gymnastics away from school but left football in" (Edwards18). What is this saying to our young women about their importance in society?

Funding cuts very directly affect how we can pursue improvements to the education system. How long will relatively progressive boards be able to hold on to positions that promote student equality and affirmative action? How will we be able to update sexist curricular materials and biased library holdings if there is no money? How will we be able to ensure that girls receive their share of a teachers' attention if class sizes are continually being increased? I am hearing of class sizes in Ontario in the mid-30s almost as a matter of course. Research clearly shows that boys generally receive more than their fair share of a teacher's time (Sadker and Sadker). If the teacher must spread this time over more students, the task of ensuring "equal time" and appropriate progress becomes much more difficult. There has also been a cut in the amount of money and time being devoted to professional development for teachers. This will limit a teacher's ability to improve her skills in ensuring equity for her students.

I would like to turn next to governance issues. Here, the corollary of the argument that the debt is out of control is that government itself is out of control. As with spending cuts, the only way to "fix" this out-of-control government is to reduce it. In Ontario, the government is working to lower the number of seats in the provincial parliament. We are also seeing a move to amalgamate regional governance systems, as well as the passing of the bill to amalgamate the local municipalities of Toronto, Scarborough, North York, East York, the City of York, and Etobicoke into one big "megacity"—Toronto.

School board amalgamations and indeed elimination of school boards has been proposed as a cost-cutting measure. Some of the effects of a reduction in the number of school boards are subtle, but they are real.

Overall, the reduction and/or amalgamation of school boards takes away or reduces local control. As I mentioned earlier, 25 of our 76 public school boards eliminated junior kindergarten programs this year. If there were fewer school boards, a one-third reduction in program provision would affect more students. It is interesting to note that it is some of the larger school boards that have cancelled JK. One has to wonder if the larger boards feel more distant from the communities that they serve.

A reduction in local governments also reduces the involvement of women; it is at this level that women are most likely to become involved in politics, more easily being able to combine work and family responsibilities with a political life.

Furthermore, a reduction in local government also reduces democracy. Any limit on democracy will limit equity.

Another area where the governance of education is being changed for the worse is with charter schools and other "schools of choice." The more I learn about charter schools, the more nervous I become. The language used is very seductive. We hear how charter schools will give parents more "choice" and how they improve "equity." Even the word "charter" has had in our recent history a positive connotation when the Charter of Rights and Freedoms was enacted, guaranteeing equality rights for women.

But what will charter schools really mean? The notion that charter schools can provide more equity is based on the false assumption that choice will lead to equity. Equity, however, is much more complex than simply a matter of choice. Indeed, there is strong evidence that such choice leads to increased social segregation. Typically, charter schools end up with a very homogeneous school population. Such a lack of diversity works to decrease equity, not increase it. Also, it has been found that more privileged groups are more active in choosing "desired" schools. If there are a limited number of spots in a school, how is it determined who will get to fill these spots? Even if admissions are based on the seemingly neutral policy of first come-first served, who has the ability to ensure that they are the first in line? Not single mothers or those who cannot afford to take a day off work. When a charter school becomes popular, the school is able to choose its students, rather than the students being able to choose the school.

Finally, I want to briefly look at the area of accountability. This is a bit tricky, because no one wants to say that they aren't accountable. But what accountability usually translates into is testing, and more specifically, standardized testing. A Canadian Teachers' Federation (CTF) paper in progress by Bernie Froese-Germain outlines the research on this issue. Quoting two Amercan researchers, "Standardized tests are constructed in ways that often guarantee biased results against minorites, females, and low-income students" (Medina and Neill 8).

Some of the major flaws pointed out by Froese-Germain are: many types of student ability are not captured by a standardized test; tests may be standardized but students are not; standardized tests designed for large numbers of students are of necessity very general in nature; standardized tests typically measure lower-order recall of facts and skills and penalize higher-order thinking; and, test performance is shaped by individual characteristics not related to content knowledge.

It should be very clear that using such biased testing is very damaging to girls and young women. Froese-Germain states:

> According to American research, despite girls receiving higher grades in high school and college, boys were twice as likely as girls to have received a college scholarship based on test results on standardized high school tests. (8)

With increasing costs of post-secondary education, such discrimination may mean the difference between a young woman's ability to attend university or not.

Standardized tests are easy and quick. They produce simple results. But they will hurt our ability to work towards equity. If the results are biased, any use we make of them will produce biased results.

Without a change in attitude, perhaps a change in heart, in government at all levels, of all political stripes, I fear our pursuit of equity has been seriously stalled.

What can we do about it? Many of us have become very good at critiquing various government initiatives. We need to be constantly exposing the agenda for what it is. Just as we have almost become used to challenging sexist and racist remarks when we come across them, I think we need to stop apologizing for our commitment to an equitable education system. Yes, it costs money, but our children are worth it. We keep hearing that we must make these funding cuts now in order to secure their future—"our children are our future"—but their future depends on how we treat them right now.

I think we need to reveal the myths and reality whenever and however possible. One of the myths that needs to be exposed is that the education system is "broken." Maude Barlow and Heather-jane Robertson's book, *Class Warfare,* exposes many of those myths. While we all know that there is room for improvement, particularly when it comes to issues of equity, there is much evidence that the education system has never been better. For example, one of our public school boards, Durham, recently won a prestigious international award for excellence in education. Not to acknowledge this award publicly is, I think, shameful. Let's be proud of our accomplishments on the individual level and on the collective level.

Also, we should not be afraid to stand up for what we believe in. Actions such as the roving days of protest in Ontario are important. They keep the issues in the public eye. And they build coalitions. While coalitions can get bogged down in meetings, they ensure that we are not working in isolated groups, pitting one group's interests against another's.

Until such time as the political pendulum swings back towards a more egalitarian society, and such time as economic prosperity is allowed to be shared by all citizens, it is incumbent upon all of us as teachers and parents, as activists for children's and women's rights, to ensure that equity stays on the agenda. We can and must find ways of promoting these goals. We need to be ever vigilant in every aspect of our lives if we are to pay anything more than lip-service to the pursuit of equity for girls and women, for visible minorities, for Aboriginal people, for those with disabilities, for everyone seeking equity.

"The problem is not one of technique, but of commitment; education is not short of advice, but of common purpose" (Barlow and Robertson 236). We must work to make equity for all our common purpose.

Excerpted from a presentation made to the CTF Eastern Regional Symposium on Women and Education held in Fredericton, New Brunswick in November 1996.

Patricia McAdie is a researcher with the Federation of Women Teachers' Associations of Ontario. She is working very diligently to raise her son to be a sensitive, caring person, one who will help to advance the pursuit of equity for all.

References

Barlow, Maude, and Bruce Campbell. *Straight Through the Heart.* Toronto: Harper-Collins, 1995.

Barlow, Maude, and Heather-jane Robertson. *Class Warfare: The Assault on Canada's Schools.* Toronto: Key Porter Books, 1994.

Canadian Teachers' Federation (CTF). "Less Adequate and Equitable Education Funding." CTF National Issues Technical Paper No. 2. Ottawa, 1996.

Edwards, Peggy. "Self-Esteem and Adolescent Women." *The A Cappella Papers.* Ottawa: CTF, 1993.

Froese-Germain, Bernie. "Standardized Testing and Educational Inequity." Ottawa: CTF National Issues Technical Paper, in progress.

Lawton, Stephen, Mark Ryall, and Teresa Menzies. "A Study on Costs." Toronto: Ontario Ministry of Education and Training, August 1996.

Laxer, Jim. *In Search of a New Left.* Toronto: Viking, 1996.

Medina, Noe, and D. Monty Neill. *Fallout from the Testing Explosion: How 100 Million Standardized Exams Undermine Equity and Excellence in America's Public Schools* (Third Edition-Revised). Cambridge, MA: National Centre for Fair and Open Testing (Fair Test), March 1990.

Sadker, Mrya, and David Sadker. *Failing at Fairness: How Our Schools Cheat Girls.* New York: Touchstone, 1994.

Canadian Health Care
A System in Peril

by Janet Maher and Monica Riutort

Is universal medicare in danger in Canada, as suggested by many of our politicians and news media? Although the history books show an initial resistance to the emergence of publicly funded health care in Canada, in a few years it has become our most treasured social program. However, the short answer is that health care in Canada has really been at risk ever since the passage of the first enabling legislation that marked the beginning of Medicare in Canada in the late 1950s and early 1960s.

The original funding formula was relatively open-ended, consisting essentially in a commitment from the federal level of government to cost-share on a 50–50 basis for services designated as medically necessary. Later, in an effort to add some predictability to budgeting, the federal government was able to limit its contribution by revising the funding formula. That formula was based on previous spending patterns and to a degree on the ability of each province to pay. In 1996, under continuing pressure to limit federal deficits, the formula was again amended to a more explicitly block-funding approach. In the form of the Canada Health and Social Transfer, the federal government has now allocated a fixed amount to be transferred each year.

The net effect of these funding changes has been smaller cash transfers to provinces, regardless of regional ability to pay. At the same time, the richer provinces have been willing cheerleaders on the ideological front. Citing health care as a provincial responsibility under the division of powers in the Canadian federal state, and in a climate of restraint, Alberta and Ontario in particular are keen to maintain maximum flexibility on expenditures, and so have been both complicit in the federal spending reductions and in resisting calls for national standards which might limit their future ability to cut, privatize, or otherwise limit services financed by the public purse, regardless of the impact on their less prosperous counterparts predominantly in Atlantic Canada.

An added problem is that in spite of very considerable investment in health care, the impetus to evaluate and systematize information and manage delivery either cost effectively or with any direct accountability to the public has not been great. While almost a third of every health dollar goes to institutions, in most provinces the majority of hospitals are privately-constituted not-for-profit corporations, most of which have associated private foundations. Increasingly in recent years the associated foundations have been used to receive private funds to support projects which are essentially beyond public scrutiny. Moreover, the structure of governance in many hospitals perpetuates a dual and parallel structure of accountability in which physicians report to the medical director, and the president of a hospital, usually a specialist in business or health administration, is responsible for all other departments, functions, and services. The result is that services are fragmented beyond belief.

Medicare and its Original Promise

Medicare, the sacred trust of Canadians, is in fact a very limited program, and has been eroded significantly over the past decade—so much so that it is likely to look very different after the current rounds of deficit reduction and global restructuring. The original vision of Medicare had two components. The first aimed at the elimination of barriers to access, and the second involved the implementation of a comprehensive public and preventive health care strategy.

Access was to be achieved through a public insurance scheme—for all services considered medically necessary. It was anticipated that the process of eliminating barriers would be gradual, and would eventually extend from essentially acute care services (those given by physicians, primarily in hospitals) to services such as dental work, eye care, and nutritional counselling—first for children, seniors, and other vulnerable groups, then for the rest of the population as resources allowed.

The past three decades have witnessed some expansion in the range of services covered for some or all of the population in one or more provinces. These include ambulance services, enhanced dental services for school children, drug benefits for seniors, welfare recipients, and other vulnerable groups. As well, in recent years, there has been a determined effort by many Canadian provincial governments, without a great deal of success, to reduce the number of services as part of a cost-containment strategy.

The second component involved the implementation of a comprehensive public and preventive health care strategy. This would include programs like seat belts and child restraint seats in cars, effective anti-smoking, anti-drug, and anti-alcohol campaigns, prenatal nutrition and other health maintenance programs, clean air and water, and better occupational health and safety. All these population-based programs have been shown to have a greater impact on improving the health status of Canadians and the citizens of other countries of the world than intervention at any level.

In the area of preventive health care, however, progress has been glacial. While some small preventive and public health measures have been implemented in recent years (such as non-smoking areas in public places, and helmet laws for motorcyclists) they are generally quite limited, not very seriously enforced, and have rarely been accompanied by the kind of public education which might realistically lead to long-term changes in behaviour. Although each provincial and territorial health budget reserves some funds for public and/or preventive initiatives, that amount is generally less than two to three per cent of total public spending on health. In other words what money we do spend on health goes to illness care, not health care.

The Canada Health Act of 1984

In the climate of economic growth and liberal social and political ideology of the 1960s and 1970s, governments were relatively content to spend money on health infrastructure (modern hospitals, research facilities, labs, and clinics) and health services. Until the late 1970s, it is fair to say that few Canadians were concerned who had responsibility for funding health care or other social programs. Even Established Programs Financing, a revision of the original federal-provincial cost-sharing mechanism, provided relatively open-ended funding to provinces. It was the Canada Health Act, introduced after several years of funding erosion at the federal level, which attempted to ensure accountability for funds designated for health care. Passed in 1984, the Canada Health Act allowed the federal government to reduce transfer payments to any province that increased barriers to access in a number of specified areas—generally acute care in hospitals.

The Canada Health Act is considered in many ways the bible on Medicare in Canada, because it enshrines at least a measure of accountability in the form of five principles for federal funding:

- •Universality: Health care must be available to all residents of Canada on uniform terms and conditions;
- •Accessibility: Health care must be reasonably available to all residents of Canada close to where they live and work and without direct or indirect charges or other impediments;
- •Comprehensiveness: Every province and territory insures a full range of services for all residents as required;
- •Portability: Coverage of health care services extends across Canada;
- •Public Administration: Our health care system is administered and operated on a non-profit basis.

Although the Act was not perfect, it did lead fairly quickly to the elimination of balance billing or extra billing by physicians—a major issue at the time—and has been the basis for limiting the spread of a parallel private sector. Seniors and social benefits recipients got greater access to drug benefit programs for a period, and home care and long-term care services were extended making community care more reliable and cost-effective, especially in urban areas.

However, it did little to address the broader social determinants of health. In fact, health and health care maintained pride of place at the top of the list of publicly funded social programs in many respects at the expense of other targeted and/or means-tested programs. Social housing, social assistance and child care are and continue to be used most heavily by those with lower incomes, insecure work, new immigrants, and those with disabilities, and it is those programs whose budgets suffered most in the budget-cutting exercises of the last decade.

Indeed, a working poor adult with a bad toothache could expect little relief until an abscess or major dental crisis landed her in hospital. Incentives to corporations to be more respectful of the environment or occupational health and safety remained low. For many Canadians, especially Aboriginal people, people of colour, the poor and immigrants, the system has been less than universal and accessible. And a further decade of restraint budgets at the federal level have resulted in a chipping away at social programs which are even less able to meet the needs of Canadians already marginalized by the system, to say nothing of ensuring equity of access to all Canadians as we look forward to the year 2000.

Demographic and Technological Change

The erosion connected with fiscal restraint coincides with and is in some ways confounded by the aging of postwar baby boomers and shifts in our orientation to service delivery.

By the year 2000, nearly a quarter of our population will be over the age of 60. While the majority can anticipate several good years after that age, advances in technology have also raised our expectations of good health in our later years. However, the drug therapies and dialysis which prolong the lives and productivity of arthritics, cardiac and renal patients well beyond what was imagined even a generation earlier are costly. Any "cost-cutting" alternatives which exclude such therapies from public funding will have the effect of further limiting accessibility to those who are poorer, older, sicker, or otherwise marginalized.

Another confounding trend in health care which has gained currency in Canada has been a significant reduction in acute hospital bed days. In part, this is the result of technological changes like laser-assisted surgery and advances in other specialties which reduce the acute period of an illness, as well as an ideological resistance to long-term institutionalization and an increase in social support for "community care." The other part, cost containment, has resulted since about 1990 in every Canadian province undertaking a relatively painful restructuring exercise with the objective of reducing the institutional infrastructure, and with it limiting the liability of public funding agencies for "surplus" capacity.

While the rhetoric has tended to take the form of restructuring to facilitate better community supports, however, the situation remains that most cases of accident, illness, or chronic disease become the private burden of the family involved. Indeed, the new-found interest of many provinces in community-based care options for seniors, people with disabilities, and chronic psychiatric patients is ironic. Given the cost containment objectives of health administrators, many current and potential patients and their traditional caregivers, namely mothers, daughters, and sisters, have reason for distrust. As acute and chronic care institutions reduce the number of beds or close down altogether, more and more of the burden will fall on women.

Furthermore, the declining role of the federal government in financing, regulating and supporting innovative programs burdens poor and other marginal Canadians and makes it easier for middle and higher income earners to lose interest in how universal health care is. Those with secure finances will be less and less likely to imagine themselves every being recipients of government financed health care.

This is particularly disturbing insofar as the trend of social legislation in Canada over the past decade or so has been to replace universal programs by "targeted" benefits, and/ or to limit eligibility. For example, what was once reasonably adequate Unemployment Insurance coverage has been significantly reduced and will be unavailable to increasing numbers of contract workers. Not only has the federal government curbed its funding for unemployment insurance, its commitment to training now comes from unemployment insurance funds requiring trainees to be eligible for or in receipt of unemployment benefits, with the result that those in marginal employment will find it virtually impossible to access job training.

Two other disturbing developments deserve notice. The first is an expansion by almost 50 per cent over the past ten years in the use of private health care insurance. However, even in the decade of AIDS and other chronic conditions where interventions are especially costly, there have been few incentives or sanctions for private insurers who disqualify potential users on the basis of certain risk behaviours. At the same time, much of the middle class, or at least those still in relatively secure employment, are turning to private insurance as a supplement or enhancement to deteriorating services.

While the cost of private insurance guarantees it will not be available to those on lower or more precarious incomes, it is sufficient to lead more and more middle-class families to feel health care as a financial burden, even though the acquisition of private insurance is voluntary. It has also been the subject of considerable debate in professional associations such as the Canadian Medical Association who are now entering their third year of lobbying for the implementation of a parallel private health care delivery system, nominally to reduce pressure on the public delivery system.

The second distressing change has been the opening and expansion of a range of commercial services outside the publicly insured system. Some others are licensed and regulated and, to the extent they provide effective and quality care options, there is an argument for including them in the basket of publicly-funded medically necessary services. Others include a growing number of unregulated and largely unevaluated counselling and similar therapies relating to such issues as eating behaviours, sexuality, violence, and incest survival. While regulation of such services is nominally covered in consumer and commercial legislation, enforcement relies for the most part on an individual complaint system which is long, complex, and reactive.

Trade Deregulation and Other International Agreements

The Canada-U.S. Free Trade Agreement, implemented following the November 1988 federal election, was significantly more comprehensive than any previous trade arrangement. Although Medicare was formally exempt, Chapter 14 on Commercial Services outlined a number of exceptions to the exemption. These exceptions included a broad range of hospital and health care management services such as general, rehabilitation, and extended care hospitals, nursing homes, drug and alcohol treatment facilities, homes for the physically and mentally disabled, and children in need of care and protection, ambulance services, home care, public health clinics, medical and radiology labs, and blood banks.

The basic provision of the 1989 agreement allows U.S. firms the same access to the commercialized or privatized market as Canadian firms. While there has not been a great increase in commercialization since the agreement, the seeds have been sown for the takeover of hospital administration, and services like laundry, housekeeping, and dietary and security services by large U.S.-based multinationals have been easy targets.

As Colleen Fuller of the British Columbia Health Sciences Association noted in her 1993 presentation to the federal hearings on the North American Free Trade Agreement (NAFTA), "Private laboratories, walk-in medical clinics, and various kinds of treatment facilities have sprung like weeds in major cities across the country." Moreover, she added, since the Free Trade Agreement came into effect, pharmaceutical and medical devices industries have grown enormously. Encouraged by the first federal extension of drug patents and interest-free government loans and grants, a number of drug companies have put big money into new plant capacity in Canada.

Fuller went on in her testimony to suggest that the only reason U.S. corporations have not moved in to the Canadian health system on a massive scale is that the Canadian Health Act has acted as an effective barrier. However, as federal funding declines, the incentive to uphold the principles of Medicare will disappear. Moreover, NAFTA sets up a process whereby, by the end of 1998, all exclusions in the areas of community, social, and professional services, as well as health and education will be reviewed. Those determined to constitute indirect subsidies to Canadian traders will be subject to elimination. Finally, the newest wrinkle in international trade agreements, the proposed Multilateral Agreement on Investment is expected to further limit the power of the Organizaiton for Economic Cooperation and Development (OECD) members involved in its negotiation.

It is also worrisome to note that the NAFTA deadline corresponds to a time when provinces will be struggling to cope with the final withdrawal of federal funds. The most likely result will be the further stripping of provincial health plans. The need for any review at all may well be pre-empted by the provinces themselves.

And if the Bill C-22 extension of drug patents from four to ten years were not enough to boost drug manufacturers' profits, the current Bill C-91, which further extends patents for up to 20 years should have brand name manufacturers laughing all the way to the bank. What the patent laws really do is give the brand name producer a full 20 years before the "recipe" for the drug becomes public property and can be used by a generic manufacturer even if it is only marginally different from another. It is hard to see how this will not mean astronomical drug prices—and the end of drug benefit plans delivered by most provinces.

Delivery and Management Issues

The Canadian governmental structure is complicated by a constitutional arrangement which locates responsibility for health care delivery at the provincial level whereas revenue generation has been a federal responsibility. Beyond this, the postwar history of the broadly based public funding of health care in Canada has meant that, by comparison with other countries with multiple payers, or multiple systems as the norm, relatively little attention has been paid until recently either to administration or to data collection that would facilitate more cost-effective use of public (or private) funds. Indeed, the recent debate on medically necessary services has gained an edge in the country at least in part because none of the legislation to date has produced a definition that would form the basis for funding decisions.

The typical provincial health budget has four main components: physician services, hospital services, drugs, and community and other services. The case of Ontario, which accounts for nearly 40 per cent of the country's population, is typical. Physician services take up approximately 25 per cent of the total allocation. Hospital services, which include some drugs, labs, and physician services are currently declining as a share of the total, but still accounted for some 40 per cent of the total in 1996. Drugs provided through the drug benefit program amount to about ten per cent, leaving about 25 per cent for everything else—administration, long-term care, and the broad category of community programs.

Moreover, as noted above, the current health care delivery system can hardly be said to constitute a system, since the funding base continues to support two major funding and delivery streams. The great majority of physicians, key players in the delivery system, work on essentially a piecework basis, are paid a fee for each service they provide, and in a hospital setting, report to a medical director. In contrast, most of the rest of the delivery system is funded on a block basis and is expected to budget accordingly. Non-medical staff take direction from physicians on matters of patient care, but are for the most part paid on a salary basis, with accountability through a separate reporting structure.

While a number of relatively comprehensive evaluation studies of health care delivery are underway, it is still early to determine whether any of the delivery reforms which have been undertaken by provinces have even begun to identify problems adequately, let alone solve them. In Ontario, a number of measures seem to be operating at cross-purposes. As part of its Bill 26 initiative, the provincial government appointed what was intended to be an arm's length Health Services Restructuring Commission with a mandate to implement the reorganization of health care delivery. However, without either a clear policy consensus in major areas, for example, women's health or access to services in rural or remote areas or by particular ethnic or linguistic communities, or a plan for the much-vaunted community support services which would replace much of the institutional infrastructure, the work of the Commission has become an exercise in cost-cutting, pure and simple, and has become intensely politicized.

An example of this has been the recent doctors' deal. After protracted negotiations with the Ontario Medical Association, the government has signed a three-year deal with doctors in which it gradually eliminates spending caps, and commits to bilateral consultation with them on any further reform, with the current fee-for-service funding pool guaranteed for the life of the deal. Aside from the fact that the financial arrangement is likely to add over a billion dollars to an already sizable bill for physician services, that settlement will eat substantially into the flexibility that would have made some improvements in community support services possible. Moreover, agreeing not to move forward on such other major initiatives as primary care reform without consulting with physicians is not only profoundly anti-democratic. It seems almost certain to take any further reform off the table until the agreement expires in 2000.

Can We Save Medicare?

Medicare, the most sacred of the sacred trusts of social programs, has been eroded so that it is now difficult to restore as a national program. It has become even more challenging to move to the second phase of public and preventive strategies that hold so much promise for reducing our overall costs of maintaining a healthy population.

There is probably no question that women, as the lower income earners and those still socially responsible for the care of children and elders have benefited from government policy initiatives like pay equity and affirmative action, and from transfer payments which make possible the expenditures on social programs. And so, it is no surprise that women have the largest stake in supporting Medicare and the allied range of social programs.

Although the situation looks bleak we still have superior health care provision for virtually the whole Canadian population while spending less than ten per cent of our Gross Domestic Product (GDP). According to the General Accounting Office of the United States, it takes 14 per cent of U.S. GDP to provide very uneven levels of service to the average U.S. citizen, and virtually none at all to some 30 million Americans.

The reform of health care in Canada is long past due. But what we should be defending is not simply a system of illness care against "deficit fighters" and commercial interests. Community-based care need not be undertaken as a cost-containment measure but as a legitimate option with adequate support systems and professional, well-paid staff in safe and comfortable working conditions. Investment in preventive and public health measures is every bit as important to the health status of Canadians as investment in new drugs and high technology medical devices.

Janet Maher is the administrator of the Medical Reform Group in Toronto, Canada, and Monica Riutort is director of Latin American Programs at Women's College Hospital in Toronto, Canada. They expect to be collaborating over the next year to pull together some international comparative material on the impacts on women of health reform and the privatization of health services.

References

Charles, Cathy, and Robin Badgley. "National Health Insurance: Evolution And Unresolved Policy Issues." Health Care Reform: International Perspectives. Eds. F. D. Powell and A. F. Wesson. Ottawa: Sage Publications, 1997.

Maher, Janet. "Health Care in Crisis." *Healthsharing* 14.2 (Summer/Fall 1993): 10–13, 36.

Report on the Health of Canadians, Prepared by the Federal, Provincial and Territorial Advisory Committee on Population Health for the Meeting of Ministers of Health. Toronto, September 10–11, 1996.

Useful Web Sites

Health Insurance — Medicare Canada
An explanation of federal contributions and payments:
http://hwcweb.hwc.ca/medicare/fedpay.htm

National Forum on Health
Final report and most of the commissioned documents:
http://wwwnfh.hc-sc.gc.ca

User Guide to the Ministry of Health of Ontario
http://www.gov.on.ca/health

Trashing Environmental Protection
Ontario's Four-Part Strategy

by Kathleen Cooper

Public health, the economy, and our children's future depend on a clean environment. In numerous polls a huge majority of citizens say they support strong environmental laws. For example, in June of 1996, Environics found that an overwhelming majority of Canadians feel that, despite government cutbacks and debts, environmental laws should be made stricter. Yet, Ontario's government is undermining the entire environmental protection regime. A four-part strategy is apparent and includes: dismantling environmental laws; weakening the role of government; shutting out the public; and privatizing natural resources.

This strategy is occurring at a time when the very concept of "the public interest" is under attack by neo-conservative voices and the corporate world. One of the important aspects of this attack is de-regulation, or elimination of public interest laws, including environmental protection. De-regulation is an international trend, as evident in the trade agreements of recent years, such as the North American Free Trade Agreement, and the General Agreement on Tariffs and Trade.

Weaker Laws

In Ontario, environmental de-regulation is in full swing. In less than two years, the government has implemented major rollbacks in environmental rules and citizens' rights in 13 laws: Aggregate Resources Act; Conservation Authorities Act; Environmental Assessment Act; Environmental Protection Act; Freedom of Information and Protection of Privacy Act; Game and Fish Act; Intervenor Funding Project Act; Lakes and Rivers Improvement Act; Municipal Act; Mining Act; Ontario Water Resources Act; Planning Act; and Public Lands Act.

In general, the many changes to these statutes have served to greatly reduce the government's role in monitoring pollution or resource use; issuing permits for polluting activities or resource extraction activities; enforcing environmental laws; and ensuring democratic access to decision-making.

The names of these laws may not immediately suggest how the environment will be affected by legal rollbacks. However, taken together with numerous additional changes to regulations and policies, every aspect of environmental protection is at risk. Controls have been weakened on air pollution, water pollution, pesticides, waste disposal and recycling, urban sprawl, energy use and climate change, pit and quarry operations, natural heritage and biodiversity protection, mining, and forestry.

For example, with weaker rules, Ontario will experience more air and water pollution including increased releases of toxic chemicals. Pulp mills will no longer be required to phase out highly toxic organochlorines. A decision to eliminate the Ontario Waste Management Corporation was not accompanied by any new powers to regulate the reduction, reuse, and recycling of hazardous wastes. Mining companies will no longer have to obtain government approval for mine closure plans, a move that will worsen the already serious problem of toxic run-off from abandoned mine sites. The lifting of the ban on municipal waste incinerators opens the door to new incinerators that generate toxic air emissions and large amounts of toxic residual ash that must be landfilled. Proposals to weaken landfill standards and changes to the environmental assessment planning process may well contribute to a legacy of toxic groundwater from landfills for decades into the future. Groundwater and surface water are further threatened by the loss of sound land use planning tools to protect wetlands, rivers and streams, and groundwater recharge areas from inappropriate development.

Air pollution will increase with the automobile dependence that inevitably accompanies more urban sprawl. Citizens can expect to see more roads, more traffic, and more traffic accidents (and continued burgeoning social costs associated with those accidents). We will face more severe smog events and a continuation of the alarming trend of increased hospital admissions for respiratory problems during smog events, especially among children. With more urban sprawl, public transit continues to be too costly and inefficient. Efforts to counteract climate change are undermined by automobile-dependent urban sprawl and the removal of energy efficiency requirements from the Building Code.

Natural heritage protection has been seriously undermined in built-up areas and in southern rural areas. It has been similarly undermined across the vast northern reaches of the province through deregulation of forestry, mining, and wildlife management.

Everyone will be at greater risk of exposure to pesticide residues because testing for these residues has been eliminated.

Voluntarism and Self-Regulation

A common thread running through the many changes to Ontario's environmental laws is the replacement of legal controls with "voluntarism" and "self-regulation." Under the guise of streamlining, government involvement in monitoring, issuing permits, and enforcing violations is being removed in many significant areas. It is noteworthy that, in cases where government oversight of polluting or potentially polluting activities has been eliminated, laws have also been changed to prevent citizens from suing the government for taking inadequate regulatory action.

Akin to the fox in charge of the chicken coop, the move to replace laws with voluntary programs raises serious concerns for the public. There are specific problems with various voluntary approaches. Three concerns are common to all of these approaches and arise from erosion of the rule of law. First, there is a lack of fair and consistent decision-making. Voluntary programs applying only to some sectors or to some businesses within a sector lack the equal and consistent standards characteristic of laws. Larger businesses with more resources (funds, lawyers, and technical advisors) will have an edge over smaller businesses.

Second, there is a lack of accountability. Without a legal standard, there is nothing to enforce. Without mandatory reporting requirements, little relevant information will be available as evidence of problems.

Third, there is a lack of public participation. The elimination of a regulatory process removes due process from the public. It is a hallmark of public interest reform groups in Canada that citizens have achieved a steady increase in rights to be involved in decisions with significant social, consumer, and environmental impacts. De-regulation and self-regulation remove these hard-won rights of public involvement in legal processes so fundamental to our democratic legal system. The majority of voluntary pollution prevention agreements concluded to date have been negotiated behind closed doors.

Weakening the Role of Government

Ontario's overhaul of environmental laws and regulations is being accompanied by huge cuts to staff, budgets, and programs concerned with environmental protection. Program and budget cuts have hit very hard in the Ministry of Environment and Energy (31 per cent of staff laid off) and the Ministry of Natural Resources (40 per cent of staff to be laid off). With the numerous moves to industry self-regulation, lay-offs are frequently in the areas of monitoring, inspection, approvals or permitting, and enforcement. Funding has been cut to a broad range of environmental protection programs, particularly those administered by municipalities (e.g., the blue box curbside recycling program, hazardous waste programs, urban public transit, energy conservation, Conservation Authorities, etc.).

Shutting Out the Public

Changed laws, budget, and program cuts also mean that hard-won citizen rights are being lost in five significant ways. First, as noted, environmental laws are being changed in ways that serve to cut off or greatly constrain public access to information and to environmental decision-making. Second, the public consultation on these legal changes frequently has been a farce. For example, in the summer months of 1996 the government held brief consultations on environmentally significant changes to four laws and over 80 regulations. Third, the move to "voluntarism" or "self-regulation" of polluters and resource extraction industries has little or no room for public involvement. Fourth, elimination of modest funding to environmental organizations, particularly the Ontario Environment Network and its caucuses, cripples a democratic and cost-effective consultative relationship between the Ontario government and concerned citizens across the province. Fifth, the elimination of key environmental advisory committees has removed important avenues for public input to government decision-making.

Perpetuating Inequality

The impacts of environmental de-regulation will be disproportionately felt by the poor, non-English speaking minorities, people on fixed incomes, Native people, and regions of the province that have long been disadvantaged, particularly the North. Pollution and polluting industries have affected such segments of Ontario society more than others. The barriers of poverty, language, distance, lack of time, and resources, will be made worse by a loss of legal tools to protect the environment and the loss of citizens' rights to obtain information and participate in environmental decision-making.

For example, with the removal of rational land use planning controls, the poor or those on fixed incomes will be hit hardest by reduced public transit and increased property taxes and/or user fees that must pay for the well-known inefficiencies of urban sprawl. Industry self-regulation of mining and forestry will perpetuate and indeed accelerate the pattern of northern "boom and bust" development. The historical drain of northern resource wealth may create some short-term gain but long-term sustainability of jobs and northern-based, value-added industries is a more remote idea than ever. The clear bias towards unregulated resource extraction in the North will also increase conflicts over Native rights and continue to marginalize Native people from control over the management of natural resources.

Privatizing Natural Resources

Finally, with weaker laws, an emaciated civil service and a loss of public rights, the fourth part of the Ontario government's anti-environmental strategy is the privatization of natural resources. The privatization of forest management (on Crown lands, i.e., over 85 per cent of Ontario's land mass) is nearly complete. Changes to the Fish and Game Act have effectively privatized fish and wildlife management and downgraded this work from conservation of biodiversity to production of game species. New powers for municipalities to dissolve Conservation Authorities and sell these public lands jeopardizes 50 years worth of land conservation efforts. The potential for this privatization of public recreational lands could impact on millions of people (often low-income) who rely upon Conservation Authorities for recreation. Also in line for privatization or public-private "partnering" is management of numerous provincial parks on a cost-recovery basis. The pressure to generate revenues could result in intensified use of parks or the introduction of inappropriate commercial activities, both of which could result in environmental harm.

An early focus on quickly privatizing Ontario Hydro apparently hit enough public opposition that plans are now on the back burner. Undaunted, proposals are now on the front burner that will facilitate the privatization, by municipalities, of water and sewer services. In January of 1997, the government announced its intention to massively restructure the means by which public services are delivered. The Province has taken over, from municipalities, the entire budget for education. In exchange, municipalities will take over the funding of numerous services, including sewer and water. Also transferred to municipalities will be responsibility for inspection and enforcement of noise and odour complaints, and for monitoring, inspection, and enforcement of rules governing the over one million septic systems in Ontario. Whether municipalities have the resources, the expertise or, in some cases, even the inclination, to take on these new tasks, is an open question.

It is unclear whether municipal property tax revenues will cover the new range of services. Many predict that the cost of the new set of services will outstrip municipal budgets, if not immediately, certainly over the longer term. Even before this new set of changes was announced, environmentalists predicted higher municipal costs due to the relaxing of controls on urban sprawl. If costs do outstrip revenues, given the difficulty of raising municipal property taxes, it seems highly likely that municipalities will embrace the notion of privatizing any number of public services.

Will Ontario repeat the water woes of Britain? Since privatization of water and sewer services in 1989, the British public has faced a litany of problems including extreme water shortages, water rationing, and alarming increases in dysentery and other public health problems. The cost of water has increased in some cases by over 100 per cent. Low-income people have had their water shut off for weeks at a time while annual salaries for water company executives have been in excess of $1 million. Ontario is extremely vulnerable to similar effects of privatization. With weaker laws and huge cuts to programs for controlling water pollution, Ontario also has no water conservation policy and no regulatory body to control the practices of private utilities.

Strategies for Change

In less than two years, both the dizzying pace and the huge volume of environmental de-regulation has been formidable. Environmental groups, such as the Canadian Environmental Law Association, have been highly critical of both the negative impacts and the lack of public consultation. In defending the changes, the government is clinging to the dubious argument that environmental regulations kill jobs. But, rigorous studies have proven that, on the contrary, environmental regulation promotes innovation and a company's competitive advantage. Environmental protection may in fact increase jobs, particularly in manufacturing, transportation, communications, and utilities.

The government knows from public opinion polling that both environmental de-regulation and water privatization are overwhelmingly unpopular with the public. Yet many changes affecting environmental protection have occurred so quickly that the vast majority of the public is unaware of them. Environmentalists have focused on public education and this work continues. Part of this effort has included the building and/or strengthening of alliances with the labour movement, health advocates, and the broader social justice community.

The common cause among these sectors is increasingly evident. The agenda of corporate globalization, de-regulation, and privatization is undermining basic features of democracy and the role of government as a guardian of the public interest. The task for the environmental movement is to continue to reveal the environmental dimensions of this onslaught and ensure this information is part of the educational and advocacy efforts of the broader social justice community.

One step along this path was taken with the organization of the "Law for the Public Interest" conference held in November of 1996. Sponsored by environmental, labour, and health organizations, this conference addressed de-regulation in these three sectors. The conference provided both the detailed analyses of changes (in background papers) and an opportunity to build the framework for working together.

Another large task is monitoring and reporting on the impacts of regulatory changes and any privatization initiatives. Much of what environmentalists have said about the impacts of de-regulation has involved making predictions on the basis of what can be expected from such wholesale weakening of the rules. The hard evidence will come in the form of future environmental damage. This monitoring task is severely constrained by the removal of significant government monitoring responsibilities and the lack of resources in the, mostly voluntary, environmental movement.

Finally, the option of simply turning back the clock and reversing many of these changes may not be possible or even desirable in some cases. Environmentalists and allies in the social justice community must develop a "reconstruction" agenda that provides the humanistic, sustainable alternative to the nihilism that we currently face. That work is just beginning.

Kathleen (Kathy) Cooper graduated from the University of Toronto in 1984 with a specialist degree in Environmental Studies. She has worked in environmental research positions for various public interest organizations and joined the Canadian Environmental Law Association (CELA) as a researcher in 1987.

The Costs of Violence Against Women to Canadian Society

by Olena Hankivsky

Violence against women affects all women in Canada directly or indirectly.[1] There is no typical victim of intimate violence; indeed woman abuse cuts across social class, education level, race, ability, and income level. Much existing research has documented important psychological effects on women that appropriately serves the immediate safety and emotional needs of Canadian women. However, in a time when competition for existing financial resources for health, social, legal, and educational services is increasing, it is essential that the issue of violence against women also be analyzed in economic terms.

In December 1995, the Centre for Research on Violence Against Women and Children in London, Ontario, published the results of the first Canada-wide research project entitled Selected Estimates of Costs of Violence Against Women, for the purposes of informing public policy and resource allocation.

The Centre examined selected economic costs of three forms of violence against women—sexual assault/rape; woman abuse in intimate partnerships; and incest/child sexual assault—in four policy areas: health/medicine, criminal justice, social services/ education, and labour/employment. Drawing on a variety of methods, including extrapolation from survey samples of Canadian women, government statistics, case studies, and examination or reports from other jurisdictions, the study distinguished between state, personal, and third-party costs of violence against women.

State costs included such things as incarceration of people convicted of rape, child molestation, or assault. Personal costs included loss of income due to hospitalization or other treatment for injuries sustained in a sexual assault or transportation and accommodation costs. Economic costs to third parties included the expense of sheltering a friend who has been abused, or an insurance company's added expenses covering benefits or claims of a woman who experiences violence.

The results show the profound effect violence has not only on the lives of Canadian women but also on government, institutions, and business. Because the data in all policy areas are incomplete and in some cases non-existent, the project was only able to capture a very selected portion of the economic costs of violence against women. Nevertheless, the selected estimated costs of violence against women and children in four policy areas were calculated as follows:

•Social Services/Education, $2,368,924,298;
•Criminal Justice, $871,908,583;
•Labour/Employment, $576,764,400; and

•Health/Medical, $408,357,041

Total: $4.2 billion (of which 87.5 per cent is borne by the state).

(Hankivsky, Greaves, and Kingston-Rieches 2)

The research also demonstrated that violence against women contributes to many other social problems and ills which affect most policy areas. The "ripple effects" of violence against women include poverty, homelessness, lost educational/employment opportunities, loss of safety and self-esteem, and difficulty with future physical contact or relationships for those women who experience violence and any dependents they may have. Directly or indirectly, these immediate and longer-term consequences of violence against women have enormous ramifications in the areas of public health, mental health, education, social services, labour, policing, courts, crime, housing, public income support, employment insurance, and income tax. Consequently, violence against women is a significant social problem which is, in no way, isolated from other areas of society.

Rationale for Investigating the Economic Costs of Violence Against Women

The need to understand more completely the impact of violence against women in Canadian society by considering economic costs was first stated in the 1993 final report of the Canadian Panel on Violence Against Women and Children prepared for the federal government, *Changing the Landscape: Ending Violence—Achieving Equality.* The panel stressed the urgent need for such documentation to accurately assess the price borne by victims of woman abuse and also, to increase awareness of the cost benefits to Canadian society and its institutions of violence prevention.

Since the panel report, and in addition to the research of the Centre, there have been two preliminary Canadian studies on the economic costs of violence against women. The first, undertaken by Tanis Day estimated the annual economic costs in the area of health to be $1,173,191,088). Second, Richard Kerr and Janice McLean have recently produced a report for the Ministry of Women's Equality in British Columbia that estimates the economic costs in that province to be $385 million dollars annually (Ministry of Women's Equality).

The economic analysis of violence against women is also a developing field outside Canada. The findings of studies conducted in New Zealand, Australia, and the United States document the importance of undertaking this type of research.

A 1994 New Zealand study estimated the economic costs of violence against women to be at least $1.2 billion dollars per year and $4,092.61 per survivor (Snively). A 1993 Queensland, Australia study investigated the lifetime figures of 50 women who had been abused in current or past relationships or had experienced sexual assault or rape.

By tracking the service accessed by these women, it was determined that the average cost per case was Cdn$23,489. Applying the average and extrapolating this amount over the female population of Queensland who might be in an abusive marital (or equivalent) relationship, the researchers calculated the total cost of domestic violence in Queensland to be approximately Cdn$481 million per year. Moreover, the study determined that eight per cent of this cost was borne by government and third parties (see Blumel *et al.*).

Thirdly, a 1990 research project, *Costs of Domestic Violence*, published by the Women's Co-ordination Unit, examined annual direct and indirect costs of violence against women in New South Wales, Australia. The results of this study indicated that most costs attributable to domestic violence are borne by the victim. Accordingly, the report calculated that at least $800 million is either paid directly by victims or lost to them and those dependent on them as a result of domestic violence. In comparison, about half that amount was counted as direct costs to governments. Overall, the study concluded that the total annual cost of domestic violence in New South Wales is just more than Au$1.5 billion.

Although no such comprehensive studies have been undertaken in the United States, there are numerous figures which also illustrate the high costs of violence against women. For example, in a 1992 study, the Pennsylvania Blue Shield Initiative estimated that domestic violence costs that state US$326.6 billion a year in health care services. Joan Zorza, senior attorney at the National Center on Women and Family Law, estimates that this would amount to at least US$6.5 billion annually for the entire United States (383). Other U.S. studies have attempted to look at specific medical services which battered women use on a consistent basis. These statistics demonstrate much higher medical costs for domestic violence than those indicated by the Pennsylvania study. According to Zorza, in 1992 the American Medical Association estimated that woman abuse alone may account for 22–35 per cent of the nearly 1.5 million annual emergency department medical visits in the United States. Marshall Rosman of the American Medical Association estimates these numbers translate to national medical costs of about $31 billion annually or US$124 per person.

Mental health care costs attributable to violence in the United States are also potentially enormous, as "up to 64 per cent of female psychiatric inpatients are abused as adults." With respect to addictive behaviour, it is estimated that "after the onset of violence, women are 16 times more likely to become alcoholics and nine times more likely to abuse drugs than women who are not abused" (Zorza 384).

Specific national work-related repercussions of domestic violence are estimated by the United States Bureau of National Affairs to be $3–$6 billion annually in loss of productivity due to absenteeism, employee turnover, and health care expenses. Studies performed in New York and Minnesota, however, estimate the annual costs to employers to be significantly higher at US$13 billion (Zorza).

Batya Hyman of Brandeis University investigated the relationship between a woman's experience of childhood sexual assault victimization and her economic welfare as an adult in *Economic Consequences of Child Sexual Abuse in Women*. By using the 1988 National Lesbian Health Care Survey by Bradford and Ryan which involved 1,925 participants, Hyman demonstrated that intrafamilial sexual assault significantly reduces a woman's education attainment and earning potential.[2] To reach this conclusion, Hyman considered information on the health status, mental health status, and demographic characteristics of the adult survivor of childhood sexual assault.

All the findings and calculations of these studies prove that violence against women in society carries with it astounding economic costs to its survivors, the state, and those who are indirectly affected by this social problem. Such research has also demonstrated that the problem of violence against women has an economic impact on virtually all sectors of society. However, further research and better refined methodologies are required to fill in the serious gaps regarding costs that have not yet been quantified and to support comprehensive, effective policy and programs development in response to violence against women.

Limitations of Economic Analyses

Economic estimates and evaluations of violence against women represent only one dimension of a very complex social problem and as such, must be analyzed as only one part of an entire paradigm of woman abuse. Considerations of violence against women from an economic perspective should also carefully take into account both the usefulness and limitations of such economic analysis.

So while the need for and potential benefits of undertaking economic evaluations of violence against women are apparent, viewing the issue in purely economic terms is problematic and the drawbacks need to be addressed. On the one hand, cost evaluations provide us with tools to analyze the economic results of choices we make and assess the value for money spent on such choices. Such economic evaluations force analysts and decision-makers to attach value to each identifiable consequence of a given service or program, raising interesting research and policy questions. At the same time, it is essential to stress it is not always possible to quantify the costs and benefits of intervention and prevention. This is especially true of violence against women initiatives, programs, and services.

The limitations of economic evaluations have been articulated by a wide range of service providers. However, the debate over the efficacy of economic evaluations is best developed in the medical field. Despite the potential usefulness of economic evaluations, many health service providers reject economic evaluations on the basis that they put dollar values on services which are essential to human health and, in many cases, human life. These individuals do not believe that economic evaluations necessarily lead to an improvement in health service delivery. Instead, they concern themselves with the potential harm to patients if important services are eliminated using only an economic rationale (Loewy 697).

The same questions also apply to the ethics of basing responses to violence against women on economic considerations. A number of studies have referred to the difficulty of attaching specific economic costs to woman abuse. For instance, when referring to the emotional and psychological effects of rape, robbery, and assault, Lithwick and Lithwick have argued that "because of the great emotional and psychological impact of such events, ... there is a strong reaction to placing a value on them" (306). Similarly, Williams and Hawkins point out the human and social consequences of violence against women by arguing that "intimate violence, including wife assault, incest, child abuse, date rape ... may generate unique costs that are less likely for other crimes" (Williams and Hawkins 697).

Economic analyses cannot adequately account for the psychosocial costs of violence against women, nor offer a complete basis for policy recommendations. So while estimated costs of violence may be represented in numerical figures, many aspects of violence against women do not lend themselves to quantitative analyses. It is extremely difficult, if not completely impossible, to put a figure on emotional suffering or deterioration of the quality of life. As Loewy points out, using economic evaluations as *the only basis* for making decisions or changes causes one to "embark on the 'slippery slope' of compromised ethics and waffled priorities" (697).

Thus, when considering economic evaluations the question becomes, "not whether such evaluations should be done, but rather how to do them in a comprehensive and useful fashion" (Wasylenki 633). To establish estimates of the economic costs of violence against women in Canada requires that a sociological analysis of violence form the basis of economic analysis and extrapolations that are required to estimate costs. In other words, the economic costs of violence against women should not be analyzed exclusive of the human and social costs linked with such calculations.

Trends in Canadian Policy Making

Despite the limitations, comprehensive economic analyses of violence against women in Canada are especially timely if one considers current trends in reducing or eliminating government spending on social services and programming. This development is the result of the current economic thrust toward deficit reduction in Canadian public policy. Deficit-cutting is driving the political agendas of all levels of government—federal, provincial, and municipal.

Providing all levels of government—and especially in the case of Ontario—with estimates of the economic costs of violence against women demonstrates its severity and impact on society in terms which preoccupy policy decision-makers. Placing the problem of violence against women in an economic context may also increase the success for economically viable and politically innovative solutions while continuing to attend to the safety and well-being of women who experience violence. Finally, the result of an economic analysis of violence against women can be used to show how both short-term and long-term state-sponsored intervention and prevention in the area of violence against women make solid fiscal sense.

Olena Hankivsky is an assistant professor in the Department of Political Science and at the Centre for Women's Studies and Feminist Research at the University of Western Ontario. She is also the current acting director at the Centre for Research on Violence Against Women and Children in London, Ontario.

[1]See, for example, the findings of the Canadian Panel on Violence Against Women in *Changing the Landscape: Ending Violence—Achieving Equality*, Ministry of Supply and Services Canada, 1993, and the 1993 Health and Welfare Canada *Violence Against Women Survey*, conducted by Statistics Canada.
[2]It should be noted that research has shown that lesbian women are no more likely to have been sexually assaulted than heterosexual women (see Bell, Weinberg, and Hammersmith 175). In addition, in measuring impact, Hyman also considered degree of "outness" of the participants of the survey since this factor has the potential of impacting negatively on earnings.

References

Bell, A. P., M. S. Weinberg, and S. K. Hammersmith. *Sexual Preference: Its Development Among Men and Women*. Bloomington, IN: Indiana University Press, 1981

Blumel, Debra K., *et al. Who Pays? The Economic Costs of Violence Against Women*. State of Queensland, Australia: Women's Policy Unit, Office of the Cabinet, 1993.

Canadian Panel on Violence Against Women. *Changing the Landscape: Ending Violence—Achieving Equality*. Ottawa: Ministry of Supply and Services Canada, 1993.

Day, Tanis. *The Health-Related Costs of Violence Against Women in Canada*. London: Centre for Research on Violence Against Women and Children, 1995.

Hankivsky, O., L. Greaves, and Joanne Kingston-Rieches. *Selected Estimates of Costs of Violence Against Women*. London: Centre for Research on Violence Against Women and Children, 1995.

Hyman, Batya. *Economic Consequences of Child Sexual Abuse in Women*. Waltham, MA: Brandeis University, Department of Philosophy, 1993.

Lithwick, Harvey, and Dahlia Lithwick. "'Liberal' Treatment of Violent Young Offenders." *How Ottawa Spends 1995–96: Mid-Life Crisis*. Ed. Susan Phillips.

Ottawa: Carleton University Press, 1995.

Loewy, Erich. "Costs Should Not Be a Factor in Medical Care." *New England Journal of Medicine* 302.12 (1979): 697–698.

Ministry of Women's Equality. *Paying for Violence: Some of the Costs of Violence Against Women in British Columbia.* Victoria: Ministry of Women's Equality, 1996.

New South Wales Women's Co-ordination Unit. *Costs of Domestic Violence.* Haymarket: New South Wales Women's Co-ordination Unit, 1990.

Snively, Suzanne (Cooper and Lybrand). *The New Zealand Economic Cost of Family Violence.* Wellington: Family Violence Unit, 1994.

Statistics Canada. *Violence Against Women Survey.* Ottawa: Health and Welfare Canada, 1993.

Wasylenki, D. A. "The Importance of Economic Evaluations." *Canadian Journal of Psychiatry* 34.7 (1989): 631–632.

Williams, Kirk, and Richard Hawkins. "Wife Assault, Costs of Arrest, and the Deterrence Process." *Journal of Research and Delinquency* 29.3 (1992): 292–310.

Zorza, Joan. "Woman Battering: High Costs and the State of the Law." *Clearinghouse Review* (1994).

Ottawa Fiddles with Child Poverty as Social Programs Burn

by Kerry McCuaig

Canadians concerned about child poverty should not take comfort in the federal government's budget. The $600 million in repackaged funding for low-income working families indicates just how banal this "attack on poverty" is. For the much-touted National Child Benefit System has little to do with child poverty and much to do with welfare reform and federal/provincial relations in a post-Quebec referendum era.

The government has found the money for the child benefit by consolidating the current child tax credit and the working income supplement and reducing payments to modest income families. It will pay a maximum of $625 additional dollars to working poor families beginning in July 1998.

As a child poverty strategy, the benefit falls short. A benefit devised to address child poverty would go to all poor children regardless of their parents' employment status. Even as a welfare reform project the benefit is fundamentally flawed. Central to its design is the supposition that denying the benefit increase to families on social assistance will serve as an incentive for them to take low-wage jobs. But the benefit increase doesn't begin to address the number one employment support parents require if they are to make the transition from welfare to work—child care. The design doesn't attempt to interest itself in the crucial issue of what happens to children while their parents work. As a result, kids already at risk due to poverty will be placed in double jeopardy by inadequate care arrangements.

The thinking behind the benefit ignores the demographic differences that contribute to one family being on welfare while another is working poor. Fifty-eight per cent of poor kids are in families where the parents work. These tend to be two-parent families, where the parents and children are older or those who can draw on extended family support. A further 29 per cent of families are on welfare, but work part-time.

By contrast the 13 per cent of families whose parents have no workforce attachment are in the main isolated, single parents, with pre-school children, or families where the parent and/or child have disabilities. Eliminating the welfare trap for these families requires more than money. It requires good child care, job training, and decent jobs.

The federal government has already relinquished any role in child care and job training—two essential levers to job creation. These and other areas of social programs are now the sole responsibility of the province. Under the child benefit deal worked out between federal Human Resources Minister Pierre Pettigrew and his provincial counterparts, phase two of the child benefit would see an increase in the amount received by all low-income families. The provinces would claw back dollar for dollar any additional payments families on social assistance receive from Ottawa. The provinces are then on their honour to redirect their welfare savings into services for the working poor. Phase two is not expected to be operational until July 1998.

It is little wonder that the child benefit has found agreement between the provinces and the federal government. No level of government has shown an interest in enlarging the funding envelope for poor kids. They are however interested in welfare reform. In today's lexicon reform means cutting welfare payments and/or redirecting money from one group of poor to another.

Which raises the inherently punitive side of the child benefit. An additional $625 a year won't even the playing field for a single parent faced with the "choice" of work or welfare. Six hundred and twenty-five dollars won't begin to buy child care nor compensate the family for the additional expenses associated with working. When the differentiated payment doesn't result in reducing the number of families on welfare, then what? More money for the working poor, or more cuts to welfare?

Reducing welfare rolls and reducing child poverty are not necessarily the same thing. If child poverty was the motivation behind the child benefit then governments, appalled by the latest report of the National Council on Welfare documenting that families on social assistance are sinking deeper and deeper into poverty, would ante-up.

These governments would pay heed to the recommendations of both the National Forum on Health and the National Forum on Crime Prevention which document that an effective way to reduce child poverty and achieve savings from two runaway areas of spending—health care and law enforcement—begins with a national child care program.

In addition, governments would acknowledge their responsibility for creating child poverty. Since 1984 when the universality of the family allowance was abandoned, payments to families with children have been reduced by over $800 million from $6 billion to $5.1 billion. Due to deindexation, payments to poor and moderate income families have fallen by $170 million a year. The $600 million allotted for the child benefit only replaces some of what this government has taken away.

Governments have increased the number of poor children by 50 per cent since 1989, by taking unemployment insurance away from their parents, by cutting welfare payments, gutting children's services, and killing decent paying public sector jobs. But instead of action on these fronts we have been presented with the child benefit, in reality a subsidy to business to mask the social consequences of poverty-level wages.

Now the government hopes it can ride into the next election claiming to care about kids. Equity advocates may be excused for our skepticism. This was the same government that last election promised $720 million in new spending on child care. That promise was scuttled, supposedly for lack of provincial interest. The child benefit also depends on provincial cooperation. Will Ottawa get a consensus this round? Quebec has shown no interest in even showing up for the talks. This gives Ontario a veto over the plan, since Ottawa has promised no new social programs without majority provincial buy-in. Meanwhile Ontario is in the process of giving away the tools it requires to participate by downloading responsibility for such programs onto the municipalities.

Canadians who are concerned about the future of social programs have much to fear. The child benefit is to serve as the template for developing standards under the Canada Health and Social Transfer and the renewed Canada Health Act the provinces have demanded. The child benefit represents the new division of powers, where the federal government transfers money directly to deserving individuals and the provinces provide a fragmented collection of targeted services. As an example of the new federalism, if the child benefit represents the best the provinces and feds can devise, our future as a nation is in real trouble.

Kerry McCuaig is the executive director of the Ontario Coalition for Better Child Care.

Struggling to Survive
Women in Families Using Food Banks

by Valerie Tarasuk, Jennifer Geduld, and Shelly Hilditch

Since the early 1980s, the number of Canadians seeking charitable food assistance has steadily grown. Food assistance programs now operate on a scale not seen since the Great Depression. Their current proliferation appears to have been spawned by the systematic erosion of social programs at both the federal and provincial levels. In the fall of 1995, following the provincial cuts to social assistance, food banks across Ontario reported increased requests for help, highlighting yet again the link between food bank usage and inadequate income supports. Currently, Toronto's Daily Bread Food Bank serves 130,000 people each month. To gain an understanding of the food problems and life circumstances of families who use food banks, a series of interviews were conducted with a sample of 153 women who sought emergency food relief from programs in Metropolitan Toronto between May 1996 and April 1997. The women interviewed were between 19 and 49 years of age, and all had at least one child living with them. Although the analysis of data from this study is still in progress, preliminary findings point to disturbing levels of deprivation and despair.

Two-thirds of the women interviewed were single parents. Household sizes ranged from two to ten persons, including anywhere from one to eight children. Eighty-four per cent of families were supported by social assistance—almost all on assistance programs whose rates had been cut in October 1995. Only 25 per cent lived in housing where rent was geared to income; many others struggled to cope with high market rents. The average household income was approximately one half the Statistics Canada Low Income Cut-offs (the "poverty line").

In the context of severe economic constraints, food selection was routinely compromised. As one woman said, "*I'm really good at making do, but I still can't buy the fruits and vegetables we need because there's just too little money.*" Fewer than one third of the women interviewed felt they could afford to provide their children with balanced meals, and only ten per cent felt they could afford to consume such meals themselves.

It was commonplace for women to put their children's food needs ahead of their own. One woman explained,

I buy milk every two or three days for my son, but I don't drink it. It is more important for my son. I wish sometimes I could buy myself an ice-cream when I buy my son one, but it is just too expensive. We go to McDonalds occasionally and my son will eat his meal there, but I skip the meal because I can't afford to buy food for both of us there.

The prospect of running out of food was a constant worry for most of the women interviewed. Fifty-four per cent of women declared that they did not always have enough food for their household. In the last year, 80 per cent of the women reported sometimes having to cut the size of their own meals and 20 per cent had gone without eating for at least one entire day because there was not enough money for food. It was much less common for the children in these families to have experienced food deprivation, suggesting that when resources are scarce women may deprive themselves in order to spare their children.

Using food banks was just one of the ways women attempted to minimize their families' experiences of food deprivation. Indeed, for many women, the humiliation of seeking charity made food banks a last resort. Over 75 per cent of the women interviewed said in the last year they had put off paying bills and over half gave up telephone or other services in order to have money for food. Other strategies women used included buying food on credit, selling or pawning possessions, and sending their children to a friend or relative's home for a meal when food was running short. As their situations became more desperate, women typically resorted to multiple strategies, exhibiting remarkable resourcefulness and determination in their struggles to ensure that their children would not go hungry.

Not surprisingly, stress was a major factor for women in this study. Forty-one per cent described their lives as being very stressful and 35 per cent said their lives were fairly stressful. Women's greatest concerns were about being able to manage payments for bills, rent, and food on inadequate incomes. As well, many expressed anxiety regarding their children's health and welfare and their own poor employment prospects. Moreover, housing issues were a major source of stress for some women who faced inadequate living conditions and the prospect of rent increases.

Compounding women's feelings of stress were their feelings of social isolation. Forty-seven per cent said they felt isolated and alone some of the time and 17 per cent experienced these feelings most of the time. When questioned about their social support in times of need, 30 per cent of women said that there was never anyone among their friends and family who could help; nine per cent felt that there was rarely someone to whom they could turn in these situations.

A number of indicators underscore the need to be concerned about the health of women and children in these families. Over one quarter of the women in this study declared that they have a long standing health condition, disability, or illness that limits their activity in some way. Furthermore, 57 per cent of the women had weights outside the "generally acceptable" range for good health; the women were either underweight or overweight to an extent which put them at elevated risk of developing health problems.

To gain more insight into the vulnerability of women and children using food banks, we asked women to recount the birthweight of their children. In total, 12.1 per cent of children born to women in this study had been low birthweight babies (i.e., infants who weigh less than 2500g at the time of birth). This is of particular concern because of the mounting evidence that low birthweight potentially disadvantages children later in life (Committee to Study the Prevention of Low Birthweight). The high proportion of low birthweight infants and the finding that approximately 20 per cent of women had their first child when under the age of eighteen suggest that a substantial number have experienced high risk pregnancies.

The preliminary findings presented here indicate the extent of food insecurity experienced by families who seek emergency food assistance from food banks and provide some insight into their social and economic circumstances. As the data analysis proceeds, the nutritional adequacy of the women's diets will be assessed and their experiences of food shortages will be characterized in more detail. As well, the role of food banks and targeted feeding programs such as children's breakfast clubs and school lunch programs in alleviating food problems will be examined. Insofar as the food deprivation documented by this study is widespread, it raises concerns about the present and future well-being of Ontario families currently living in poverty.

Valerie Tarasuk, Jennifer Geduld, and Shelly Hilditch are members of the research team which undertook this study. The study participants were recruited and interviewed by Sheri Fogarty and Sandra Bailey. The study was funded by the National Health Research and Development Program of Health Canada, and conducted with the support of the Daily Bread Food Bank. For more information about this study, please write to Valerie Tarasuk at the Department of Nutritional Sciences, Faculty of Medicine, University of Toronto, Toronto, Ontario M5S 3E2.

References

Committee to Study the Prevention of Low Birthweight, Division of Health Promotion and Disease Prevention, Institute of Medicine. *Preventing Low Birthweight.* Washington, DC: National Academy Press, 1985.

Statistics Canada. *Income Distribution by Size in Canada.* Ottawa: Statistics Canada. (Catalogue 13-207). 1995.

ACTEW's Top 8 Reasons Why Workfare Won't Work

by Advocates for Community-Based Training and Education for Women (ACTEW)

8. Workfare is expensive

Let's face it, one of the big reasons governments are interested in workfare is to reduce their welfare costs. Workfare can cost more than welfare when you add to the basic welfare payment the costs of: more subsidized daycare spaces (25,000 on the waiting list already) for the possible 198,000 sole support parents on welfare in Ontario (90 per cent of whom are women); increased bureaucracy to administer the program; and, increased people on EI because jobs are being taken up by workfare recipients.

7. Workfare doesn't create long-term economic stability

Studies in the U.S. have shown that workfare works best in those areas where there is low unemployment. Even where workfare has supposedly worked (the SWIM program in California) 51.3 per cent of participants in the program were on welfare at the end of year two and 58.7 per cent of the control group were on welfare. SWIM participants were only making a few dollars more than before—they were still poor. In Ontario the unemployment rates are high. The reason the welfare rolls are so high is because many people have become unemployed and moved onto welfare. Without jobs, workfare will be another financial burden on an already overburdened government.

6. Adults cannot be forced to learn

Unless people are paid and treated decently we cannot expect them to be responsible workers. People are humiliated and depressed working at jobs that are meaningless. The same is true of training. The government can force adults to take training in order to receive their welfare cheques, but they can't force adults to learn. One of the basic tenets of adult education is that learning must be voluntary.

5. People should not be punished for being poor

These are two sides to this issue: those who believe the poor are lazy and defrauding the state and those who believe that the poor are as honest as anyone else and would rather work. ACTEW believes the poor would rather work. ACTEW knows that: there is very little welfare fraud (losses due to fraud amount to between two per cent and four per cent of total welfare payments); 38 per cent of people on welfare in Ontario are children and will be negatively affected by parents working at meaningless jobs to receive welfare payments already too low to maintain their households; and, that people are on welfare because they are unable to work or because they cannot find work, not because they won't work.

4. Workfare does not enhance people's employability or work skills

Very few participants in workfare programs actually receive appropriate training to enable them to find work which raises them out of poverty. Where there are voluntary work programs for welfare recipients, there are already too many people for too few spaces. Voluntary training programs with appropriate assessment and support services can make a difference to poor people's lives in the long term, but they require a large monetary commitment up front.

3. Workfare can shift the burden of support from one level of government to another

Many workfare programs have placed people in temporary government subsidized jobs only to see those people laid off at the end of the subsidization period (PAIE program, Quebec). These people are then eligible for EI and when that runs out, for welfare. In Michigan the workfare program caused 82,000 people to lose their benefits. A Ford Foundation study revealed that few of those people became self-sufficient and the homeless population grew dramatically in Detroit, at an enormous social and monetary cost to the city.

2. Workfare can displace employed worker's jobs

In Sweden the workfare program was successful as long as unemployment figures were low. As soon as unemployment started to rise in the 1990s the government had to start subsidizing jobs in the private sector. This led to longer-term employees losing their jobs. In Alberta one hospital laid off nursing assistants and replaced them with subsidized labour. Employers may not hire new workers (which supplies living wage jobs for the unemployed) when subsidized labour is available (as was the case with Quebec's EXTRA program).

1. Workfare erodes our values

Workfare is a system that punishes poor people and offers no compassion and respect for those people who find themselves scrambling to feed themselves or their children. This system can erode our humanity and decency and teach our children to doubt that most people are honest and hardworking. ACTEW believes that workfare will stretch our social fabric to the ripping point.

Advocates for Community-Based Training and Education for Women (ACTEW) is a provincial umbrella group representing over 4,000 women across Ontario in pre-employment training programs. ACTEW distributes information regarding training and labour force development policy, advocates for women's access to training, consults with various levels of government, and networks among women's groups and training/education providers.

Confronting the Cuts: One Woman's Story

by Pat McDougall

I am on Family Benefits. My ex-husband has been in jail since April 1996 and has charges outstanding in Durham, Peel, York, and Victoria County Regions. We receive no support payments.

My benefits were cut by 21.6 per cent in October 1995. A total of $401 per month was taken off my cheque. I was only given two months notice. This was not enough time to make up the difference to pay my taxes and water and sewer bills.

In April of 1996 I lost my home. My monthly mortgage payment was $804.88, realty taxes were $100 per month, water and sewer bills were $33 per month, car insurance was $57 and house insurance $25.60 per month, hydro was $180 to $200 per month depending on the need for heat. Wood for the wood stove, groceries for the five of us, toiletries, gas and maintenance for the car, birthdays, Christmas, school trips, etc., are extra.

I lost my $6,000 down payment on the house, $2,000 in lawyers' fees for closing the purchase of the house, and four years of mortgage payments which totalled a little over $40,000. This was totally disheartening.

On September 1, 1996 the government implemented a policy that eliminates Family Benefits if you wish to go to college or university. You are put completely on OSAP instead. It costs about $6,000 per year to attend college full-time. After two years in college I would be $12,000 in debt. How can someone in my position consider going to college for more than a couple of years? How would you be able to start making monthly payments to the government on the small income you might earn. Even a job paying $30,000 a year would not be enough once you calculate income taxes and the cost of working. Once off the system, I would not receive a drug or dental plan nor the two clothing allowances I get each August and November for my children which I desperately need to dress them for school in winter.

When things go wrong like the car breaks down, which mine did this December 1996, how do you pay for repairs when you don't have any money? You cannot survive in a rural area without a car and and garages want cash and lots of it.

As of October 1995 I have to pay $2 for every prescription. This has really added up since my middle son has an ulcer and has needed several prescriptions. My daughter is also sick a lot. She has struggled through four years of high school with bouts of mono (the worst case her doctor had ever seen), strep throat, tonsillitis, irritable bowel syndrome, bowel and bladder infections, sinusitis. She is determined to finish her Grade 12 through correspondence courses. I have purchased over 64 prescriptions. Some were not covered at all.

I have four extremely positive and bright children. One wants to be a doctor. Another wants to be a teacher. The other two will also have the marks they need to go to university. But, how will I help my children with even the small things? I can't afford the school trips which are anywhere from $60 to over $100 per child: *Phantom of the Opera*, Niagara Falls, Toronto Zoo, Science Centre, meal money, spending money, etc. Each time I have to go to the school and tell them that I can't afford it.

When a mother does not receive support payments or have a part-time job to supplement her social assistance cheque, school should be offered free-of-charge. We should have to attend in order to keep collecting the assistance. The long-term benefits would be the ability to get a good job and come off the system, as well as a better feeling overall for the parent, a better example for the children, and a better picture financially for down the road.

Another positive aspect of being off the system is that renting isn't so difficult. When you are applying to rent a place they always ask where you work. I have to say I am on mother's allowance which is embarrassing. You are always worried that they will not accept you.

Pets are also a problem. I don't think it is fair to my children to tell them that they have to get rid of their cat and dog because of mom's situation. How much do the children have to give up? As it is we never go on any family trips like most of their friends still do (for example, bowling, skiing, movies, or even McDonald's). My children have always been extremely talented and used to take dance lessons, swimming lessons, and gymnastics. All this stopped in 1990 when the marriage broke down. I ended up in the hospital with pneumonia. Later it got worse when I could not eat for being so scared all the time as creditors and the police were constantly at the door.

I am extremely frustrated because it seems so simple. Getting an education would get me off the system as I am very outgoing, personable, intelligent, and positive. I have an excellent resume. I have worked for A. E. Williams Insurance Adjusters in Oshawa; the Oshawa General Hospital; the Bank of Nova Scotia, Head Office, Toronto; Campeu Corporation, Toronto; for professors and lecturers at the University of Western Ontario, School of Business; the Department of Neurosurgery, University Hospital, London; and North American Life Insurance Company, Oshawa. I have secretarial experience as well as experience in public relations and marketing. I have taken computer courses in Haliburton at Sir Sandford Fleming College. Right now there are no jobs in Haliburton.

I want to go ahead, not backwards. I want to be proud of myself and help my family. When you believe you can do anything and you hit brick walls every time you turn around it is very discouraging. You keep saying to yourself, "if only the government would see it my way, if only they would listen to me and give me this big chance I need, I could do it. I could go to school full-time, work very hard, feel exhilarated, feel positive, make plans with my children, bring hope into the home, be lifted up instead of always lifting your children up, I could be lifted up too."

When you have no money it seems like all the doors are closed, especially in the '90s. I would like to start enjoying life. I'm always worried about the future and angry because one break—free education—could open the doors for me and at least I would have a chance!

Lastly, I would like to mention something that happened to me this past winter and spring. Every other Wednesday the ladies from the Women's Safety Network would drive me from Haliburton to Lindsay to appear before a judge for support hearings. The ex, most of the time, didn't show up. When he did appear he was told he had two weeks to make his support payments or he would get 30 days. Three court dates went by and the judge kept threatening him with jail. The ex finally sent a cheque and two weeks later it bounced. This time a different judge sentenced him to 60 days in jail. But it was too late.

The ex had already served me with papers to appear in a Peterborough court. He wanted to get full-time custody of my children. He stipulated that because I was on mother's allowance I could not afford my four children. To me this was insane. This person was in and out of court and jail all the time. Why was it allowed to go this far, especially in a court of law? All he was doing was buying time. He figured that if he got custody of the children, no judge would send him to jail for not making his support payments.

I was scared to death. A professional con artist was trying to avoid going to jail by taking my children away from me. Not knowing what was going to happen, I was pretty frantic.

I was denied legal aid but I found a lawyer in Peterborough. When this lawyer found out that I had been denied legal aid she called the office in question to find out why. They told her that because I had custody of my children and the ex hadn't seen them for more than two months during the past five years, that he didn't stand a chance of winning. My lawyer was appalled and told the office that they shouldn't be playing lawyer. She thought it was terrible that I was denied legal aid. They blamed it on cutbacks. We had to appear in court anyway. I was nervous wreck. I thought my world was coming down on me. I thought the ex might at least gain visitation rights but the children did not want to see him. The lawyer selected by the attorney general's office interviewed the children and the ex was denied access.

How could the legal system have allowed this to happen? The courts should have intervened long ago. He has never paid us any support money; it will be six years this spring. Why did I have to go through that horrible month of waiting for the court date, wasting the lawyers' time, the court's time, taxpayer's money, the Women's Safety Network's time and money? No one in my situation and especially my children, after what they've been through, should have had to go through all this.

What is going to happen when the ex is out of jail? The children and I always wonder if he is going to show up in the neighbourhood as he did three years ago, driving right up beside my daughter and scaring her.

I am worried about more cutbacks. I am moving to Oshawa with my children and I don't know how I will be able to afford the higher rents plus utilities. But there is more opportunity there with regards to Durham College, access to transportation, and more available for the children (like jobs). What lies ahead when I have been cut back $401 per month? There is no future in Haliburton either. There are no jobs.

I want positive changes for my children. I am hoping for a brighter future.

Pat McDougall has four children: Sarah, Gordie, Michael, and Matthew. They have recently moved to Oshawa.

Before and After
A Woman's Story with Two Endings ...

by the Metro Toronto Committee Against Wife Assault & Metro Woman Abuse Council

June 1995: Before the Cutbacks

A woman, who has immigrated to Canada from South America, has three adolescent children and is living in downtown Toronto. She speaks limited English and has never worked outside of the home in Canada.

The woman goes to the doctor after receiving serious injuries from her husband. He has been increasingly abusive to her, both emotionally and physically over the last ten years.

By attending training sessions at the Centre for Spanish Speaking Peoples, the doctor has learned how best to detect and deal with women patients who are being abused by their partners.

The doctor discusses the woman's situation with her and reinforces that abuse is a crime. He discusses various options for her protection and safety, including referring her to a women's shelter. He also urges her to visit the Centre for Spanish Speaking Peoples, which offers counselling programs for Spanish speaking women. The doctor schedules a follow-up appointment to check her injuries, and continues to encourage her to take some action to protect herself and her children.

The mother and children go to the Centre for Spanish Speaking Peoples, and by attending counselling sessions and a support group, she gains the strength and information to make the decision to leave her husband. She has learned what she needs to do to end ten years of emotional and physical abuse.

Once she has made the decision to leave, a staff person provided through the Multilingual Access to Social Assistance Program (MASAP) helps her with the welfare application process, which would otherwise be difficult given her limited knowledge of English.

The MASAP Program was completely eliminated in the first round of massive cuts to social spending in October 1995.

The mother and her children go to a shelter, where they receive support, referrals, advocacy, and information. They all attend counselling groups, where they each continue to gain the strength and self-confidence to legally leave an abusing husband and father.

Due to cutbacks in funding and changes in agency mandates, shelters are now being told to focus on food and housing needs only. Emotional needs, including counselling, are seen as luxuries.

The mother is referred to Legal Aid, where she qualifies for a legal aid certificate and is able to get a lawyer to start divorce proceedings. At the same time, the mother and children get on the Battered Women's Priority List for Metro Toronto Housing, and they are offered housing within three to four months.

The mother attends English as a Second Language classes at the Centre for Spanish Speaking Peoples, where she also continues to get support and information. Once her English has improved, the Centre refers the mother to Dixon Hall for employment retraining. She completes a six-week course and has two job interviews as she prepares for the next stage of her independence—a job.

The Legal Aid System is currently in a state of upheaval. Women are being given legal aid certificates, but lawyers are refusing to honour them because payments are not assured.

Every one of the 4,000 hostel beds in Toronto was occupied on October 20, 1995. This was unprecedented at this time of year, before the winter weather.

Over the past year, the number of single mothers using hostels has increased by 53 per cent—from 639 to 965. Hostel use by single mothers and their families rose faster than any other homeless group.

The job retraining program offered through Dixon Hall, like others across the province, was closed down due to cuts in social spending.

January 1996: After the Cutbacks

A mother with three adolescent children speaks limited English and has never worked outside the home. The woman goes to her doctor after her abusive husband has seriously injured her.

Her doctor had been a participant in a community education project at the Centre for Spanish Speaking Peoples. Through this project, physicians were trained in how to detect and respond effectively to women patients who are experiencing abuse at the hands of their partners. However, the project at the Centre took place over a year ago, and was not funded for a second year. There has been no follow-up, and the doctor does not remember much of the information, only the basic principles.

The Statistical Story

Several studies of hospital emergency room patients have demonstrated that 25 to 35 per cent of all women attending emergency rooms are there because of injuries/illness resulting from domestic violence.

Physicians often estimate that one or two per cent of their female patients are assaulted by their partners, but conservative estimates indicate that at least one in eight women in Canada are assaulted by their partners.

In one Ontario hospital, the number of reported wife assault cases increased 1,500 per cent after policies and procedures were implemented to deal with women abuse.

The doctor treats the wounds, gives the mother the number for the Centre for Spanish Speaking Peoples, and suggests that she contact them.

In the meantime, the doctor urges her to do whatever is necessary not to antagonize her husband and to keep him happy so that her wounds can heal and that she will not be hurt further.

The woman does not call immediately, fearing what will happen if her husband finds out that she has talked to someone about the abuse. However, after much consideration, and after seeing how upset her children are, she does call the Centre.

The Centre for Spanish Speaking Peoples has reduced staff as a result of cuts to community service agencies, and the woman is put on a waiting list. The Centre used to get Purchase of Service funding to provide counselling to low-income people, but this program has been cut entirely.

She is mailed brochures in Spanish about social assistance, shelters, subsidized housing, and the Legal Aid System. Because of budget cuts, there is not much more the Centre can do.

Two weeks later, after the woman has received the brochures, her husband finds them and assaults her again for daring to take "family problems to a stranger."

After the second assault within one month, the woman begins to feel desperate enough to take action. She phones the Metro Toronto Housing Authority, and with great difficulty given her limited English, she gets the message that there is a three-year waiting list for subsidized housing.

She then phones four shelters and discovers that there is no room—two shelters have started up a waiting list and say she should call back in one month, while the other two shelters suggest she contact a housing co-op.

At this point, the woman tries to call welfare, but can't get through on the general number. This is especially hard for her, because she is limited in when she can use the phone safely.

On October 6, 1995, the provincial government announced the cancellation of the Multilingual Access to Social Assistance Program (MASAP) along with massive cuts to ethno-specific, multi-service community agencies and support services for battered women.

Still unable to talk to someone on the phone, she hears on the radio about the massive cuts to welfare. The woman fears that even if she gets through on the phone line she still won't be eligible, so she makes no further attempts to call.

Almost two-thirds of separated or divorced women have suffered sexual, physical, or emotional abuse. Many of these women end up on social assistance.

The 21.6 per cent cut to social assistance means that a single parent with one child will receive $7.76 a day per person. Two adults with two children receive $5.01 a day per person.

Children represent 40 per cent of all people receiving social assistance.

People on social assistance (40 per cent of whom are children), will be required to subsist on incomes that are more than 40 per cent below Statistics Canada's low-income cutoff (Ontario Social Safety Network).

The mother leaves with her three children to stay with her sister. The living situation is crowded, and gets difficult very quickly with two families sharing a small apartment. Tensions between the sisters emerge, as do tensions between the children.

The husband knows where the mother is living. The mother and her children have no income, and can only look forward to continuing to live in these crowded conditions. In fact, they will wait up to three years for subsidized housing.

The mother tries to find a job, but with few work skills and limited English, she is unable to find work.

The JobsOntario Training program has been cut by $86 million, and the program is being terminated.

In the end, the mother and her children return to the violent home. The children avoid being home as much as possible as the tension increases daily. They feel helpless to support their mother, yet are angry at her for returning to such an abusive man. The mother is further isolated, given that the husband flaunts the fact that she tried to leave and could not "make it on her own"—and has come "crawling back" to him. The father's violence escalates and begins to be directed at the children as well.

In a Canada-wide study of assaulted women, significant numbers of women reported that their partners had abused their children physically (26 per cent), psychologically (48 per cent), and sexually (7 per cent) (Ontario Women's Directorate (OWD) "Wife Assault").

In some studies, up to 50 per cent of young offenders charged with crimes against people were found to have been exposed to domestic violence as children (Ontario Women's Directorate (OWD) "Dispelling the Myths").

It has been shown that there are more serious child adjustment problems related to witnessing domestic violence than to the separation, divorce, or loss of parents.

*****

The two stories in this article have offered a glimpse of the life of one woman and her family, and their first-hand experience with abuse. More and more women and families across Ontario could tell similar tales. Amid the stories of cost-cutting and reducing deficits, we must also consider the social deficit, and take steps now so our society won't be paying in the years to come.

This article has been reprinted with permission from the Metro Toronto Committee Against Wife Assault and the Metro Woman Abuse Council.

The Metro Toronto Committee Against Wife Assault (MTCAWA) is an umbrella organization of service providers, agencies, and front line workers. The objectives of MTCAWA are to identify problems related to the present service system and to develop and facilitate implementation of strategies to eliminate these problems, and to monitor government policy and program initiatives in the area of wife assault. The goals of these objectives are to improve the response of existing service systems and to decrease the incidence of wife assault in Metro Toronto.

The Metro Woman Abuse Council is an inter-agency organization, under the auspices of the Metro Chairman's Office, with a mandate to develop and coordinate Community Response to Woman Abuse in Metro Toronto.

References

Ontario Social Safety Network. "Welfare Rate Cuts: Backgrounder #2." Toronto: Ontario Social Safety Network, 1995.

Ontario Women's Directorate (OWD). "Wife Assault." Toronto: Ontario Women's Directorate, 1994.

Ontario Women's Directorate (OWD). "Dispelling the Myths." Toronto: Ontario Women's Directorate, 1994.

The Changing Face of Shelters

by Kathryn Robertson

This article looks at how work within shelters for abused women is changing in Ontario. This is by no means an exhaustive discussion, and considers the impact of these changes in only one area of the province. The strategies presented are suggestions, not conclusive answers. Changes are taking place so quickly that we will need to continually develop new strategies. We must try not to let the pace and breadth of these changes overwhelm us. Instead, we must critically analyze the changes which are taking place, so that we can develop appropriate strategies.

Note: For the purposes of this article, "abuse" will encompass physical, sexual, emotional, psychological, environmental, verbal, and financial abuse of women, within intimate relationships. Many abused women are mothers, and their children are also victims of woman abuse. The cuts will have a detrimental impact on children, and will permit the intergenerational pattern of abuse to continue. For ease of wording, the article may not always mention children explicitly, though their presence and needs are implicitly recognized.

Impacts

The government's simplistic and short-term approach to social problems is betraying abused women and their children because it ignores the social and systemic issues which contribute to the abuse of women. By withdrawing financial support for many programs, the government is indicating that society does not have a responsibility to deal with the issue.

Shelters were one of the few programs under the Violence Prevention Initiatives not to receive a massive reduction in funding; funding for prevention oriented programs such as second stage housing, voluntary counselling for abusers, Wife Assault Month, and public education was completely eliminated. The government does not seem to understand that women and children leaving abusive relationships are in complicated situations, and therefore often require support from a variety of programs—of which shelters are but one. Instead, it has cut away essential programs which complement the work of shelters and provide ongoing support to abused women. Changes like reduced social assistance rates, cuts to community-based services, and a freeze on public housing have meant that oppression does not end for women when they leave their abusive relationship.

Women are increasingly anxious about their ability to survive, so an increasing amount of time is spent counselling women on issues of housing, budgeting, etc., rather than dealing with women's emotional issues. This will likely have a significant impact upon their ability to heal and create an abuse-free life for themselves and their children. Conversely, if a women does not have adequate resources to feed her family, or to furnish her home, she will be unable to attain the stability which is an important part of the healing process. Cuts to Legal Aid have meant that women have less time with a lawyer, and that staff are desperate for lawyers who will accept Legal Aid, even lawyers who do not typically work with abused women. As a result, many women are not receiving proper legal representation.

For many women, cuts to essential programs like social assistance and child care have a significant impact on their decision to leave. Some women feel that they cannot leave, and some will live with the abuse for a longer period. This is the harsh reality of today's Ontario—women and children remain in life-threatening situations while others enjoy a tax cut, paid for by the elimination of social programs.

There is an increasing demand for shelter space for women who have become homeless. Many of these women (and their children) are homeless because they are unable to secure adequate housing with reduced social assistance rates. An alarming number of women in housing crises are women who have left abusive relationships and have never stabilized because they have been unable to access supportive services.

As government funding decreases, organizations are increasingly dependent on the good graces of the community. Shelter staff now spend more time seeking donations in order to maintain services within the shelter, and to help women establish independent accommodations. As a result, staff have less time and energy to work with women on emotional issues, or to work on broader issues such as political advocacy. Many shelters are hiring fundraisers. While the generosity of donors must be commended, I would argue that such a charity model is problematic, because it focuses on "deserving" individuals, as opposed to broader societal change. In addition, revenue from donors is less predictable than government funding.

Many organizations fear that if they are too political, too outspoken, or even too "feminist," their funding will be threatened. As a result, abused women are losing advocates. Shelters have less time and no funding to engage in the public education efforts that are essential to the prevention of woman abuse. Some women even have the impression that shelters are no longer operating.

In December 1996, women's advocates were faced with the challenge of a government-sponsored consultant's report which presented a new framework for all violence against women program. The McGuire Report, as it was called, was clearly biased against women-run programs such as shelters and rape crisis centres. It also did not represent an accurate picture of the kind of work that these programs do with women. The legitimacy of the report was questioned by those who were consulted but did not see their opinions reflected in the findings. The public became concerned after the media presented some of the most controversial recommendations, i.e. that shelters could become temporary holding places while women obtained restraining orders in 24–48 hours (those who work with women know that legal orders are often not available so quickly and that restraining orders cannot protect many abused women—not three weeks before the report was released, a woman in Mississauga was killed by her partner, though she had a restraining order against him).

This report led to a convergence of opposition which has not been seen for quite some time. During the meeting when the report was presented to women's advocates, the audience became so frustrated by a seeming lack of understanding and concern regarding the situation of abused women, and an apparent unwillingness to share the findings of the report, that the report was taken from the consultant and thrown into the audience. This instantaneous act of resistance forced the report into the open and began a concerted process of organizing to have the report shelved. The report also made many realize that our existence cannot be assumed and that we will need to fight to maintain our programs and services, and especially services which are women-run.

In July 1997, the provincial government released its own plan for violence against women programs. While the government did not formally denounce the McGuire report, it did not adopt the report's more controversial recommendations. This is primarily due to the work of women's advocates across the province to expose the problems with the McGuire report.

The new plan announced $5.5 million in "new" spending on specialized domestic violence courts, prevention programs, and support for front-line emergency services. This "new" money in fact represents approximately half of the amount which had been previously cut from violence against women programs. Much of the funding is committed to institutionally-based services such as hospitals, courts, schools, and Children's Aid Societies, rather than to women-run organizations such as shelters and women's centres.

The Future

Because shelters are regarded by this government as the primary service for abused women and their children, shelters will have to take on more responsibilities (particularly in the areas of counselling and community outreach) as other services are reduced. Some shelters are already finding themselves offering food bank-type support for their ex-residents. Shelter staff will spend more time finding resources to fulfill women's material needs. We will be housing more homeless women, particularly as rent control is lifted and there are fewer public housing units. This will change the nature of work in shelters, since these women typically have a shorter stay and present different issues. There will be fewer services for referrals, especially for long-term counselling and ethno-specific programs. Proposed changes to social assistance could mean that women will be disentitled for long periods with absolutely nor esources and fewer rights of appeal, making their situation even more complicated.

Funding will be an ongoing problem. The provincial government will almost certainly make further cuts to shelters. There is a fear that funding could be completely eliminated for shelters with low occupancy rates. Shelters also receive municipal funding through a daily rate paid for each occupant (per diem). This funding mechanism has always been problematic and unstable. If indeed fewer women see leaving their partner as a realistic option, shelters will experience financial shortfalls. As municipalities receive more funding cuts, there may be other problems with per diem funding, as well as funding for "extras" such as personal needs allowances and transportation costs. In an effort to control costs, municipal social assistance staff may put pressure on shelter staff to move women through the shelter more quickly.

During "mega-week" in January 1997 the provincial government shifted further funding responsibility for welfare and other programs onto municipalities. This will affect funding available for shelters, in that welfare will now be competing with more programs for increasingly inadequate municipal monies. "Poorer" municipalities with a less lucrative property tax base will experience a greater impact.

There was concern that responsibility for core funding for shelters for abused women would also be shifted. At this point, the responsibility remains with the province's Ministry of Community and Social Services. This arrangement is preferred because it means that advocacy and consistency across the province is more feasible. There have been hints though that shelter programs could be moved into another ministry, and the impacts of this are uncertain.

The handling of woman abuse within the larger agenda of support for victims of crime will mean there will be a concentration upon short-term crisis intervention and criminal responses. This certainly does not meet the long-term needs of women who have been abused and ignores the fact that most of them never involve the criminal justice system. The government has shown a great deal of support for specialized domestic violence courts and will establish six new courts. We will need to monitor these courts to determine their effectiveness and build working relationships with court staff.

Since the government emphasizes accountability, services will need to prove their effectiveness like never before. Coordination of services is also emphasized. Shelters will probably be expected to coordinate and/or harmonize with other more mainstream community services which may not share the feminist or grassroots orientation of shelters. It will be a struggle to protect the philosophies and practices which have distinguished the work of shelters. We must also be cautious that we do not slip into the business mentality of fiscal imperatives which currently pervades both society and government.

Many agencies are struggling with the sense that we need to fill the gaps created by reductions in government spending (whether through increased fundraising, use of volunteers, or increased workload), and the awareness that this is exactly what the government wants us to do. This struggle cannot be easily resolved. In the future, it may mean communicating the impact of the changes, even if it seems no one is listening. While shelters are becoming increasingly wary of being political, we must not ignore that being political and fighting for social change is part of our heritage as women in the anti-violence movement.

Strategies

Working from solutions: This government responds best to groups which present solutions along with concerns. It is helpful if solutions are expressed in terms which the government would support or understand. Better that we propose the solutions, rather than bureaucrats or government officials who have little or no experience in this area.

Visibility: Those who manage to talk to government representatives are remembered when it comes to later funding decisions, or when opinions regarding policy or program changes are needed. Government members are usually eager for public engagements, and these may provide an opportunity to increase visibility and to advocate for your program.

Other avenues: Another way to attempt to influence the government is through local MPPs. They are concerned about returning to office, so they may take the concerns of constituents more seriously. As well, they may be more aware of the important role that shelters play within their community. The Ontario Association of Interval and Transition Houses has used this strategy in the past. Women can also ask their MPPs to advocate on their behalf to provincial bodies such as the Family Support Enforcement Plan. Members of the Opposition, and the Critics in particular, are also able to pressure the government on issues.

Applying direct pressure: While it is important to educate local MPPs, we will also need to apply direct pressure to ministers and the premier. There were rumours that the premier's office took notice of the consultant's report when it got media attention. We need to constantly remind ministers of our existence, our expertise, and our concerns. This may mean making a concerted effort to be visible to them and to hold them accountable. When ministers are not willing to meet with us, we will need to use other strategies.

Cost arguments: Financial imperatives and ideology are driving this government. They emphasize the need for personal responsibility and for families and communities to look after their own. But by cutting social programs, we are in fact creating a huge human debt. In December 1995, the Centre for Research on Violence Against Women and Children published a study which estimated that violence against women and children in Canada costs approximately $4.2 billion annually (through costs such as policing, medical intervention, and lost days at work), and that the costs are borne primarily by "the state" (i.e. taxpayers). Can we not then argue that shelters, which help women to escape abusive situations are in fact cost-saving measures? Specific programs can make this type of cost argument by comparing what it costs to support women to what it might cost to allow their problems to continue.

Enhancing the support of donors: We need to move our supporters beyond the charity-based mentality which focuses on "good deeds" and relieving the problems of individuals. We should be very intentional and explicit about asking donors for support, because they may not know what we need. For example, women in shelters need more than donations of used toys or a once-a-year financial contribution. Supporters could write a letter to their MPP regarding the importance of programs for abused women and their children. They could encourage employers to provide work opportunities for women and property owners to provide affordable, adequate housing for women. This government is adamant that the "community" can pick up the slack created by funding cuts. We must, then, hold the community (and those who elected the government) accountable to do this. We must be cautious, though, that our ethics are not compromised by the donations we accept.

Meeting women's material needs: While recognizing the problems associated with workers spending more time attempting to meet women's material needs, we must still respond to these needs. Some of the ways that this has been handled is through "Good Food Box" programs or community kitchens (the assumption being that buying or cooking in bulk is cheaper) and a skills sharing list so that women can assist each other and trade services (i.e. budgeting, child care) without exchanging money. Programs like these can be run by the participants themselves and can allow them to develop new skills. Community economic development is an area we should also explore. We will also need to become more involved in housing issues and advocacy in this area since housing is becoming even more difficult for women to find

Alliances within "the system": It is to our advantage to ensure that bureaucrats and other government officials working on women's issues have relevant and meaningful information about the situation of abused women. We may, then, need to establish working relationships with these people, so as to have a route to bring concerns and information.

Proving effectiveness/outcomes: We will need to create our own measures of effectiveness, because, as we know, traditional theories and measures do not fit the reality of women's lives. For example, if a woman decides to reconcile with her abusive partner, has the shelter failed in its work? Or, has it done its work, in that the woman has returned with more information and more of a sense of her choices? These measures should be based upon feminist principles, including giving voice to users.

The McGuire report criticized shelters for providing few measures of their effectiveness. This may be an argument which we could pay some thought to. Putting more effort into evaluating effectiveness could also benefit abused women if we find that our approach needs to change in order to be more effective.

A new framework: The government's plans for violence against women often propose generic services to deal with an issue which is clearly gendered. Feminist services will need to defend themselves and explain their importance in order to survive. This will prove challenging since the government is clearly anti-feminist and feminism is generally facing a backlash within society. Women's advocates and organizations will need to think about how far (or if at all) they are willing to compromise in terms of their approach and ideals.

Collaboration: Some shelters in Ontario are looking at ways to collaborate in order to cut costs. For example, shelters could share administrative staff, e.g. bookkeepers or could buy in bulk together.

Conclusion

Our society is undergoing fundamental changes. It is anyone's guess as to where this change will take us. Despite burnout and discouragement, we must not stop our fight to eliminate the abuse of women. We must continue to make the case that woman abuse effects us all, and that society has a responsibility to deal with women abuse in a comprehensive manner. As feminists, we situate the issue of woman abuse not within individuals, but within a society which is patriarchal, racist, and based upon unbalanced power relationships. It is dangerous when we forget this, and we must not allow ourselves to get caught up in the prevailing trend towards individualism and conservatism. Shelter workers ask abused women to be courageous and to take risks everyday. We must, then, ask the same thing of ourselves.

Kathryn Robertson has worked with abuse survivors in Victoria, Kelowna, and greater Toronto, and on policy issues within the provincial government. She has studied social work at the University of Victoria and the University of Toronto, specializing in women and social policy. The author wishes to thank all those who provided helpful feedback for this article.

"In the Basement"
Child Care's Uncertain Future

by Wendy J. Atkin

"Fight the Cuts," "Support Non-Profit Day Care"—protest signs bearing these and other slogans have become almost commonplace in Ontario politics. In fact, since the rise of the child care movement over 20 years ago, Ontario parents have had to go to the line repeatedly to lobby for social resources to be directed towards providing quality child care for their children.

In recent years, the situation has worsened, as the industrialized workforce has seen a retreat from the so-called welfare state that emerged under the postwar influence of Keynesian economic theory. Seniors' pensions, health care, and broadened access to post-secondary education are social spending items which are assumed today to be a right of citizenry, although they have not escaped the cuts. Access to high quality, affordable child care designed to meet a variety of parental needs and fulfill a range of child development goals, is by contrast an unrealized dream. Why, when it comes to our children, is the political discourse so unyielding?

Child care in Ontario has a chequered history, from its origins in the day nurseries established to provide custodial care so that low-income mothers could go out to work, through the diffusion of modern child development theories by way of nursery school and specialized child care facilities, to the "nine-to-five" daycare centres that grew alongside women's labour force participation from the late 1960s to the present day (Friendly). Although there are many child care options available to families today, restrictions on access, low wages for child care workers, and the threat of cuts, rather than growth under the current provincial government, seem to quash the dreams of child care advocates. If you look around your own community, chances are you will find a place where children are thriving in a quality child care setting that is, for now at least, very real.

There is a non-profit child care centre located on a university campus in eastern Ontario. Founded by faculty and students over two decades ago, the university community has, more or less, supported the centre through all of its growing pains and successes. Most recently, the centre was the recipient of one of the last of the JobsOntario construction grants and is housed in a state-of-the-art new building, with charming colours and storybook symbols integrated into the architecture. Strong volunteer commitment by the parents, essential services provided at a discount or under the sporadic goodwill of successive university administrations, combined with a relatively stable workforce, provide the centre with a relatively secure base. The staff, although underpaid, command higher wages and better benefits than most women working in the child care sector (and they are mostly women). This reduces staff turnover. In the infant room alone, the three full-time teachers have among them over 40 years of combined experience.

Under the current wave of cuts, this child care facility, like others of its calibre, is particularly vulnerable. The government's agenda hinges on privatization and workfare. This threatens the fiscal foundation of the centre. The university, under pressure to slash budgets as its transfer payments shrink, will withdraw some of the services it used to provide. The regional government has difficulty affording subsidies for low-income parent fees, and is proposing changes in policy that include eliminating centre-based care for infants and closing the centre during the summer months. As the staff and parents receive more and more bad news, morale begins to wane. The atmosphere becomes tense. Parents and staff mobilize. By late 1995, middle-class parents who have never held a picket sign in their lives, march with their children alongside child care workers during a one-day walkout.

Yet, the cuts keep coming. A parent at the centre penned the following story and said to the director, "please use this in any way you can." This is how she envisions her days if she loses access to the non-profit child care centre where both her infant daughter and toddler son can receive care under the same roof:

> You set the alarm for 5:30 a.m. so that you can manage to leave your home at 6:30 a.m. after waking and dressing your two children under the age of three. There's barely enough time to give the younger child a bottle, and your toddler doesn't eat much because he's so sleepy. You have to drop the baby off at a sitter's, who takes care of four other babies under the age of eighteen months. You have written a note to the sitter to make sure that your baby's diaper gets changed more frequently, because her diaper rash is getting worse as the week goes by. After dropping your baby off, you rush to the child care centre with your toddler, who craves the stimulation and socialization that the centre provides. By the time you get to work at 8:00, you realize you forgot to leave the baby's bottles at the sitter's. And it's only Tuesday. (Surman)

Now, several months later, we have the result of the government's child care review in Ontario and it is part of the general unbundling of traditional provincial government responsibilities for social services, which the government has fobbed off to municipalities that can scarcely afford them. The province, in turn, has been cut loose from historic ties with Ottawa. The Canada Assistance Plan, albeit a flawed apparatus that was never intended to administer child care policy, died on April 1, 1996. In its place, the Canada Health and Social Transfer (CHST) passes responsibility for spending fewer social dollars onto the provinces, no strings attached.

Let us dissemble these twin devolutionist innovations. Much of the policy debate surrounding the sloughing off of social spending powers from one level of government to the next has occurred without public scrutiny. Yet, together they represent the abandonment of the social client—the resident of Ontario—you, me, and most importantly, the children who are ultimately our collective responsibility.

In August 1996 the provincial premiers released their report, "Issue Paper on Social Policy Reform and Renewal: Next Steps," which expands on the notions they put forth in the 1995 Ministerial Council Report on Social Policy Reform. These documents provide the framework for the Federal/Provincial/Territorial Council on Social Policy Renewal to go about its work of unpacking the historic jurisdictional divisions by way of sectoral council studies in the areas of health, social services, labour market matters, post-secondary education, social housing, women's issues, and Aboriginal peoples. The "work" of this council and its related working groups has proceeded steadily, much of it consisting of closed-door meetings of politicians and bureaucrats commissioned to write working group reports which remain confidential. To date, there has been little open public discussion about this process which has resulted in the dismantling of social programs and will lead to a revised Canada. It is remarkable that constitutional issues have received so much public debate in official forums, yet the issues which are, literally, life-threatening, are treated *in camera*.

Child care spending in the form of subsidies to low-income families had been provided under the Canada Assistance Plan since 1966, within provincially and municipally-run child care programs. The Canada Assistance Plan also contained the incentive of matching funds for new program innovations. Since the implementation of the Canada Health and Social Transfer, the picture has changed dramatically. The Caledon Institute estimated that social spending would diminish by $7 billion in the first three years of the CHST. Already, the Canadian Council on Social Development says families are receiving $800 million less support from federal child benefits in 1996 than they did in 1984, and the rate of coverage has dropped to 80 per cent. This loss is particularly significant as both federal and provincial politicians are currently preoccupied with the "children's benefit" as a means of fighting child poverty. The children's benefit, aside from isolating children from the economic context of low-income families, serves the national unity goal—no one can argue against federal fiscal responsibility—but does little to provide essential services such as child care.

I trace these devolutionist trends—from the federal government to the provinces and, in Ontario recently, from the provincial government to the municipalities—to provide a backdrop for the current crisis in child care. The reasons why we need child care are well-documented. Starting with the Royal Commission on the Status of Women (1970); the Royal Commission on Equality in Employment (1984); the Task Force on Child Care (1986); the Report of the Special Committee on Child Care (1987); and the Social Security Review (1994), as well as numerous provincial/territorial studies, inquiries, and commissions. Today, the need for quality child care in the early years is highlighted by both the National Forum on Health and the National

Crime Prevention Council. The federal government's own election document promised to increase child care spending to create a maximum of 150,000 new child care spaces.

Quality child care has social value as an early childhood development strategy, a support to parents at work or at school, an aid to families and children living in poverty, and a key tool in pursuing women's equality. Statistical changes in female labour force participation and birth rates seem to suggest a reduced need for child care. Nothing could be further from the truth. In 1991, the last year for which reliable figures are available, only 15 per cent of children 12 years or younger requiring care for at least 20 hours per week had access to licensed care arrangements. Furthermore, child care is a significant factor in labour force attachment, especially for women. The *Labour Force Survey* identified 3,680,000 persons in Canada not in the labour force who were otherwise able to work in 1992; over 2.6 million of them were women. Of those who had children, 60 per cent cited child care responsibilities as the main reason they were not currently looking for work.

Children born in Canada today may never be able to access quality child care in the same numbers as the cohort preceding them. The scene across the country is mostly bleak; even slippages in standards, service erosions, and threats to child care workers' jobs and wages are becoming commonplace. We could hold child care up as a poor example of a "devolved" social program, but the reality is that this key children's service has never benefitted from federal legislation that would have strengthened its infrastructure to weather the current climate of cutbacks. Every major social program in Canada, from seniors' pensions to medicare, has required strong federal leadership and gradual provincial participation in order to become established. Yet where children are concerned, we have not yet been able to clear the fiscal, policy, and jurisdictional hurdles.

In Ontario, parents and child care workers participated in an extensive child care review conducted by the previous government. Unfortunately, no legislation emerged from that process. On January 14, 1997, the province announced that municipalities will be required to pick up half of the costs of the provincial child care budget. Licensing for child care programs will fall under municipal jurisdiction, with no clear indications on what quality indicators will guide regulation. Profound concern exists in the child care community that municipalities that cannot afford child care will focus cuts first on the most vulnerable forms—infant care and programs for children with special nees. Although the full impact will not be realized until the province releases its plans to restructure child care we may see the collapse of the regulated child care system in Ontario.

In December 1996 parishioners at a local church asked for my participation in a roundtable on child poverty. I thought that it ironic that this church was rumoured to be attended by a prominent federal government cabinet minister. At the last minute I begged off the roundtable in order to spend time with my children on that snowy

Sunday afternoon. They called again last week. "I know we are a small group of families involved here, but we are really concerned about the news on child poverty and want to do something." I agreed to speak to them but stressed that my strong support of a social infrastructure as prerequisite to any income transfer strategy for fighting child poverty would undoubtedly provide contrast with the views of the other speaker, many of the parishioners and, if the rumours were true, by the cabinet minister in question.

"But we really want you to come," the speaker at the other end of the phone persisted. "You see, child care is not far removed from what we find ourselves doing here. Over the past couple of years, homeless women have been sleeping in our church basement. It was only a few, at the start, and we had a strict rule that the doors would be shut behind them each morning at 7:00 a.m. Then, we gradually became aware that there were hardly any places for the women to go during the day and many were without food. So we initiated breakfast, and that was soon followed by a lunch program." I was surprised, although I should not have been given the dismal state of the region's economy. But what she said next gave me a start. "The fact of the matter is, we have found ourselves to be in the child care business, also on the sly, as many of the homeless women bring their children. So—we have to provide child care in the basement, too."

Wendy Atkin is coordinator of the Child Care Advocacy Association of Canada. She has been a parent and advocate for non-profit child care for the past eight years and is also completing a PhD dissertation entitled "Raising the Next Generation: Child Care Politics and Practices in Canada, 1950–1990" (Carleton University, Department of History).

References

Canadian Council on Social Development. "Integrating Children's Benefits: What Will Result?" Ottawa: Canadian Council on Social Development, Jan. 1997.

Friendly, Martha. *Child Care Policy in Canada: Putting the Pieces Together*. Don Mills, ON: Addison-Wesley, 1994.

Surman, Kerry. "Memorandum." 6 Nov. 1996. Unpublished personal communication distributed to public.

Statistics Canada. *Labour Force Survey*. Ottawa: Statistics Canada, 1993.

The Effects of the Cuts on Poor Women and Their Families in Thunder Bay

by Emily Scott

When monthly benefits for families on social assistance in Ontario were cut by 21.6 per cent, many families, especially those with young children, subsequently found themselves living below a bare subsistence level. Diane, a young single mother of two, depicts her plight in the following excerpt taken from a letter she wrote to the Thunder Bay Coalition Against Poverty:

> Once upon a time not so long ago, there lived a single mom with her two children in a city called Thunder Bay. Recently she had been financially devastated by the government cutbacks to social assistance recipients. This mom doesn't work—or should I say—doesn't get paid for the work she does. She is a full-time student at Lakehead University, and is maintaining a home, raising two young children. Not long after the cutbacks, this mom had a limiter put on her hydro. This meant that the Naughty Mom who only paid $100 on her hydro bill instead of the $236 she was suppose [sic] to, would not be able to use her stove to cook meals, and Naughty Mom could only have one or two lights on at a time. But Naughty Mom was even naughtier than this. See, Naughty Mom did not phone the hydro company this time to say she was keeping $136 for food for the month to feed herself and her children. You see, this happened once before and when Naughty Mom phoned to say she could only pay part of the bill, she received a lecture. What she needed was compassion, understanding, and someone to believe in her. Well, Naughty Mom struggled to meet her children's needs for the month with the very little money she had. She bakes bread but how could she now? A spaghetti dinner was out of the question. Even Kraft dinner could not be made without a stove....

It is left to non-profit agencies and other volunteer groups to help individuals like Diane maintain a little dignity. One such organization is the Thunder Bay Coalition Against Poverty (TCAP), which came into existence as a direct result of the cuts to welfare. From a first meeting of eight women, the organization has grown and amalgamated with other activist groups, as well as formed partnerships with labour groups and church groups. According to TCAP's coordinator, Christine Mather, before the cuts, people were finding it tough, but could basically manage. Now, they're just not getting by; in some cases it has been a downward slope from poverty to privation. Examination of an actual budget showed that in the case of a couple with two young children, before the cuts, from a monthly allowance of $1,546, the family was left approximately $104 per week for groceries and other expenses, after paying such costs as diaper and personal care bills, rent, and telephone. After the cuts, with all other expenses remaining the same, the family now has to make do with $43 for food. Compare these figures with those of a survey done by the Lakehead Social Planning Council, which indicated that it cost $450 to feed a family of four in Thunder Bay in December 1994. It is therefore not surprising that food banks have proliferated. As Christine Mather remarked, "The most visible and early effect of the cuts was an increase in the use of the food banks." When housing costs almost half of the monthly allowance, there aren't many options left to provide growing children with the basic necessities of food and clothing. As TCAP found out through a recent questionnaire, food, housing (including payment of utilities), and transportation were the greatest concerns.

Hydro costs are a big problem during the winter in Thunder Bay. As a result of persistent lobbying by TCAP and similar groups, an Anti-Poverty Task Force was established by the city to look into various poverty issues through a number of subcommittees. One of these, the housing subcommittee, met with a hydro spokesman to see what could be done to alleviate the situation for people like Diane. There was plenty of sympathy, but no change in Hydro policy regarding limiters or payments. Limiters would continue to be installed in meters during the winter months, even though some households which should have had limiters were being cut off altogether. (Limiters are circuit breakers which allow enough power for a furnace, a refrigerator, and a light or two.) While arrangements could be made to pay arrears in instalments, monthly payments would still be determined, not by the customer's ability to pay, but by the total amount of arrears; as a result, it is estimated that as many as 800 people would have disconnections or limiters during the winter because of non-payment of hydro costs.

There are other consequences to the cuts in social assistance as well. Activities like job hunting are severely limited because of problems with transportation, loss of child care subsidies, and housing. Appropriate clothing is also a concern for some families. Poor people are often not very well outfitted for our harsh northern Ontario winters, and some find even the Goodwill store prices higher than they can afford. Measures like a clothing co-op, where families can take whatever they need and recycle other items, have helped somewhat.

Furthermore, the cuts have an incremental effect. As families are forced to borrow from the next month's budget to meet their current costs, they never quite catch up. Moreover, cuts lead to loss of jobs, and families who were previously directly unaffected are finding themselves caught in a domino effect. For example, Brenda cooked for a private daycare centre. Three fathers were laid off and had to withdraw their children from the facility; as a result, she also lost her job. As her husband's job is casual and by no means secure, this young family is looking at the future with some dread.

The experiences have been much the same, whether women have been receiving welfare payments for an extended period, or whether new circumstances have changed their situation. And helping agencies, never very secure in their funding bases, have found themselves stretched in trying to preserve a basic level of service. For example, the Faye Peterson Transition House, which was established in 1983 as a refuge for battered women and their children, feels very constrained in the current provision of services to its clientele. Although its capacity is 15 women and children, there are usually more, and never fewer than 15 at any time. There are two other women's shelters in Thunder Bay, but the Faye Peterson Transition House is the only regional centre. According to Roberta Crouch, the coordinator, the cuts have had some immediate negative effects. Over the past eleven months, this has been reflected in changes in operation. They have lost only one of their full-time staff but this individual was also the sexual abuse counsellor, and a public educator, so public education programs have been severely curtailed.

Crouch has also seen negative effects by way of changes in outcomes for many of the women who seek refuge there. For example, since cuts in legal aid have meant a lack of representation in court, many women, unsure of the legal intricacies, nevertheless have to represent themselves in court and feel very intimidated. Crouch concludes that fewer abusers are being charged, and cases are taking longer to come before the courts. Also, the transition house used to be an acceptable place for children while their mothers were trying to sort out their situation, but lately, more and more often, judges are awarding custody to fathers if the mothers have taken refuge there. Many of the women who go to the transition house are forced to apply for welfare benefits and since the monthly payments are inadequate, a large number of them resort to the food banks. Their choices are few; either bear the privations of their new situation, or return to an abusive home. Some women, despairing of getting the assistance they need to ensure their safety, take the latter option in order to meet their children's basic needs.

These are the visible effects; more subtle are the attitude changes of the public and the fear these mothers feel. Diane, the young mother mentioned earlier, was fearful of being turned away from the food bank because her friend had taken her there in her car. This underscores the point that people in her situation have to face a number of demeaning attitudes, not only from some individuals in public service, but also from landlords, the public at large, and even from the media. Poverty affects the whole community, in a literal as well as psychological sense. The comforting insulation that was supposed to protect our most vulnerable citizens—the poor, children, the elderly, people with disabilities—the social safety net has disappeared.

The growing poverty in our society leads one to question the central purpose of government. It seems unjust that welfare recipients, already existing at a bare subsistence level, suddenly lose 21.6 per cent of their monthly cheque, while the cost of essentials—food, clothing, and shelter—have either remained the same or increased. Looking at the larger picture, one wonders how both the provincial and federal governments can justify allowing companies huge tax breaks or deferrals, or giving massive grants, while dismantling social structures. Most people want to work, but the governments have done little to create jobs.

Yes, things have been tough for women and poor families in Thunder Bay, as elsewhere, but despite these problems, one strong element that is apparent is the resilience on both the part of the agencies and the women who use the services. Greater involvement has made many ordinary citizens more aware of the larger picture—how deficits are created, who is paying the larger share of costs in our economic predicament, and who gets the tax breaks. TCAP, labour groups, women's groups, and other marginalized groups within the province are determined to continue the fight for social justice and put an end to the retrograde policies that are unravelling the social safety net. As Roberta Crouch said of agencies like the Faye Peterson House, "Government did not open these shelters, and government is not going to close them."

Emily Scott has worked as a classroom teacher and coordinator of services for students with special needs at the primary, secondary, and tertiary levels. She is currently providing educational services on a private basis, and volunteers on a number of committees and multicultural organizations concerned with social issues. She represents racial minorities on the North Superior Training Board in the Thunder Bay region.

References

Lakehead Social Planning Council. "Human Service Needs Data Base." Thunder Bay: Lakehead Social Planning Council, 1996.

Thunder Bay Coalition Against Poverty. *Survey of Needs Priorities of Food Bank Users.* Thunder Bay: Thunder Bay Coalition Against Poverty, 1996.

A Report on Hunger in Peterborough

by the Peterborough Social Planning Council

I've always worked hard to feed my family, but after 22 years of employment I was laid off. We may soon lose our home or have to sell it, and have to go on welfare. If this could happen to us it could happen to anyone.

This report is based on a study of hunger and food security in the City and County of Peterborough. It builds on food security research conducted in other Canadian centres over the past four years.

The results clearly demonstrate that a vast majority of households in the study sample are food insecure. Children make up a high proportion of the individuals in the households which are food insecure. This study points to the possibility that many of the 32 per cent of individuals and ten per cent of families who are living on low incomes in the City and County of Peterborough are food insecure.

"Food insecurity" more accurately describes food access and availability issues in Canada. The term food insecurity refers to the inability to obtain sufficient, nutritious, personally acceptable food through normal channels (i.e. grocery stores), or the uncertainty that one will be able to do so (Ontario Public Health Association Food Security Work Group; Davis and Tarasuk; Kalina; Campbell, Katamay, and Connolly; and Campbell, Katamay, Oram, and Berchem).

The findings reported herein are based on the results of interviews with randomly selected clients of two local agencies. The sample consists of the respondents and their families, or other household members, totalling 329 people (203 adults and 126 children living in 138 households). Only those respondents living below the Statistics Canada low-income cut-off are included in the analysis.

Through the experiences and voices of people in Peterborough who live on low incomes—the best witnesses to food insecurity—this Report seeks to contribute to the existing body of evidence and to document local issues of food insecurity. Through this study people experiencing food insecurity were given the opportunity to challenge prevailing dogma by talking about the reasons for their food situation and to provide their own thoughts on workable solutions.

Food security was an issue for the majority of the 138 respondents, with 87 per cent reporting they had experienced at least one of the four aspects of food insecurity in the last year. Eighty per cent said that they worried about running out of food; 63 per cent said that they had run out of money to buy food to make a meal; 75 per cent said they had eaten less than they feel they should; 75 per cent felt they could not always afford to eat properly; and 31 per cent said they had experienced an episode of severe hunger.

Households with children had particular problems meeting their food needs compared to households without children. Among households without children there were 15 per cent fewer occurrences of food insecurity.

Household size appeared to have little bearing on whether or not households living on low incomes experienced, in the past year, at least one of the four aspects of food insecurity. Similarly, household size had little influence on whether or not respondents had run out of money to buy food to make a meal. There was, however, a marked difference in the number of households reporting one or more incidents of severe hunger in the past year. Forty-three per cent of single member households compared to 25 per cent of multiple member households said they experienced severe hunger, having gone without food for a day or more.

Having someone in the household employed did help, but was no guarantee of food security. Among low-income households with employment earnings, 75 per cent reported experiencing at least one of the four aspects of food insecurity. The risk of food insecurity was increased when no one in the household received earnings from either full- or part-time work. Among households that relied solely on government transfer payments for their livelihood, 92 per cent were classed as food insecure.

What Are the Barriers to Food Security?

I'm forced to choose between living in a good area for kids and eating properly.

When asked why they had run out of money to buy food to make a meal, the majority of respondents (68 per cent) cited insufficient income as the cause.

Housing costs are a major budgetary expenditure, and for most households in the sample, a significant barrier to food security. Among our sample, housing costs were the most common expense cited for running out of money to buy food to make a meal.

Most households ranked unexpected expenses as the second most common expenditure responsible for the household running out of money to buy food to make a meal. Households with employment earnings are vulnerable to running out of money to buy food to make a meal, as a result of being laid off or having their work hours reduced. Twenty-five per cent of this subgroup had experienced food insecurity because of job loss or reductions in hours of work.

What Would Help?

Rents are too high for houses. Where are families supposed to live?

From a list of nine possibilities, respondents were asked to identify all options they believe would help them have enough good food to eat. They were then read back their choices and asked to select the one that, over the long-term, would make the biggest difference. Fifty-nine per cent of the sample said having wage earning employment, a better job, or higher wages would make the biggest difference in helping them have enough good food to eat. Respondents ranked lower cost housing and/or utilities followed by higher welfare benefits as the next most important long-term solutions for mitigating their food insecurity problems. Solutions identified included: having a job; having a better job/wages; lower cost housing/utilities; higher welfare benefits; more education/training; help with money management skills; help with cooking/shopping skills; access to food stores; and drug/dental coverage.

Discussion and Conclusion

I've been visiting my doctor regularly. He feels I'm not eating properly. My kids are fed three times per day whereas, I eat three times per week. I've lost 60 lbs. in the last year.

The results of this study clearly demonstrate that a vast majority of the 32 per cent of individuals and ten per cent of families living on low incomes within the County and City of Peterborough are food insecure (Peterborough Social Planning Council). The problem may even be more widespread in the City of Peterborough, where 37 per cent of individuals and 13 per cent of families are living below the poverty line. A high proportion of the individuals in the households that experienced food insecurity were children.

Food insecurity can be conceptualized as a linear continuum (Donovan, Clemens, Payne, and Kosky). It begins with worry about running out of food before getting money to buy more, followed by shortages of caloric and nutrient intake. If money shortages persist, periodic episodes of going without food for a day or more may occur.

This concept of a continuum was supported by the results of our study. Eighty per cent of the sample reported experiencing anxiety about running out of money to buy food. Slightly fewer respondents said they sometimes ate insufficient food quantity and quality, and still fewer, but more than half the sample, said they had run out of money to buy food to make a meal. Finally, almost one-third of the sample reported periodic and episodic severe hunger. These households were the most food insecure.

Increased employment opportunity represents the single most important strategy to alleviate hunger and food insecurity. In Peterborough, unemployment rates during the period of our study (1996) were 10.2 per cent in July, 11.1 per cent in August, and 10.6 per cent in September (Human Resources Development Canada), representing 4,300, 4,700, and 4,300 people unemployed.

Known job vacancies for these months were 493, 385, and 400. Assuming an additional 80 per cent hidden job market, vacancies may have been as high as 2,465,

1,925, and 2,000. Therefore, without even considering the "fit" of the unemployed people to existing vacancies, there was a shortfall of 1,835, 2,775, and 2,700 jobs during the period of our study. In other words, there were not enough jobs for everyone who wanted to work.

The fundamental barrier to food security was poverty. Households were forced, by inadequate income, to make choices that put them at risk of developing any of a wide range of debilitating behaviours and conditions linked with energy, protein, vitamin, and mineral deficiencies. These consequences include, but are not limited to, slow or stunted physical and mental development, fatigue, listlessness, apathy, lowered resistance to sickness and disease, and development of negative attitudes about self and society (Campbell, Katamay, Oram, and Berchem; Badun, Evers, and Hooper; Davis; Welsh; and Community Development Council of Belleville and District).

The level of risk is dependent on the duration, severity, and frequency of hunger, as well as the life stage of the individual affected (Campbell, Katamay, Oram, and Berchem). Although all age ranges are at risk, it is pregnant women and infants (0–4 years) who are most vulnerable to the health implications of food insecurity. Some physiological and social consequences may even persist on into adulthood, affecting educational achievement, employment opportunities, work performance, overall mental and physical health, and life expectancy (Ontario Public Health Association Food Security Work Group; Campbell, Katamay, Oram, and Berchem; Community Development Council of Belleville and District).

Obtaining adequate food quantity and quality was a particular challenge for low-income households with children. Of households with children, 94 per cent are food insecure. Households with infants, young children, adolescents, and/or youth face expenses not experienced by adult households. For example, a child in school requires additional money for outings, supplies, and clothing. In our study, the majority of adults with child dependents reported putting the needs of their children ahead of their own needs, by depriving themselves to provide food for their children. Even if caregivers are successful in shielding their children, by doing so they may harm their own health. Mothers may also jeopardize the health of their future children (Campbell, Katamay, Oram, and Berchem).

Study participants, many of whom were social assistance recipients, were making major efforts to cope with poverty and their food situation. In attempting to obtain all the calories and nutrients critical to their well-being, respondents used a wide variety of strategies, including a self-reliant approach, one based on informal cooperation and exchange, and one centred on the attainment of food items through formal economic and social support systems.

Peoples' first line of defence against hunger is to try to cope on their own, using strategies such as buying less expensive food, cutting back on essential non-food items, and choosing not to pay bills on time. These ways of coping allow people to retain a measure of personal pride and dignity (Tarasuk and MacLean).

The most widely used coping strategies were the options of buying less expensive food, and buying and serving food that was less nutritious than wanted. Fewer respondents preferred options such as selling or pawning personal possessions, choosing not to pay bills on time, and cutting back on essential non-food items. Gardening was also not widely used, possibly because most people living on low incomes do not have access to land.

A second line of defence against running out of money to buy food to make a meal is to participate in informal cooperation and exchange. Results of our study show that many respondents who have run out of money to buy food turn to the traditional sources of social support; reliance on family, friends, or neighbours for money or food. Twenty-one per cent, however, did not turn to either family, friends, or neighbours for assistance. Reasons for this include social isolation, economic constraint of family, friends, or neighbours, or loss of social networks (Ontario Social Safety Network).

Borrowing money to buy food is not an option for social assistance recipients. The Ministry of Community and Social Services requires these loans to be reported as income. The value of the loan is deducted dollar-for-dollar from the next month's disbursement, thus, forcing the recipient to borrow again to try to meet food needs. If the recipient fails to declare the value of the loan he/she is considered to have committed "welfare fraud" (Ontario Social Safety Network).

Respondents' apparent lack of preference for neighbourhood food security initiatives such as community gardens, collective kitchens, and food buying clubs was most likely due to issues of awareness, accessibility, and availability, rather than a reflection of respondents' willingness to participate or level of need.

Other studies have found that people seek formal help outside of the home and their network of friends, relatives, and neighbours usually only when the food shortage reaches a critical stage (Olson; Tarasuk and MacLean; Campbell and Desjardins; Katamay).

By documenting the budget of a minimum wage earner, it is perhaps easier to understand the relationship between low wages and a person's ability to feed him/herself. Assuming UI, CPP, and income tax deductions of $218 per month, a worker paid $6.85 per hour over 40 hours per week has a net monthly income amounting to $969 (Donovan, Clemens, Payne, and Kosky). Using monthly expenditure estimates based on the cost of a "Nutritious Food Basket" ($178.68 for a male 19–24 years old), and rent for a one bedroom apartment including utilities ($559), the monthly cost of bare essentials comes to $737.68 (Peterborough County-City Health Unit). Add to this $58 for a monthly adult bus pass and the worker has left at the end of each month $173.32, or the equivalent of $5.77 per day; what many people may unthinkingly spend on a coffee, bagel, and a newspaper each day (City of Peterborough Transit).

Out of the remaining $173.22 per month, the worker needs to pay for other core expenditures including clothing, laundry, personal care items, telephone, and health and dental care. Since this amount is clearly insufficient to meet all needs, the worker is forced to make difficult choices.

There are only two areas from which to take money; the rent or the food budget. If the person chooses not to pay rent, he/she is evicted. Therefore, it is often the food budget that is seen as flexible (Kalina; Katamay; Ross, Shillington, and Lockhead). The income of a person out of work and living on welfare allowance is inadequate to ensure food security. For example, the maximum monthly allowance for a single man (19–24 years old) living on General Welfare Assistance (GWA), without wage "top up," is $520 (Peterborough County-City Health Unit). After calculating expenditures for a bachelor apartment ($392), and food ($178.68), the individual is left a monthly deficit of $50.68 (Peterborough County-City Health Unit). A single GWA recipient does not have enough money to house and feed him/herself. Clearly he/she has no money for job-finding expenses such as transportation, telephone, stamps, or newspapers.

Among social assistance recipients are people permanently or temporarily disabled, and displaced older workers near retirement age, who face particular barriers to employment and thereby have reduced ability to access food security. The City of Peterborough Social Services reports that there were, on average, 595 people deemed unable to work and receiving GWA from June to October 1996, inclusive (Statistics Canada).

Also, among social assistance recipients are many lone mothers and fathers who cannot work without the availability of child care services; another barrier to food security (Olson; Task Force on Food Banks). The total income of a single mother (25–49 years) with a nine-year-old son, living on Family Benefits Allowance (FBA) and receiving a Child Tax Credit is $1,042 (Peterborough County-City Health Unit). If they share a bedroom or one person sleeps on a couch in the living room, the family can perhaps manage with a one bedroom apartment costing $559, including utilities. Add to this the cost of a food basket ($254.50), and the family has left $227.50 a month to cover child care, school expenses, telephone, insurance, and other essential non-food items (Peterborough County-City Health Unit).

In addition to anything that limits a households' financial resources such as inadequate wages or social assistance benefits, barriers to food security include anything that limits the portion of money available for food acquisition (Campbell). The primary expense for most households is the cost of housing and utilities. This expenditure was the most common non-food cost responsible for the household running out of money to buy food to make a meal (Donovan, Clements, Payne, and Kosky; Community Development Council of Belleville and District; Olson).

This study also found that on average, households were paying nearly twice the proportion of income for shelter that is recommended by the Canada Mortgage and Housing Corporation. If shelter costs were lower, there would be more disposable income for food and other essential non-food expenses.

People sometimes blame the poor directly for their food situation. Some exhort the poor to manage their money better. Among financially constrained households, however, constant attention is paid to planning and keeping track of money spent on food and non-food items (Campbell and Desjardins). Even those households with incomes approaching Statistic Canada's low-income cut-offs have to, after shelter, make careful choices between a proper diet, and other essential needs such as transportation for work or job searches, clothing, and telephone. Although education about money management has its merits and therefore, has a role to play in achieving food security, it is poverty, rather than ignorance that is the root cause of the problem.

A common myth is that low-income persons do not know how to shop for and prepare a nutritious meal. Studies indicate, however, that even though low income households spend a greater amount of their income on food than more affluent households, they get more calories and nutrients per dollar (Horton and Campbell; Maxwell and Simkins).

Some people have the misconception that people who are food insecure lack education/training or language skills to lift themselves out of the mire of poverty. An inquiry into food security in Belleville in 1992, however, determined there was no statistically significant difference in education levels between households who did and did not report running out of money to buy food (Community Development Council of Belleville and District). More education/training or better language skills does not necessarily translate into improved food security through finding a job, or finding a better job with higher wages. It is not uncommon, however, for people to be trained and re-trained for jobs that may never exist.

People unemployed are sometimes stereotyped as lazy and not wanting to work. Among the sample there was a high level of willingness to work indicated by a vast majority of respondents identifying the single most important long-term solution as having a job, having a better job, or higher wages. Thus, it can be concluded that it is not a lack of willingness to work but rather, a lack of employment opportunities and adequate wages that are the root causes of food insecurity.

To build food security it will be necessary to change economic and social policy at local, provincial, and national levels, to ensure that people have opportunities to obtain adequate incomes for themselves and their families. Actions, however, that concentrate solely on long-term solutions condemn the children who are food insecure today. Thus, there is also a need to reform the delivery of direct food aid, to permit dignified access to safe, nutritious, and adequate quantities of food.

Many people living on low incomes may feel there is little they can do to change their present situation. For example, they know that no amount of searching can help them find jobs that provide an adequate income. In addition to feelings of despair over lack of employment opportunities, they may feel stigmatized and inadequate if they are on social assistance and/or using food banks (Riches). It is not surprising, therefore, that approximately half of the respondents held no optimism for their future

Reduction in welfare has hurt the family to the core. There wasn't enough before, but now we feel like nobody gives a damn whether we live or die. I can't work as I am ill and have no skills that anyone wants. I want to work. I despair for my child, and her future. God help us!

This article has been excerpted with permission from the Peterborough Social Planning Council. For a copy of the report in its entirety please contact the Peterborough Social Planning Council at 257 Stewart Street, Peterborough, Ontario K9J 3M8. Telephone: (705) 743-5915. Fax (705) 743-3318. Email: pspc@knet.flemingc.on.ca

The Peterborough Social Planning Council (PSPC) works to build a strong community through research, community development, and public education. The PSPC is a United Way Member Agency.

References

Badun, C., S. Evers, and M. Hooper. "Food Security and Nutritional Concerns of Parents in an Economically Disadvantaged Community." *Journal of Canadian Dietetic Association* 56 (1995): 75–80.

Campbell, C. "Food Insecurity Nutritional Outcome or a Predictor Variable?" *Journal of Nutrition* 121 (1991): 408–415.

Campbell, C., and E. Desjardins. *Managing Limited Food Resources: Strategies Used by Families with Limited Incomes.* Toronto: Department of Nutritional Sciences, University of Toronto, 1987.

Campbell, C., S. Katamay, and C. Connolly. "The Role of Nutrition Professionals in the Hunger Debate." *Journal of Canadian Dietetic Association.* Proc. of "National Conference on Hunger." 1986.

Campbell, C., S. Katamay, B. Oram, and P. Berchem. "Hunger, Poverty, and Malnutrition: The Nutritional Implications of Food Security in Canada." *Journal of Canadian Dietetic Association.* Proc. of "National Conference on Hunger." 1986.

Canada Mortgage and Housing Corporation. Toronto, Ontario.

City of Peterborough Transit. Personal communication. October 1996.

Community Development Council of Belleville and District. *Hunger in Belleville: Task Force on Hunger Report.* Belleville, 1992.

Davis, B. "Children at Risk: Poverty Taking its Toll." *NIN Rapport* 6.3 (1991): 1–3.

Davis, B., and V. Tarasuk. "Hunger in Canada." *Journal of the Agriculture, Food, and Human Values Society* 11.4 (1994): 50–57.

Donovan, U., R. Clemens, J. Payne, and S. Kosky. *Thames Valley Region Food Security Survey*. Middlesex-London Health Unit, Elgin-St. Thomas Health Unit, Oxford County Board of Health. August 1996.

Horton, S., and C. Campbell. "Do the Poor Pay More for Food." *Food Market Commentary* 11.4 (1989): 33–39.

Human Resources Development Canada. *Statistics Canada Labour Force Survey*. Media release. 6 Sept. 1996 and 11 Oct. 1996.

Kalina, L. *Building Food Security in Canada: A Community Guide for Action on Hunger*. Kamloops, BC: Kamloops Foodshare, 1993.

Katamay, S. "Nutrition and Food Security: A Presentation to Region 5 of the Ontario Dietetic Association." 26 Oct. 1992. Unpub.

Maxwell, C., and S. Simkins. *Background Paper on Nutrition for the Disadvantaged*. Ottawa: Health and Welfare Canada, 1985.

Olson, K. *Food Security in Edmonton: Organizing for Action*. Edmonton, 1992.

Ontario Public Health Association Food Security Work Group. *Food for Now and the Future: A Food and Nutrition Strategy for Ontario*. Toronto: Ontario Public Health Association Food Security Work Group. March 1995.

Ontario Social Safety Network. *Ontario's Welfare Rate Cuts and Anniversary Report*. Toronto: Ontario Social Safety Network c/o Social Planning Council of Metropolitan Toronto, 1996.

Peterborough County-City Health Unit. *Nutrition Matters* 12.2 (June 1996).

Peterborough Social Planning Council. *Peterborough Profile 1994*. Peterborough, 1994.

Riches, G. *Food Banks and the Welfare Crisis*. Ottawa: The Canadian Council on Social Development, 1986.

Ross, D., E. R. Shillington, and C. Lochhead. *The Canadian Fact Book on Poverty*. Ottawa: Canadian Council on Social Development, 1994.

Statistics Canada. *Statistics Canada Labour Force Survey*. July-September 1996.

Tarasuk, V., and H. MacLean. "The Food Problems of Low-Income Single Mothers: An Ethnographic Study." *Canadian Home Economic Journal* 40.2 (1990): 76–82.

Task Force on Food Banks. *Not by Bread Alone: A Strategy to Eliminate the Need for Food Banks in the GTA*. April 1991.

Welsh, J. "Hunger in Canada: Consequences and Challenges." *NIN Rapport* 6.3 (1989): 1–2.

Parkdale Community Audit Project

by Anne O'Connell

Late in 1995, a handful of residents and workers in community centres in Parkdale embarked on a research project committed to documenting and communicating the rapid changes taking place in their neighbourhood. These changes are the result of profound shifts in public policy, with the most dramatic examples being introduced by the government of Ontario, changes such as the 21.6 per cent reduction in welfare rates of assistance, and the proposed 30 per cent cut in personal income taxes. The magnitude of the welfare cut alone translates to an annual loss of $7.6 million in incomes of residents living in South Parkdale. Clearly the entire local economy would be affected by this single policy change. This report is the product of interviewing 200 households in South Parkdale, between August and October 1996, and tells the story of what the people of Parkdale say is happening to their lives after a year and a half of deep and widespread cutbacks.

The overall purpose of the community audit project was to provide a view from "both sides of the fence," from the business sector and the consuming sector, from middle-income and low-income households. Asking for and recording people's opinions presents much richer possibilities for establishing meaningful cross-sectoral dialogue, which in turn provides a solid base from which to develop new approaches for action. We hope these will range from community forums, to joint ventures in advocacy, to local economic initiatives.

Though the results may differ from community to community, we believe the model created through this project offers a thorough and robust tool that any community can apply. It can provide answers about what is the impact of public policies which "downsize" our social infrastructure by examining changes in: consumption and spending patterns; quality of life issues; survival strategies; people's capacity and interest in making change at the political level; and people's capacity and interest in making change at a community level.

Community Profile of South Parkdale

All ways are gone for poor people, every corner.

The 500 people whose lives are reflected in this survey represent over two per cent of the total population of South Parkdale. These residents live in 200 households in a low-income neighbourhood in Toronto. In our sample we interviewed an equal number of men and women. Our sample also mirrors the breakdown in the rent/own category for the census data: only seven per cent of households in South Parkdale are homeowners compared to 37 per cent in the City of Toronto.

In 1990, census data show that 36 per cent of residents in South Parkdale were living below the poverty line. A minimum estimate tells us that five years later, 52 per cent of residents in South Parkdale have incomes below the poverty line, a dramatic increase and disturbing comparison to the national poverty rate of 18 per cent across Canada.[1] Out of the 200 households in our sample, 183 informed us of their total household income per year. Of those who responded, we found that 108 households (59 per cent of the households) live below the poverty line. Calculating the number of people living in each of these households—(269 people out of a total of 500)—54 per cent of South Parkdale residents in our sample are living below the poverty line. Of the households that have children under the age of 18 in our sample, 74 per cent, or three out of four children live below the poverty line.

This is a staggering number in light of a recent announcement that one in three children in the City of Toronto live below the poverty line.[2] The situation worsens for single-headed households with children, in which all but one household lives below the poverty line. In our sample 94 per cent of single adult households with children are female-headed. While only 27 per cent of households with children live above the poverty line, 51 per cent of households of adults without children and 46 per cent of senior-only households in our sample live above the poverty line.

What is a community audit?

Community audits can assess the impact of cuts to public provision of services and supports and can assess the capacity of communities and individuals to respond with useful alternatives to these services and supports. Furthermore, they are useful for:

•providing a benchmark or inventory of currently existing public supports and services

•monitoring and tracking the evolution of their provision

•providing tools to develop an inventory of current capacity to respond

•creating a forum for community/civic development

•creating a feedback loop for agencies to systematize, develop, and coordinate response mechanisms to emerging needs

•offering a methodology and/or clearinghouse of information to assist national/regional/umbrella organizations better track and represent local issues and concerns

•creating a repository of ideas, innovations, and strategies which could be adopted in different communities

• describing and monitoring the health of a local economy.

Furthermore, in our sample, 44 per cent of households spoke a home language other than English, with the three highest language groups being South Asian languages, Tagalog, and Vietnamese. Statistical testing revealed a significant relationship between levels of poverty and the language most often spoken at home. Of those that speak English at home, 51 per cent of households live below the poverty line compared to 71 per cent of the households that speak a language at home other than English. This means that non-English speaking households have a 20 per cent higher incidence of living below the poverty line. *"We have to live in one room, can't maintain ourselves, [TTC] tickets are too expensive, can't look for a job ... on waiting lists. Come to this country to build a future, want to go back but don't have money for ticket."* Length of residence also had a relationship with poverty rates in South Parkdale. Of the households that have been in Parkdale for less than five years, 67 per cent live below the poverty level versus 51 per cent of households that have been established in the area for five years or more.

This connects the issues of poverty and high mobility, though it does not define the causality. Parkdale is a place where new Canadians come to settle. Since we asked for "home language" and not when people came to Canada we cannot make direct inferences about immigration patterns. Yet, the necessity for ESL programs, settlement services, equitable employment practices, and a commitment to challenging discriminatory policies that have an impact on income, appear to be supported by these figures.

Local Economy

In the spring of 1996, we interviewed 47 retailers in Parkdale about the impact recent policy decisions have had on business. In particular, the welfare cut and the 30 per cent tax break have been put forth as a strategy to stimulate the economy, which should be good news for business. However, we learned from local businesses that: half of the businesses experienced a decline in business volume in the last year, with three quarters of these indicating a loss of 21 per cent or more in business volume; 41 per cent stated the tax cut will have no effect or may negatively impact their business; 64 per cent of businesses are worried about their business for the coming year.

In the survey of retailers, we asked businesses to estimate the percentage of their sales that are purchased by local residents. Of the 43 businesses who gave an estimate, 72 per cent stated that over half of their business comes from local residents. In order to build a dialogue around local versus external spending patterns we asked each household to tell us the amount of consumer spending they make in the neighbourhood or outside of Parkdale. Of the 197 households that responded to this inquiry, 57 per cent stated that over half of their purchases are made solely in South Parkdale. These numbers show that residents nearby contribute heavily to the local economy and the interdependence that exists between business and community is significant.

Change in Spending Patterns

We asked residents if the cutbacks in the last year have had an impact on their spending patterns or levels of consumption. Of the 200 households we spoke with 56 per cent stated that they now purchase fewer goods and services. *"I pay extra money for some medication, buy less food and clothing which is necessary for the baby ... less money so have to spend less for everything."* Given that over half of our sample shop locally, this marks a serious hit to businesses in the area within the last year. The significant drop in local spending power dates back to the 21.6 per cent cut to welfare in October, 1995 which represented an annual loss of 7.6 million dollars to the income of Parkdale residents.

In particular, we learned that from those who do buy less it is most prevalent in the areas of groceries, clothing, restaurants, hairdresser, and home furnishings. On top of buying less, 26 households (13 per cent of total sample) stated that within the last year there are items that they can no longer afford. These data strengthen the findings in our retailers' survey that half of the businesses in South Parkdale experienced a decline in business in the last year. It is also no surprise that all of the grocery stores reported a loss of business, along with half of the restaurants and clothing stores in our sample.

Of the 63 households that are now purchasing less food, 75 per cent live below the poverty line establishing a significant relationship between a drop in food purchasing and income level. Similarly for the 53 households that have reduced their clothing purchases, 70 per cent are living below the poverty line. Income level was not significant when purchasing fewer home furnishings or trips to hair salons and restaurants; these are non-essential goods and services in which those living above and below the poverty line have cut back on.

How the Changes Affected Families

> *I want a better job than what I have now. The cuts are affecting my chance of getting a good job. More pressure, more tension, more yelling in family due to economic pressure.*

Responses from 163 households showed us how the cutbacks have affected their daily lives. The most common response was that people now felt their income was insufficient to live on. People spoke about not being able to cover their expenses, buying less food and clothes, constantly looking for deals, and finding it hard to live in the current economic climate.

A lack of sufficient income erects further barriers, shown in the next most common responses: an inability to afford the high cost of public transportation and the loss of life chances. *"More money for the TTC. Tuition went up. I used to go to university. This year it is too expensive and I need to work instead.*" People stated that lost opportunities are a consequence of the cancellation/reduction of adult education and children's programming, the increase of tuition fees in the post-secondary education system, an increase in classroom size; and how the lack of daycare spaces makes accessing education/employment opportunities increasingly unattainable.

People also pointed to the stress of the health cutbacks and the extra costs for medication, and how employment problems are having serious effects on the survival of their families. Employment problems included job loss, cuts to job training, increase in workloads, and the lack of available jobs.

Furthermore, the reduction of services in the last year provided by legal aid, homecare, housing, immigration, and community centres adds to the new day-to-day barriers people in South Parkdale are now faced with. As one individual commented: "*It feels like there is a stranglehold on you and there is nowhere to turn.*"

What Are People Doing Differently?

Significantly, more than a quarter of the entire sample is altering the way they shop: budgetting more constantly, buying less food and fewer big purchases, buying cheaper qualities of food, using more coupons, going to food banks, shopping at second hand stores, and handwashing their laundry. *"More than ever I look for work, decrease expense on meat from four kilos to two kilos/month, no more fruit and vegetables. Now pasta and some sauce is what I eat.*"

Perhaps most alarming, a full 20 per cent of the households surveyed reported that they felt increasing social isolation. Many people now go out less frequently, households are cutting off their cable and/or telephone service, and people have described how inaccessible the simplest opportunities are becoming: "*Never go out now, cutback on food, little money, don't buy clothes [except] cheap discount clothing, buy less books, go to library, want lessons for the kids [but] can't afford it, summer camp is too expensive.*"

What's Happening to The Neighbourhood?

People have upset faces, like a mirror, faces tell everything.

In addition to the experience of individual households the findings show that 60 per cent of our respondents have noticed a dramatic impact on the Parkdale neighbourhood. Income was not a factor in measuring whether residents stated a community impact had been suffered or not. In order of importance, households noted: an increase in homelessness, panhandling, and food bank use; increase in illegal activity; suffering and stress about future; deterioration of public space (dirty parks, less activities at community centres); people spending less, business going down; serious housing problems.

Regardless of household wealth, residents in Parkdale are disturbed about what is happening to their community. This finding establishes common concerns for organizing community forums that deal with the emerging issues in our neighbourhood.

Just as retailers in the spring observed a decrease in purchasing power of Parkdale residents, residents in turn spoke of the noticeable impact on local business. *"People are buying cheaper things. Garage sales are on front lawns everywhere."* Based on a mapping of businesses in the area conducted in October 1995, we learned in the survey of retailers that six months later ten per cent of the businesses had left the area. A recent updating of the map shows that after a year of welfare cuts, close to 20 per cent of businesses had left the area, with half of those locations now having another business operating out of them.[3] *"Everyone's complaining there are no good stores left."*

Political Literacy of Parkdale Residents

In this section of the survey we were interested in learning how people respond to, understand, and fit into the existing political system. We asked residents what they thought the number one issue should be for the provincial government. A total of 182 households responded to this question, offering 204 responses. The highest occurring response is that government should be concentrating on the issue of employment and job training (87 occurrences). Surprisingly, the next highest category did not focus on what government should be doing; residents instead expounded on how angry they are with the current policy direction and governing style of the provincial government (41 occurrences). Of these 41 responses, half believe people who are poor have been targetted unfairly, with some calling for the reinstatement of the welfare cut and a review of cutbacks generally, while the other half of these respondents point to a governing style that refuses to engage in consultative processes with anyone. The next most common responses involved: strengthening our health, education and child care systems (16 occurrences); dealing with our housing problems, i.e. homelessness, affordable housing, and reconsidering the rent control bill (15 occurrences); and that government should have a role in managing the economy (13 occurrences).

The Tax Cut and the Deficit

In our survey of retailers "lower taxes" was the most common request made by respondents, yet only four households in our survey stated that it was an issue the government should address. Given the business community's stated desire for lower taxes, we expected retailers to then favour the 30 per cent tax cut—part of an election promise that ushered the provincial government into power. The tax cut has been promoted as a measure that will stimulate the economy. Business people in Parkdale, however, strongly question the promised windfalls of the tax cut, with 41 per cent stating it will have no impact on their business or may negatively affect their customer base as a whole.

In our sample of households 84 per cent of residents stated "no/don't know" to the tax cut as a positive influence on the economy. While higher income households will benefit more from the tax cut, we found that both those below and above the poverty line voiced their disapproval or uncertainty about this policy.

In an attempt to measure the economic significance of the tax cut, we asked residents what they would do with the money they received back. The single most common answer (43 per cent) showed that households would pay bills/debts with money received from the tax cut. This finding tells us that the majority of money would address old consumption patterns versus new spending that could invigorate the economy. Given the public focus on the urgency of deficit reduction, we find it remarkable that neither business people or residents identified it as a priority for the government. Here we see a disjuncture between what gets named as a "public issue" as opposed to the issues people want the government to attend to.

Political Influence

We learned from the retailer survey that over half of the business people in Parkdale do not know who is their city councillor or MPP. In the household survey we added Metro councillor to the list and found that: 46 per cent of households know their City councillor; 20 per cent of households know their Metro councillor; 34 per cent of households know their MPP.

While the residents in our sample are least familiar with the Metro councillor, the tenure of each representative seems to be a relevant factor. The Metro councillor has been in power for three years, compared to our city councillor—in office for the last 15 years and our MPP representing Parkdale now for 18 years. Given that one third of residents in South Parkdale cannot vote, they likely have less influence on elected officials. Political influence is further captured by the number of respondents that have ever contacted a level of government for assistance: ten per cent of respondents have contacted their City councillor; five per cent of respondents have contacted their Metro councillor; nine per cent of respondents have contacted their MPP.

These data show that a considerable disengagement exists between residents, politicians, and the political process. The figures were higher for business people in the area, with 36 per cent reporting some contact with their city councillor and 27 per cent relating to their MPP.

When we inquired about their influence on government, 64 per cent of households stated that they had no influence on the decisions government make. Of the 96 households that explained why, one-third stated that government does not listen to or consult with people which precludes any chance at influencing policy making. Another

19 per cent of respondents thought that groups have more power than they as individuals do. Residents spoke positively about the influence and power groups can have, reflected in their own experiences of membership and volunteerism across a variety of sectors.

Community Capacity and Civic Engagement

We asked residents to tell us if they volunteer or have memberships in any associations, trade unions, political parties, religious organizations, clubs, groups, boards, or agencies. Of the 193 households that responded, 43 per cent stated that they participate and volunteer in their community. This primarily included participation at their school or church, active membership in community centres, ethno-cultural groups, and seniors' organizations.

Notably, income was not a factor for those that volunteer their time to a wide range of interests and social causes. In the current environment of cutbacks the government has encouraged volunteerism as the route to alleviate the strains on programs that focus on those "less fortunate."

What these findings tell us is that people living below the poverty line are themselves contributing to supporting our social infrastructure. Low-income residents in Parkdale contribute to the "social" economy, breaking one of the tired and destructive myths of the poor "living off the system." The three highest areas of participation can be found in community-based organizations and agencies, cultural groups, and in the public sector, i.e. schools, centres, and hospitals. These results build on the findings of the Community Agency Survey of May 1996, that reported 78 per cent of the "workforce" in community-based social service agencies are volunteers.[4]

What we found most encouraging is that residents feel they have a high level of influence within their respective groups, compared to their ability to affect government decision-making. When we asked people if they thought they had some decision-making power through their group membership or volunteer work, 71 per cent of the respondents stated they had some influence, a powerful contrast to the 17 per cent that stated they had some influence on government decision-making.

The lack of political influence is found in the numbers of those that ever participated in a political party—only five per cent of all respondents. The contributing factors that led to meaningful participation was that the group was small and that influence was an understood aspect of membership. The groups that residents participated in allowed them to be active, vocal participants.

Next Steps

The future of this project is perhaps the most difficult to formulate and launch. In a section of the survey not featured in this report, residents in Parkdale point to a number of positive features that make it a vibrant, diverse neighbourhood equipped with good facilities that are close at hand. A strong level of interdependence between business people and residents exists, with common concerns and interests. This establishes some ground work in bringing together the various stakeholders in developing ventures and initiatives, both social and economic, that will serve the well-being of Parkdale.

The challenge for us is twofold. First, a meaningful coalition (business and resident being represented, different income classes being represented, different ethnic groups being represented) needs to have one or more achievable and concrete projects for action. Which leads to the second challenge. Most people and small businesses have a severe time deficit. A project like this takes time to build momentum. Momentum builds enthusiasm. Enthusiasm attracts more of people's time. And so the first steps of articulating a cooperative venture will make or break this project. Wish us luck! And if you have any experience with this kind of thing, get in touch with us.

Participating Organizations

St. Christopher House, Sistering, Parkdale Intercultural Association, Parkdale Community Health Centre, City of Toronto Public Health Department, and the Social Planning Council of Metropolitan Toronto.

For More Information

Enquiries about the entire report, questionnaire development, tips on interviewing, and recording can be directed to Armine Yalnizyan, Social Planning Council of Metropolitan Toronto, Suite 1001, 2 Carlton Street, Toronto, Ontario, M5B 1J3; telephone: (416) 351-0095, fax: (416) 351-0107.

Excerpted from the "Parkdale Community Audit Project Report No.2—A Survey of Residents, March 1997," a joint publication of the City of Toronto Public Health Department and the Social Planning Council of Metropolitan Toronto.

Anne O'Connell decided to return to school after four years of front line support work with homeless and low-income men and women. This change coincided with a 30 per cent tuition hike for post-secondary studies, while financial support for students has dwindled. Participating in the Audit Project helped her to understand how we connect community knowledge and academia, in a way that remains committed to learning and action.

[1] The 52 per cent includes those living below the poverty line based on the 1991 census

plus the increase in those on social assistance since that time period. These numbers do not take into account any increase of those who are working or are unemployed and may also live below the poverty line.

[2]This statistic comes from the City of Toronto, Public Health Department.

[3]Mapping of businesses from Dufferin St. to Roncesvalles Ave. on King and Queen St., courtesy of Parkdale Intercultural Association, contact Gilmar Militar.

[4]The Community Agency Survey is conducted by Metro Community Services, the Social Planning Council of Metropolitan Toronto and the City of Toronto Planning and Development Department.

Feeding Kids on Tuna and Bologna
The Impact of the Cuts on Single Black Women in Toronto

by Karen Flynn

Given the current economic situation, the picture that emerges for women in the province of Ontario is a bleak one, especially for those from racially and ethnically diverse backgrounds. Single black women and their children, who are dependent on some form of social assistance, have already begun to feel the impact of the recent cuts to welfare benefits. Already doubly disadvantaged, single, poor, black women on social assistance are stigmatized by racist stereotypes that classify them as "lazy, illiterate, baby machines, drug dealing, and promiscuous." During December of 1995, I interviewed five poor, single, black women and learned from them how the cuts have affected their physical and emotional well-being, how they cope with welfare cuts, and their views on the future.

Women's Response to Cuts to Social Assistance

Prior to the introduction of the cuts, the media frenzy heightened feelings of fear and uncertainty among people, particularly among women who utilize some form of social assistance or service. The women I spoke with worried about the financial implications of the cuts and how these changes would affect their ability to purchase the basic necessities required for survival. They worried about cuts to daycare, public transportation, and education. These services are essential for women who attend school or are in the process of job hunting. Deseree, a 24-year-old university student, and the parent of a five-year-old daughter comments: "I felt very concerned, very afraid, very worried. I don't think people realize what a struggle it is already. There are women out there who are working hard, and trying to make a change in their lives."

Nicole, a 25-year-old university student, with two children adds:

> *More than anything, I was worried about child care. I was worried about the money they give me each month, but child care was more important. I have always wanted to work. I figured if they did cut me off, and I had to leave school, it would be hard to find a job, but as long as I had child care then I would be okay.*

These women were already having a difficult time surviving on social assistance. Once the cuts were implemented, the women worried more about cutting back on food than cutting back clothing and other necessities. Nicole comments: "Kids need a variety of foods daily. I don't think my kids should have to eat any worse than say someone not on welfare."

Barbara, a mother of three in her late 30s, recently cut down on food "just to make ends meet." She worries about the mixed messages her children will be receiving in school as to what constitutes a suitable diet. "How are you going to raise your children on tuna? [At school] they tell your kids they have to be healthy. They need to eat good. They tell them in school what's good and what's not."

Some women attempt to locate supermarkets where food prices are cheaper, but they are still faced with problems as far as daycare or transportation is concerned. Barbara adds: "Not everyone has a car. Especially in this weather, who can go from store to store and look for deals? I try my best to go from store to store, but I can't reach them all."

Strategies for Survival

Even though, theoretically, the welfare system is designed to help those who need financial assistance, in practice, it maintains poverty among people, especially women. Social assistance by itself is barely enough for women and children to live on and employment that may be used to supplement welfare payment is prohibited. Furthermore, incentives once in place to encourage job training have been eliminated. In response, black women develop or find alternate means of surviving. Mona, a 33-year-old mother of one, states: "… I had to find something else to do to make some extra money. People don't want to collect welfare but there are no jobs out there…. I would go crazy if I had to sit around and wait for welfare."

Mona cleans another (white) woman's home for $50 a week, a task traditionally associated with black women. Even though it is out of necessity that Mona performs these domestic duties, her employer benefits more from this arrangement than Mona. The employer, for example, does not have to register with Employment and Immigration Canada or even pay Mona the average fee for a domestic worker. Race continues to determine, to a large extent, the type of job opportunities available for black women.

The common perception of women who work and collect welfare is that they are "abusing the system." The reality is that social assistance is inadequate to meet the needs of its recipients. Extensive reductions to welfare and social benefits compel many to find other ways of sustaining themselves, even if it is illegal.

Another survival strategy employed by some women is to move in with family and friends. For example, although her sisters provide no economic support, Mona notes:

I know that if I was living by myself it would be hard, it would be tough. My sisters don't do anything for me to make my life easier. The only thing they are good for is splitting the rent. If I had money I would live by myself with my son. But right now I can't afford it. Right now it's easier.

Black women turn to their mothers, sisters, friends, and, in the case of one woman, the children's father for support. But many, like Barbara, don't have a support system.

[If I have] no money, there is no one to turn to for help. I have no friends, no family. It's difficult for me and other people who don't have relatives to turn to. I am here alone. I don't have no mother, father, sisters, or brothers. I can't go to my neighbours because they are probably worse off than me.

Moving in with family and friends reinforces the current governments' position that family and community should fill the gap created by the cutbacks. This will deflect attention from the state and its role in perpetuating inequality. Furthermore, the state will cease to allocate resources to individuals and institutions who need them.

A number of coalitions have been formed and countless demonstrations have been organized throughout Ontario to protest against budget cuts. When asked whether they participated in any type of activist work, the women interviewed expressed concerns about the validity of activism, whether activism actually works, the benefits to be gained, the exclusion of certain groups from activist work, and the inability to participate in activist work due to lack of time. Mona states:

If I get involved in activist work how is it going to benefit me? A lot of people get involved and it doesn't benefit them at all. Most people in these groups are looking out for themselves [and] most of them are white people.... You don't see any black people getting involved. Don't you know why? Because [white organizations] keep black people out.

Poor black women have been, and continue to be, marginalized by the feminist and labour movements. Organizations need to reach women who are illiterate and poor, and women who have no concept of what feminism is. An organization such as the National Action Committee on the Status of Women (NAC) needs to take the feminist agenda into the homes of black women who do not have the time to attend meetings. Strong alliances and coalitions are counterproductive if they refuse to acknowledge how racism and poverty coexist for non-white women. Moreover, they will fail if they continue to privilege the interests and needs of middle-class white women to the detriment of non-white women.

Additionally, involvement in any form of activism should be viewed as acts to ensure survival. Women may engage in different forms of activism that do not always involve demonstrations or involvement in a union, or other political groups. Deseree contends that her "form of activism is talking, writing an article, doing poetry, and getting involved, in perhaps, forums."

For some black women the daily struggle of surviving in a racist, classist, and sexist society is their method of activism. Daily activism to guarantee survival is applicable in all women's lives, especially those who live in poverty. As the well-being of children is contingent upon a mother's emotional and physical health, these women work at surviving daily to assure the survival of future generations, instead of participating in political activism.

We are witnessing the erosion of the welfare state in the industrialized world which will only intensify the feminization of poverty. In the interest of competition, reducing the debt, and attracting investors, the needs of women and the poor are no longer central to political debates.

Black women want to provide for their families, and they want job opportunities that provide them with a respectable standard of living. These women would rather have decent paying jobs and provide their families with adequate housing than endure the embarrassment, humiliation, and stigma attached to black women on welfare.

Despite the obstacles, however, these women are optimistic about the future. They see education as the key to creating a better life for their children and themselves. Jackie, a 21-year-old mother of two, reflects the sentiments echoed by some of the women:

> ... I think our future is looking up. I have made certain changes in my life. I am going to make sure [my children] are well taken care of. That they will have food on the table, clothes on their backs. At the same time, I understand that there are a lot of extras that I may not be able to give them now. I know that when I am finished my education then I will be able to do that.

For black people in North America, education has always been perceived as the route to success despite the paralyzing effects of institutional and systemic racism and sexism. Unfortunately, cuts to education and yearly tuition increases will make it more difficult for poor, black women and their children to pursue any kind of education. Although these women are worried about the long-term effects of the cuts, there is no doubt that these women will continue to rely on traditions of resistance and survival that are characteristic of people of African-descent. They will continue to network, share, and exchange resources among family and friends and, outside of the family institution, use whatever mechanisms available to guarantee the daily survival of their families.

Conclusion

The ongoing debate regarding the cuts to welfare and social programs continue to resonate throughout the province. Feminists unanimously agree that as the principal recipients of social assistance and social programs women and children will suffer the repercussions of these cuts. However, what they fail to construe is that in the same way that these cuts are not gender-neutral they are not race-neutral. Black women as a group are significantly poorer than white women and will experience the cuts in ways that are different from white women. As these interviews illustrate, black women are concerned about the destruction of social programs, the cuts to welfare payments, and lack of job opportunities in a racist, sexist, and hostile Ontario.

Karen Flynn is a Jamaican-born feminist and community activist, host at CHRY Community Radio, and is currently a second year PhD student in Women's Studies at York University.

Supporting Society's Marginalized Groups

The cuts have augmented my struggles against the constant pressures of economic survival, part-time attendance at the University of Toronto, a part-time job, and full-time work as a single parent. I really can see no sense in cutting funding for subsidized child care, funding for the Ontario Student Assistance Program, and funding for the Family Benefits Act. For women like myself, such increased economic and emotional stress only makes it more difficult, if not near impossible to imagine a successful future for myself and my child.

These hard times effectively create a need for the development and maintenance of support services for society's marginalized groups. I hope to play a part in advocating for minority women as well as creating and sustaining the much-needed support services for these women. I believe it is imperative that the faces and experiences of the researchers and advocators adequately reflect the communities in which they research and serve. I am convinced that this type of service, or lack thereof, impacts greatly upon the social and psychological development of women, and their families—especially women of colour. I believe in giving our children, our future, every possible advantage. As well, I believe in our power to lobby, protest, and vote for positive change.

—Diane Aiken has recently completed her four-year Honours BA in Women's Studies and Cultural Anthropology at the University of Toronto. She is currently a first year M.Ed. student at the Ontario Institute for Studies in Education/University of Toronto, where her focus is on Cross-Cultural Feminist Counselling. Diane is a divorced mother and sole support parent of a ten-year-old daughter, Dominique.

What the Education Cuts Mean to Me
A High School Student Speaks

Many of my friends have lost their jobs due to cutbacks. Single mothers I know have had a very tough time surviving on an increasingly unstable social assistance program. Wonderful teachers at my school have had to leave. Job security has become a thing of the past; this has left many people uneasy, scared, and tense. The Ontario I once knew is changing at a rapid pace. The education system I once knew, with kindergarten and Grade 13, has been eliminated and its future seems uncertain.

When I graduated with my Grade 12 diploma in June of 1996 I graduated short of two Grade 13 credits. I opted to enrol as a part-time student for September of 1996, so that I could work part-time and save money for university. When I returned to school everything seemed fine until about a month and a half into the semester when I was approached by my vice-principal. She informed me that I was an "illegitimate" student because I was only taking two courses. She told me that if I did not take another class I would be kicked out of school. I was completely unaware of this new policy. I found out that the decision to no longer allow part-time students within the system had been made over the summer. Fortunately, this policy was implemented after I had finalized my plans and I was able to work the situation out with the administration at my school. For other students I know, who were affected by this policy, its impact was far worse. The reasons for being a part-time student varies: some students can only afford to be a part-time student; some students have children and therefore do not have the time to be a full-time student. These are the students most affected by this policy. Many of them had to quit school or were forced to become a full-time student, which made it harder for them to survive.

This policy to eliminate part-time students may seem like a small change when compared to something like the amalgamation of Toronto or the millions of dollars being cut from social programs but it is a policy that affects people who are vulnerable and need support. It is a policy that affects people's basic rights, in this case the right to an education. It is a policy that favours those who are financially secure. It is a policy that has been implemented with no consultation with the community.

These changes have left me with a feeling of deep hopelessness and have made me question my future. What repercussions will these changes have ten to fifteen years from now? Change is not an instant process; it is a gradual one. One can only imagine how severe the impact of these changes will be in the future.

—Amy Slotek is a recent OAC graduate from Monarch Park Collegiate in Toronto. She has aspirations to go on to university and become a lawyer.

Stories About Women and Housing

by Susan Bacque

The other day I went to a daytime drop-in to meet Casey. I met her sitting in the dark church sanctuary of the Open Door drop-in at the corner of Dundas and Sherbourne in downtown Toronto. She was visiting friends at the church while her partner made some extra cash at a job for the day. They have no home.

Outside the telephone poles are littered with signs of opposition to the current government. "Some cuts just don't heal" is the eye-catching headline on a poster for a protest rally at Queen's Park. "Join the march against poverty" urges another.

Inside the Open Door, every pew is occupied by a sleeping person, stretched out for the day, safe and comfortable for the first time since the previous nights' wanderings. It smells of urine, cigarettes, and unwashed bodies. If poverty had a smell this would be it.

The provincial government has cancelled 27 new non-profit housing projects where the people at the Open Door could be living, slashed welfare cheques by 22 per cent, and eliminated the job training programs which held out hope for future employment.

One thousand nine hundred and ninety-five new non-profit housing units will not be built; $8 million per month in welfare payments is gone; $0.5 million for advocacy organizations is gone; $130 million for legal aid is slated to go; second stage housing for women is gone. Furthermore, rent control which protects Casey from "economic eviction" and rent gouging in the private market will be phased out, probably at the end of 1997. What real choices does Casey have?

The one obvious choice she makes is to live the best way she can. She chooses community and support. In fact, Casey copes well with homelessness as she searches for better options.

Casey is 29 years old, a mother of four, well-groomed, and well-dressed in designer jeans which she got for free at a clothing depot. She has a few friends at this drop-in and more at the overnight drop-in where she lives and works on weekends. Does she know that this overnight refuge will close at the end of April as it is only a winter relief program?

A middle-aged man greets her and touches her shoulders affectionately. He is part of her community, her family, her support, her connection to life. He and others like him have taught her how to live without a home.

Casey uses a food bank and carries the canned goods she gets there to the social services agencies where she knows people who will let her heat the food. Occasionally she will buy fresh food including milk. While she was pregnant Casey ate food retrieved from selected dumpsters and heated it over makeshift burners on outdoor barbeques.

Frozen pizzas with recently expired "best before dates" were a favourite.

Casey's baby boy was born six months ago and she proudly shows me a picture. C.J. has big cheeks and looks healthy. But he also looks scared. And he has reason to be. Like Casey's other children he will be moved from his grandmother's, to his parent's, to a foster home, to a friend's, and back through the cycle. Perhaps a well-meaning social worker will intervene. There will be fights over who cares for C.J. since the several hundred dollars in income his presence adds every month to the social assistance helps everyone.

There will also be fights because Casey is desperate to raise her own child. She has buried the pain of three children already lost to her and the pain of her own lost childhood. The pain is deep and entangled in a web of partial disfunction and some addictions. Her fragile self-esteem however is anchored by well-honed survival skills. Like me, and most women I know, having children gives Casey a purpose. Being pregnant gets her attention, care, and food. Casey may continue to have babies because in many important ways, this is the easiest, healthiest, most readily available way for women to take care of themselves.

Casey is gradually learning other ways too. She is part of a "Breaking the Cycle" pregnancy program for parents who have or are addicted to drugs. She has been drug-free for over a year. At the Open Kitchen, parents cook for other parents and learn about nutrition and shopping on a budget. At 416 Dundas, Casey has started anger management classes where she can work off years of resentment; working the streets and dancing naked in front of drunken men in bars takes its toll. She receives mail from her correspondence course at 416, the Open Door, and her aunt's. She also works at a private agency which helps street youth.

Casey can be successful in maintaining positive relationships and finding appropriate ways to maintain her self-esteem. Right now she is depending on friends in the street community as well as government-funded agencies for support. As we sit together and chat she explains that the next step for her is finding an apartment. Her goal is to find and maintain a stable home.

She stoically searches the newspaper classified section. I think her task is impossible as most apartments are unaffordable, unavailable, or unsuitable. She has looked at an apartment at Shaw and Adelaide—$750 for a two bedroom. She insists that she needs two bedrooms if she is going to be able to keep C.J. and live with his father.

Securing a place does not sound likely. Her income is $223 per month although this will rise to $1,030 if she and her partner find a place to live with C.J. She has no references and her partner has a poor credit rating. The vacancy rate in Toronto is 0.9 per cent. Landlords are being choosey about who they rent to. Casey's options are extremely limited.

Edel knows pain and poverty too. She is 48 years old, a single mother, has a Master's degree and many years of work experience, most recently with a government-run housing provider. She was laid off in anticipation of budget cuts. After her unemployment insurance ran out and she had no success finding new employment, Edel turned to welfare. She is not optimistic about ever getting back into the workforce.

Last fall she realized that her welfare was insufficient to cover her expenses. A brief stint with a boarder proved to be a nightmare of confusion amidst welfare's changing rules about renting to roommates, especially those of the opposite sex. Her welfare cheques were mistakenly reduced; she fell into rent arrears for the first time in her life. Her landlord began eviction proceedings.

When she shopped, Edel was choosing between Kraft Dinner and toilet paper. Medical expenses for her son's severe asthma were mounting. She moved to a less expensive apartment ($700 for a two bedroom). There are guard dogs at the entrance to the building to deter drug dealers. A bullet hole appeared in the lobby window shortly after Edel and her son moved in.

Two months after she moved, Edel spent a weekend in anxious anticipation of bill collectors the following Monday. Late Sunday afternoon, she had a heart attack. After one week in hospital, she got home to find additional bills; one for the ambulance and one for the phone she didn't use in her hospital room. She thought she wasn't going to make it.

Edel is resourceful and has a good support network. An east Toronto community health centre has been pivotal in her recovery, as has a group of mothers who exchange services, information on bargains, and coping strategies. She says now, "I will get through this; life goes on and you have to make the best of it." But she is scared by what she sees.

"There are so many people all around me now, so many professionals who are not working. People are making very scary choices between living and suicide, between keeping their kids and placing them with the Children's Aid Society (CAS). People who have never stolen before are stealing so they have money left over to pay rent. Some people are behaving irrationally just because of the stress. The stress eliminates all my creativity and all my hope."

In a different part of town, in her apartment subsidized by the provincial government, Jane talks about her life. She says she has found inner peace and joy after a seven-year struggle which almost claimed her life. At 45, after years of productive employment and self-sufficiency, her life fell apart. Jane spent 18 months hospitalized for depression after several suicide attempts. She shows me the scars—on her neck.

To recover from her depression, Jane got help at a provincially funded psychiatric unit, sought support from her mother, searched the Community Information Centre's Blue Book to find providers of assisted housing, and used a myriad of other support services. She found a unit which she loves although the three-storey climb is difficult. Her asthma is so severe that she pauses every few steps. Fans gently blow on her face as we relax in her sitting room. Jane continuously and conscientiously fights to maintain her health and her sanity. Some days her only goal is to get out of bed.

Jane is cherub-like and brings cheer to her many friends. She is a collector of videos, music tapes, children's books, and porcelain French clowns. These are all displayed in her crowded bachelor apartment in this old brick apartment house.

Her rent is $410, and will gradually increase until it reaches 30 per cent of her income which was fixed seven years ago when she went on long-term disability.

Jane isn't a worrier but she says the threats of the provincial government "getting out of the housing business" are anxiety producing for her. She has spoken to her MPP who has assured her, at a community meeting, that public housing will be sold to a "caring manager." Jane wonders who she can talk to for clarification.

Jane spends her time on community boards, volunteering and speaking at conferences about housing, poverty, the mental health system. She finds it hard to be on the receiving end of kindness and needs to give back to her community. Charity, she says, feels good for the giver but not for the receiver. And she is right. Her volunteer involvement managing non-profit housing and in speaking out on issues which are important to the tenants gives her power, energy, and a sense of worth.

Poor people with skills, a voice, and legitimate ideas about their own needs are no longer needed by the provincial government for their contribution. They are needed to pacify the guilt of the wealthy. They are needed to receive charity. They are needed for their compliance and their silence. They are needed to quietly offset the upside of the economic ledger.

It is unacceptable to claim prosperity and economic improvement when an entire segment of the population is, in fact, less well-off than before. People will be visible, will be heard, and will create their own solutions regardless of their level of income, or where they live or where they do or do not work. The provincial government has a responsibility to work for all people of Ontario. No more kidding around.

Susan Bacque is a community housing worker at the City of Toronto, where she works with agencies and other governments on programs for homeless people. She is also co-producing "View from the Street," a documentary about people living at Street City in Toronto.

"Nonsense" Revolution Hits Indian Country

by Kim Anderson

An often quoted expression in our communities is "our children are our future." Traditionally, Native leaders made decisions with serious consideration to how their actions would affect people seven generations down the line. I have a hard time believing that any of us, Native or non-Native will survive that long, given the blows we are currently taking with the short-sighted decisions emanating out of the current political climate. With cuts to half the provincial environmental laws, I wonder what water our grandchildren will drink, what air they will breathe, how they will find anything to eat when the plants and animals are no longer able to sustain themselves and the people of our battered planet.

Perhaps our grandchildren will be able to buy their way to survival; the strategy is so far unclear. What is clear is that those children currently deemed less worthy, the poor, are already suffering deficiencies basic to their survival.

With a 21.6 per cent cut to social assistance payments, the growth of our future generations is being hindered from sheer lack of food and nutrition. Welfare administrators on reserves are reporting "lots of food shortages near the end of the month." In the city, Native social agencies note an increase in demands for supplies from the food banks, and requests for assistance to feed Native families through food vouchers. This increase comes at a time when food banks are themselves suffering shortages because of cutbacks. In turn, donations have been more conservative from a belt-tightening general public. Michelle Murphy, executive director of the Native Women's Resource Centre of Toronto (NWRC) adds that, increasingly, the kinds of foods available are "starchy foods that fill one up, but don't provide adequate nutrition."

On reserve and in the cities, absenteeism of Native children from school is on the rise because, if lack of food isn't the problem, inadequate supports for clothing, shelter, and family services are also a result of cutbacks.

School is not a priority when you have no home. According to Native Child and Family Services of Toronto (NCFST), in this time of crisis "rent is always the last thing to get paid." This has resulted in numerous evictions. Middle-of-the-night moves into shelters have become commonplace for the Native urban poor.

Anishnawbe Health Toronto (AHT) has seen their street patrol assistance to the homeless more than double during the last two years. Notably, they are seeing more women, and, for the first time, women with children. AHT executive director Barb Nahwegahbow comments that, unlike those that have been living on the street for many years, the newcomers to the street lack the skills and knowledge for survival in this milieu.

For those poor children who narrowly miss the street, there are other options. There are shelters, but they are filling up. To cope with the overflow, some shelters are buying up rooms in low grade hotels. Colette Deveau of NCFST comments that our future generations are thus being raised in "ex-hooker trade hotels."

Degenerate housing and social conditions have also resulted in increased incidences of violence in our communities. "The explosions in a relationship happens a lot faster now than it used to," notes Deveau of NCFST, adding that supports for things such as custody cases, legal aid, and family services are unable to meet the increasing needs of families in distress because of cutbacks.

No Life for the Lifegivers

It is clear that our children are suffering. What about the women? As Native people, we have a traditional respect for our women because of the heavy responsibilities they carry for the future of our nations. Our women are honoured for their role as lifegivers. As mothers, they are tremendously significant because of their role as teachers of the upcoming generations.

It begins with birth. Whereas mothers used to be given a few days reprieve at a hospital following childbirth, they are now released within 24 hours. Although I am an advocate of homebirth—of moving away from these institutions that govern the sacred—I realize that this is not an option for mothers without adequate child care, housing, or partner/family support. As in other areas of health care which have moved from hospital care to home care, who will pay for all those extra costs, for supplies, and drugs that have heretofore been covered by the hospital? Health care and health support is becoming increasingly costly to the individual.

Right from the start then, we are expecting our mothers to conduct their responsibilities with fewer and fewer tools. Public health nurses no longer visit mothers with newborns. Follow-up care for new mothers is essential for the health and well-being of both mothers and infants, yet this is seen as a disposable extra in a society that values neither the lifegivers nor the future.

In their role as teachers, women are, likewise, increasingly unsupported. First of all, women who are worried about whether their children will have enough to eat, a place to stay, or a violence-free home, have little time left to foster their own education, and that which they can share with their children. They need to get this through adequately funded programs. This means, for instance, literacy programs that can still rub a few dollars together to provide transportation and study supplies when the tight budgets of their students do not stretch that far. Across the province, Native literacy programs are reporting a decrease in enrollment rates because of the inability to provide supports to get people into the class.

In Toronto, funding has been cut to one of the most effective programs at the Native

Woman's Resource Centre (NWRC). The now defunct student advancement program allowed women to upgrade their education to Grade 12. Executive director Michelle Murphy reports that the loss of this kind of program is felt more broadly than solely among those students who participated. This program had an impact on a whole circle of people, from female relatives who would discover other programs at NWRC, to children who benefited from literacy assistance. "Most of the women would go on to college, university, or work," reports Murphy. "Now they can't go on because of lack of support."

I don't have to look far to see the impact of the current agenda on our present and future generations. What are some of the "nonsense" solutions the provincial government is proposing in its vision of a healthy province?

Family Values

It has been suggested that extended family and community support can and should fill the gap of costly social programs. This is a bitter pill for Native people. Traditionally, we operated with strong extended family and community support systems. These systems have been eroded and attacked through state policies such as the institutionalization and abuse of Native children in residential schools and the provision for generational family dysfunction via the displacement of children to the child welfare system. The "nuclear family" model, enforced over the centuries through state pressures, "educators," and missionaries have hit our communities with the impact of the nuclear bomb. What we are left with in many cases is, as Sioux author Mary Brave Bird sums up, "neither [extended family systems], nor white style nuclear families, just Indian kids without parents."

In spite of these attacks, Native people have been remarkably resilient. We have maintained the flicker of community and extended family support. This has been helpful in battling the cuts, as exemplified in communities such as Garden River. In this community, welfare administrator Doreen Lesage reports that families have been able to share the moose and fish they manage to procure from traditional lifestyles. This might have been a more viable, sustainable, and cost-effective solution to social assistance for Native people, had the rivers not been poisoned, the land clear cut, and Natives robbed of traditional hunting and fishing territory and rights.

Back in Toronto, Native single moms have turned to the community organizations that our people have developed to supercede the loss of extended families, communities, and economic systems. Yet with doors and services closing because of cutbacks, the supports that remain are increasingly stressed. Organizations working directly with women and their children are hardest hit. For example, all core funding to the Native Women's Resource Centre of Toronto has been cut, leaving an organization that provides 2,000 women and their children each month with health, education, and social service programs with a few grants and a paltry $45,000 "stabilization fund" that is, not surprisingly, extremely unstable.

How Many Times Can You Clean a Graveyard?

Native people have always worked for the welfare of their communities, and would like nothing better than to earn a living for it. "Give us money to work, and we will work," say the clients of Garden River welfare administrator Doreen Lesage. But, as Lesage points out, "at least you could provide minimum wage."

Furthermore, workfare make-work projects will be hard to scratch up in communities where work of any sort is hard to find. "How many times can you clean a graveyard?" asks Lesage. "It's a natural thing here, we do it yearly—it's something we all go out and do [as a community]." In such communities, no one gets paid for this kind of community effort.

Prior to the introduction of workfare, First Nations in Ontario had been developing "Innovations," a program that recognized the systemic barriers to employment on reserve. They were working on solutions to meet the various needs of social assistance recipients as they struggle with avenues to support themselves and their families. Yet, there has always been little support in government for this kind of holistic initiative. Sandy Porter, executive director of the Ontario Welfare Administrators' Association remarks that barriers such as the lack of industry, job opportunities, training, and transportation in rural communities are overlooked. A welfare administrator in northwestern Ontario concurs, relating that the cookie cutter approach designed for urban centres will fall flat in the many First Nations communities who lack the prerequisite infrastructures.

Accountability

What the government wants in our education and social programs are *clear links to employment*. The oversight is that there are no jobs, particularly on or near reserve communities.

So we must measure up. "They are talking about accountability like it's a new thing," says Priscilla George, a consultant working with Native literacy groups in Ontario. "We have always been accountable, not to funders solely, but also to the communities and learners that we serve."

In short, though the government is quick to co-opt the language of community development, they do not adhere to any of the principles. Programs and services that are designed, developed, delivered, and evaluated by communities according to their needs are now accountable to the provincial coffers alone. "We are 30 to 40 years back" reports Nancy Johnson, a social policy analyst with the Chiefs of Ontario. Significantly, all of the "development" across the sectors undertaken by the provincial government has been without consultation with the First Nations.

Can We Talk?

We'd like to talk to the government about this but we do not have any means of doing so. We might as well turn our framed, parchment paper "Statement of Political Relationship" documents (signed by the government with the intent to respect and operate on a government to government relationship) to the wall. "There is no Aboriginal agenda," reports Linda Commandant of the Chiefs of Ontario, "no process to resolve issues.... You can't deal with them ... you can't even get to the table."

It is certain that the education we have done, and the relationships we have built over many years with senior bureaucrats are now of little worth. Those civil servants who have kept their jobs no longer have any answers for us. Either they don't know themselves what is happening, or they are party to what Nancy Johnson calls "the cone of silence."

In Native literary and cultural tradition, we have figures like the trickster or the sacred clown. Sometimes they operate in a way that is crazy and out of whack. They turn everything upside down with the purpose to instruct, and to remind us of the responsibilities we carry to walk the good road. As we struggle to survive these cuts, we can only hope that these clowns are here but temporarily to turn it upside down, so that we can set it right again.

Kim Anderson is a Cree/Metis, raised in Ottawa by parents from Manitoba and British Columbia. She has worked in social policy and education for a number of Native organizations. She currently lives in Toronto with her partner David and their children Rajan and Denia.

How Do We Organize?
Coalition Building

by Ethel LaValley

How do we organize? What works and what doesn't and why? What kind of models could be used for grassroots organizing among and between organizations, individuals, and even sectors?

My experiences as a community and union organizer have shown me that to organize you have to have a focus, a willingness to listen to all points, a respect for all viewpoints, and an understanding that each person speaks for a space they know.

I believe one of the most effective models of organizing is coalition building. A coalition is simply several groups working together for a particular cause. Each individual group may have very different goals, structures, and values but, as a coalition, they all share a common interest in a single issue or in achieving a particular goal.

Groups may contribute to coalition efforts in various ways, in the form of people, funds, services, information, endorsements, or contacts. We know that one individual group, working alone, will be less effective than several groups working together. The more groups that support an issue from a variety of perspectives, the greater their power. An employer, a legislator, or the media might ignore an issue supported by an individual or single group. But the same issue might merit new interest if it is supported by a broad-based coalition.

Coalitions bring long-term rewards. If you build a successful coalition around your issue, it will be easier to gain support from some of the same groups on other issues of importance to you.

Building a Coalition

Building a coalition requires planning. The first step is to outline what you want the coalition to accomplish and how member organizations might contribute to that end. Determine what type of relationship you want to develop with other organizations.

Endorsement

You may want to use other groups or individual names, with their permission, to endorse a particular project or to support a piece of legislation. Such endorsements can persuade reluctant administrators, legislators, or even potential supporters. An example would be the "Ontario Women's Declaration," a document which has over 200 supporting groups, and which will serve as an organizing and mobilizing tool over the next several years. Petitions are another way of organizing both groups and individuals.

Short-Term Alliance

You could band together to achieve a specific short-term goal. This means that you must clearly define that goal, the tactics, time lines, and strategies to be used, and the role each organization will play in achieving it. We have seen this model in actions such as the fight to keep a daycare centre from closing, educational forums, rallies, or organizing of community events such as International Women's Day. And short-term alliance can and do lead into long-term commitments on issues and actions.

Informal Coalition

This is an ongoing coalition with broad goals, such as educating the public on your group's goal or keeping the issue on the agenda of your legislature. There is no formal structure and no new organization is formed. Member organizations assign and undertake specific tasks to support the goals of the coalition.

This is the kind of model that is used by the Ontario Federation of Labour (OFL) in our Fight Back Campaign. When we choose a community day of action and protest, our staff assist both unions and community groups in organizing the day. The key to these actions are the co-chairs, one from labour and one from the community. They serve as the main spokespersons. Leading into the day we work closely together on public education through community pamphlets, forums, and the media. The key to the success for these actions is the decisions and the organizing is community-based.

Formal Coalition

A formal coalition actually creates a new organization with a formal structure. The coalition acts and speaks for its member organizations. Groups contribute pre-determined funds or services. Some might donate financial resources, while others provide volunteers or in-kind services such as printing, postage, or computer services.

There are a number of successful women's coalitions, such as the Ontario Coalition for Better Child Care (OCBCC). The Coalition's membership is made up of child care community activists, labour, and child care workers. Member groups pay a member-ship fee based on the size of the organization. Education and policies of the Coalition are used by the member groups within their membership. That's to say the OFL's policies and educational programs on child care mirrors that of Ontario Coalition for Better Child Care.

The Coalition also links with other coalitions, such as the Equal Pay Coalition. The example of low paid child care workers was used to demonstrate the need for legislation on equal pay and the need for government funding for wage adjustments.

Maintenance Work

Like all relationships, coalitions need maintenance work. Here are a few tips on what doesn't work and on how to keep things running smoothly: Encourage coalition members to be flexible and open-minded. Every group need not agree on every point, but it is important to be able to listen to other perspectives and to be willing to compromise. Try to avoid unnecessary conflicts among members by keeping coalition meetings and activities focussed on the common goal. Do not let the coalition become a forum for conflicts over other issues. When possible, be supportive of member organizations' activities in other areas. Visible signs that you support each other help build trust and strengthen the coalition. Try to avoid "reinventing the wheel." Always ask what has been tried already and what has not worked before.

Be open to expanding coalition membership as your work and the issue evolve. Keep an eye out for new sources of support. Be aware that some organizations may have "competing" agendas, in their own interest, that can complicate coalition efforts. Try to identify these interests early on. Where possible, relate them to the overall coalition goals, using them as a motivating force. If this becomes an obstacle, you may have to discuss the problem privately with the organization in question before it blows up in a coalition meeting or activity.

Ensure coalition work is distributed equitably. Try to keep each organization involved to its maximum potential. Be generous with praise. Recognize members' contributions within the coalition and in external publicity.

Other Forms of Organizing

Organizing can take many forms. Coalitions are one way. However, there are others, such as newsletters, mailings, phone trees, fax networks, the Internet, kitchen table discussions. All forms can work, be they community actions such as demonstrations at Queen's Park, or two or three women meeting with their local MPP on government cuts, or fax networks to share information, or a women calling a local politician to voice her views on an issue, or a letter to the editor of a local paper.

The larger challenge for organizing is the ability to listen to all points of view, respect the experiences, be opened to ideas. How women who are white, able bodied, heterosexual, or employed organize and mobilize on an issue can be different from women of colour, aboriginal, lesbian, have disabilities, or are poor. All of us have skills and knowledge to offer. We need to provide the space to build on all of our voices.

I will close by quoting Adrienne Rich's "'Going There' and Being Here" *(Blood, Bread, and Poetry)* on social change: "If you are trying to transform a brutalized society into one where people can live in dignity and hope, you begin with the empowering of the most powerless. You build from the ground up."

To organize, we have to do just that—build from the ground up.

I learned about racism and organizing many years ago when I decided to enter political life. In the mid '70s, I decided to apply for a grant of $2,400 to get my grandmother hydro. She was in her 70s and never had what we would term "essential" today. By that I mean inside washrooms, hydro, etc. At that time, government grants were being given to upgrade homes (i.e. drilled wells etc.). My grandmother didn't fit the guidelines because she didn't "own" her land. I felt guidelines were just that— "guidelines," and that she qualified over other projects.

I decided to run for municipal council to further my cause, since that was the decision-making body. What an experience! My ex-husband told me I couldn't run, because women shouldn't be on council. The council of the day discouraged me first by pleasantness and then anger. When I gained momentum, they tried to stack the deck by running more candidates—all men.

I had to do something quick. I talked personally to many people about why I was running. I was seen as this "militant" woman in a community of 300 families and a threat to the present council. One of my co-workers came up with a slogan "Vote for Ethel, she's not just one of the guys." We put these signs around town (organizing and I didn't know it). We just did it. We had meetings at local restaurants, became very visible, and stuck to the issues. We campaigned on a positive front—that I could make a difference.

The night before the election, I received a call about midnight, advising me that the council didn't need a woman or a squaw. That call determined my future—to be the community leader one day. I won the election (fourth spot) in 1974 and in 1985 became the first female Reeve of that Township.

The next year, my grandmother received hydro and died shortly after.

My grandmother was an inspiration, and I owe her and my parents a lot of gratitude for sticking by me and believing in me. I've always stayed on the high road and believe that is the key to completing any goal.

This story is not intended to relive the past, but to inspire people to stay on the high road and always believe that, while you can't change yesterday, you can work together today to build a better tomorrow.

These remarks were originally presented to the Women of Action Day, January 23, 1996, at Metro Hall in Toronto, Ontario.

Ethel LaValley was elected secretary-treasurer of the Ontario Federation of Labour (OFL) in 1995. She is the first Aboriginal to be elected as an officer of the OFL. She has also been vice-president of the National Union of Provincial and Public Employees and became the first Aboriginal elected to the Canadian Labour Congress in 1994. She is currently Reeve of the Township of Alry and vice-president of the Association of Municipalities of Ontario (AMO).

How to Conduct Your Own Community Audit

by Anne O'Connell and Armine Yalnizyan

In November 1995 the Parkdale Community Health Centre approached the Social Planning Council to help design a methodology for a community audit to assess the impact of the 21.6 per cent welfare cut on all residents of Parkdale. The Parkdale Community Health Centre then organized the participation of three other community-based groups—St. Christopher House, Sistering, and Parkdale Intercultural Association—and solicited seed money for the project from the City of Toronto Public Health Department.

A group of agency staff and local residents worked together to outline the objectives of the project, design the survey tool, facilitate the training day, conduct door-to-door interviews, and contribute to the development of the report. Early on it was decided that we would do face-to-face interviews of retailers, then residents, of South Parkdale, which is defined by census tracts four, five, and seven. This area has a population of 19,945 people in private households and 1,060 in institutional/collective dwellings.

We wanted the people we interviewed to represent the local community as closely as possible so we created the sample of households to interview in the following way.

A Representative Sample

We divided the neighbourhood into six approximately equal areas—one for each of the size interview teams. The target number of interviews was 50 for each team. We counted the number and listed the addresses of high rises (five or more stories) and walk-ups (under five stories) and listed the streets of houses in each of the six areas. From census information, we knew that 60 per cent of residents lived in high rises, 30 per cent in walk-ups and ten per cent in houses. We obtained a list of private rooming houses (collective dwellings) so this population would also be represented in the survey. From our information we determined the percent of interviews that needed to be done in each of these housing types. In order to interview people throughout the whole neighbourhood, the interview teams randomly selected from each of the building types. We put the addresses of the apartment buildings and the names of streets with houses into a hat to select where we would do the interviews to get the target number of 50 interviews (60 per cent from apartments with five or more stories = 28 interviews; 30 per cent in apartments under five stories = 14 interviews; ten per cent in houses/apartments/duplexes = five interviews; and three interviews were to be done in collective dwellings). For example, the research team counted up the total number of floors in the five apartment buildings that were randomly selected from the list in their area. We wanted to do the number of interviews in each of those buildings that corresponds to the number of floors that each building makes up in the total. This way the interviews are spread throughout the whole neighbourhood (vertically and horizontally). We staggered floors and apartment numbers so we would get a variety of household sizes (eg. apt. 101, 402, 803, 1104, 1405). We selected every third house on those street names which were drawn from the hat.

We also used information from the census to determine the percentage of South Parkdale residents who were seniors, children, one person households, family households with children, adult only households as well as the percentage who moved in the past five years, language spoken most often at home, and the percent with incomes below the Statistics Canada low income cut-off. We had information that showed the percentage of persons on social assistance as of October 1995. We aimed to get a sample that was representative of the demographic make-up of the area (particularly the first five characteristics above).

The Process and the Participants

One of the overall goals of this project is to involve local residents in the development and implementation of the research. This allows people in the community to gain research skills, while grounding the research in the experience of living in Parkdale. Residents and staff involved in the first (retailers) survey could apply that experience to the second stage of the project, as new participants joined the research team. The vast language skills of the participants in this project allowed interviews to be done in Tagalog, Vietnamese, Amharic, Tigrinya, Tamil, Spanish, and English.

Along with living in the community, the ethno-racial diversity of our research team was integral to the project. The perspectives and experience brought to the table informed many aspects of how we asked questions and identified the pertinent issues. At the same time, interview teams had to deal with how some households were responding to them. All interviews were done in pairs which was essential for dividing the tasks of interviewing and recording, establishing the comfort level of teams and residents, and for the safety of our research team. An ongoing issue during the interviews were the overt and subtle forms of racist attitudes, that some residents expressed. In one situation, a superintendent of a large apartment building spoke openly of how she refuses to rent apartments to people of colour.

Notes were prepared for each interview team on working with your partner, rules on how to do a random sample, how to get into apartment buildings, tips on interviewing and recording, and recording sheets. Meetings were held during the interview process to discuss how things were going and to share information on what worked best (such as how to approach superintendents for permission to interview in the building) and to strategize on problems (such as how to deal with refusals and racist comments).

The project coordinator entered the results as the questionnaires were completed and matched the respondents with the census information. The target for households with children was met three-quarters of the way through, so interviewers were asked to restrict future interviews to households with adults only in order to get more seniors and singles in the sample.

In total, 200 households were interviewed. There were 500 people in these households, over two per cent of the total population of South Parkdale. We knocked on many doors to reach this sample size, having to compensate for a number of refusals, call backs, and households where no-one was home. We found the ideal times to interview people were early morning and between 4:00–8:00 pm.

The households we interviewed were very similar to the South Parkdale population as profiled by census data. The estimate for percentage of low income in 1995 based on census adjustments was 52 per cent; in our sample it was 54 per cent. The percentage of respondents who said they were affected by the social assistance cuts was equal to the percent in the population overall that were on social assistance in 1995 (35 per cent). Our respondents were less likely to have moved, but this may be because we had a greater proportion of households with children and fewer single person households. Our respondents were more likely to speak a language other than English but this may reflect the growing diversity of the neighbourhood since the last census. Also we were able to conduct the interview in seven languages.

Because our sample matches the best available information on the current make-up of the South Parkdale population, we generalize our findings to the South Parkdale population when we summarize our findings. We also looked to see if responses differed according to income or home language. We used a chi-square test of statistical significance to obtain the probability that this difference occurred by chance and only where these tests show significant relationships (i.e., less than five per cent probability that this relationship would occur by chance) we use this information in the discussion of our findings.

Our budget for the project was developed with a view to pay local residents for their time for training, meetings, and doing the interviews. Seven community residents did the interviews in teams of two, often with an agency staff person. Other resources for the project included the staff time and in-kind contributions of the community agency partners. Most importantly for the well-being of this project was the time provided by the project coordinator, Anne O'Connell, who at the time was a graduate student in the Faculty of Social Work, University of Toronto.

Excerpted from the "Parkdale Community Audit Project Report No.2—A Survey of Residents, March 1997," a joint publication of the City of Toronto Public Health Depart-ment and the Social Planning Council of Metropolitan Toronto. Enquiries about the entire report, questionnaire development, tips on interviewing, and recording can be directed to

Armine Yalnizyan, Social Planning Council of Metropolitan Toronto, Suite 1001, 2 Carlton Street, Toronto, Ontario, M5B 1J3; telephone: (416) 351-0095, fax: (416) 351-0107.

Anne O'Connell decided to return to school after four years of front line support work with homeless and low-income men and women. Participating in the Audit Project helped her to understand how we connect community knowledge and academia, in a way that remains committed to learning and action.

Armine Yalnizyan is the program director at the Social Planning Council of Metropolitan Toronto. She is the author of several publications on the restructuring job market and the transformation of social security. She is currently working with a variety of local groups documenting social change at the community level, monitoring the fallout from the withdrawal and restructuring of the welfare state.

Types of Community Audits

Benchmarking—the macro view

This type of audit is time-consuming and heavily research-oriented, which may limit its utility in some communities. Benchmarks would be established in different sectors: health, education, child care, income supports, transportation, community supports (libraries, pools/arenas, community centres), social housing/shelters, immigrant/integration services, etc. For each sector a series of parameters would be developed that are specific to those supports/services. The resulting inventory could be imagined as a huge before-and-after grid.

For example, under housing, at any given time in a community, there may be x shelters for the homeless, servicing y people for z period of time. Different types of shelters, servicing different populations, could be identified. Social housing units could be identified. Housing help centres and their services could be identified. The number of renters versus home-owners could be identified. The proportion of social-assistance recipients making up the renting population could be documented. Having established a benchmark timeframe, the provision of these supports and demographic changes could be monitored on a periodic basis, i.e. two months after the cuts, a year after the cuts, etc.

Agency-based community audits—public service delivery

This could be coordinating and pooling of existing data, survey information, and group sounding information already collected by agencies regarding use of the agency and emerging needs and/or unmet needs. Alternatively it could be a new tool, particular to this exercise, jointly developed among a broad cross section of agencies or by sectors of agencies.

In Metropolitan Toronto the Social Planning Council, City of Toronto Planning and Development, and Metro Community Services designed a survey tool to be used annually on the known "universe" of human services—about 1,800 different agencies. Thus far there have been two years of "audit" in Metro as to how human services are being restructured. This tool has been widely used in communities across Ontario.

General grass-roots community audit—the people story

Designed to be a social development tool, a small handbook of user-friendly questions that promote an understanding of how a community utilizes the public supports and services which exist, which ones are most problematic when scaled down or back, and helps develop an assessment of what capacities exist in the community to respond to the gaps between need and provision. This type of audit could be a tool for community/civic development in the broadest sense and should, ideally, be able to be utilized in the widest variety of neighbourhoods (i.e., classes). The handbook could be designed to correspond to general clusters of public goods as identified in a "benchmark" type document with multiple choice questions such as: what kind of housing problems do you have? how do you get to work? what kind of day care arrangements do you have/do you need? if doing paid work, what income source would you rely on if you lost your job? These are questions regarding what services and supports people rely on or need.

A second set of questions or discussion points would centre around developing capacity and identifying agents of change: who do people turn to when they need something done? what are the voluntary agencies, community based agencies, school boards, churches, etc. around which resource clusters can be developed? Can a new business be started up to provide an emerging need? Who might not be able to avail themselves of this? Can it be provided collectively? Are there ways of levering resources to meet those needs?

Sector-based grass-roots community audit—how we do things

This type of audit would be more issue-specific, possibly a more organic way of people coming together in a community audit. Education, child care, transportation, housing, food issues, health, the elderly, income support etc. Each handbook would ask a more in-depth range of questions specific to these areas, geared to doing a thorough inventory of a community's needs and knowledge of existing supports, and geared to developing a deeper understanding of resources/capacity to address these concerns. It would provide a solid basis for developing concrete and relevant solutions for local problems as well as being a natural forum in which to organize strategies to advocate and push for broader, more systemic change.

Prepared by Armine Yalnizyan, Social Planning Council of Metropolitan Toronto.

Disrupting Corporate Rule

by the Metro Network for Social Justice

The leading edge of strategy discussions in many social movement organizations at the moment is that of confronting corporate power. Many of us are in the first stages of studying the multi-faceted dynamics of corporate power and its political, economic, and cultural dimensions. But there are a number of direct action strategies that social movement activists can take to challenge corporate power.

Tony Clarke of the International Forum on Globalization calls this "Disrupting Corporate Rule." Here are some of his suggestions:

Rethinking action strategies

We need to take a closer look at strategies and tactics for non-violent resistance.

Recalling resistance heritage

We can learn some important lessons from the struggles for resistance. Indeed this heritage has often been the foundation stones for mass protest movements of workers, environmentalists, women, peasants, indigenous people, and peace activists throughout the world.

Practicing non-violence

What we need are multi-level action campaigns which are designed to make creative use of various strategies and tactics for non-violent resistance.

Challenging corporate charters

By doing research on state charters and evaluating the performance of targeted corporations, citizen groups and social movements can put themselves in a position to legally challenge the charters of transnational corporations (TNCs) or their certificates of authority on grounds that they have been misused or abused. In other words, the corporation's right to exist is being challenged by the people.

Generating economic leverage

Strikes and boycotts could be used as effective tools.... There are pools of capital, such as worker-controlled pension funds, that could be harnessed.... Various strategies for community-owned enterprise and economic self-reliance can be used.

Deploying litigation tactics

Some of the relevant legal skills and expertise that has been developed over the years by various social movements and progressive institutions, not only in addressing corporate power but also in defending the rights of people and the environment, could be pooled and redeployed for the fight against corporate rule.

Mounting political pressures

Whatever strategies and tactics are utilized by social movements to disrupt systems of corporate rule they must be accompanied by lobbying activities demanding political support for our struggle and insisting that the state must not be used to repress the fight for democratic control.

Building popular resistance

Unless a "culture of resistance" is developed among people at community and regional levels, the capacity to challenge and disrupt structures of corporate domination will be limited. This calls for "deep organizing" in which people cultivate a long-term commitment to "community-based resistance" and "community-based alternative" to corporate rule.

Developing global solidarity

Developing international links of solidarity is imperative.... One of the cardinal features of transnational corporations is their capacity to shift their operations from one country to another.... The critical importance of developing solidarity links with social movements in other countries is inescapable.

In thinking about social change strategies, some questions should be kept in mind. For example, is corporate behaviour the issue? Do we want to encourage corporate owners and managers to behave ethically, to make them "good corporate citizens"? Proponents of this view pressure corporations to behave better in terms of labour and environmental standards, how they treat local communities, fair trading practices, and a number of other issues. Consumer boycotts and buycotts (supporting products or services produced by exemplary companies) and public exposure of bad practices all help to pressure companies to abide by their own corporate policies or claims.

Alternatively, there are strategies to directly challenge the concentration of economic and political power. Rather than reforming corporations as they exist, this way of thinking seeks to create new forms of capitalism.

For example, in unionized workplaces, workers can bargain for greater participation in management or ownership, as is more common in Europe. There have also been cases recently—such as Algoma Steel in Sault Ste. Marie—where failing companies have been taken out of corporate ownership and put under the ownership of the workers themselves.

Finally, some activists argue for local community economic development and local food security through the development of co-operatives and credit unions as a way of challenging corporate power.

They believe the issue is creating local, collective alternatives to meet basic needs. The field-to-table movement is one such example, where social change workers organize food centres for low-income people providing produce purchased directly from farmers. This eliminates private wholesalers and retailers, delivering fresh, healthful food direct from the farm to the consumer.

Community-based strategies for survival and strength must be seen as part of a long-term social change agenda. In the context of deep government cutbacks, communities and social agencies all across Ontario are beginning to develop new initiatives for local survival. While these are being born out of duress and suffering, they also hold the seeds of a new future.

In some sectors, or geographical areas, new coalitions are forming to share information, advocacy work, and resources to help meet needs and create networks to replace the gaps in services caused by the withdrawal of the government.

What is Community Economic Development?

What is community economic development? Community economic development (CED) is a people-oriented approach to economic development, one which fully recognizes the multi-faceted context of a community, including its cultural, social, religious, and economic aspects. CED aims to increase community and individual self-reliance through self-help and community participation. More than anything, the success of CED depends upon broad community participation and co-operation between individuals, organizations, businesses, and government. In North America, CED has roots which have either lost or have yet to establish a sustainable economic base. Activities have ranged from very small business development initiatives to larger, more ambitious projects, all aimed at self-reliance and the empowerment of marginalized communities. Several general objectives characterize most CED projects:

- •CED involves marginalized groups and individuals in promoting long-term, sustainable development;
- •projects develop the kinds of resources that allow all people access to economic opportunities within their communities; and
- •they address the root causes of economic impoverishment. In this way, CED goes beyond traditional approaches to economic development, focusing on

the development and enrichment of people and communities first, before corporations and industry.

　　—CED *At Work in Metro Toronto*, Ontario Community Economic Development Secretariat and the Social Investment Organization, 1995

While this is a new arena for many social movement groups to consider, there is considerable history to build on. There are established community economic development networks, local initiatives around food security, local barter networks, and others. CED groups are involved with economic development, political education, and building the capacity of people to organize collectively.

In terms of economic development, CED does have some risks. For example, because it is based on the idea of economic development, it does contain the same possibilities as the neo-liberal economy for producing technological unemployment, and the downward spiral in income and living conditions. In other words, CED does not necessarily get us out of the hole of the neo-liberal economy. In the short term, however, it puts economic resources back in the hands of local communities.

To make CED work, political education is needed. Political education can cultivate a broad-based critical consciousness. Part of how activists understand "community capacity building" is building capacity for popular voice in political debates.

The biggest challenge is in addressing the question of organizing: how to challenge the isolationism and individualism that characterizes most people's lives. It is hard to reach people and persuade them of the value of networking or organizing, yet organizing collectively will be even more critical for survival and strength in the future.

Deepening need in communities may encourage people to participate in community projects that seek to address direct needs before they are ready to do anything explicitly political. Community gardens and barter systems may be the arena for local organizing.

The challenge of inspiriting people is to move beyond their isolated individualism toward a vision of community interdependence that is at the heart of the work of social transformation.

This article has been excerpted with permission from "Hope in Hard Times: An Economic and Political Literacy Primer," published by the Economic and Political Literacy Working Group of the Metro Network for Social Justice (MNSJ). To reach MNSJ, or to order a copy of "Hope in Hard Times" ($12.00 each at time of publication), please call (416) 351-0095.

Rich in Resources
Women in Community Economic Development—A Training Kit

by Advocates for Community-Based Training and Education for Women (ACTEW)

The following is excerpted from *Rich in Resources: Women in Community Economic Development*, a kit prepared by Advocates for Community-Based Training and Education for Women (ACTEW). ACTEW's interest in Community Economic Development (CED) came out of a strategic planning exercise with ACTEW member programs in 1993. Programs asked for information and training resources in the area of women and community economic development. Finding there was very little material in this area, ACTEW applied for grants to support research and the development of materials about women and community economic development initiatives.

This resource kit is the result of a project generously sponsored by Levi Strauss Inc. of Canada, the Ontario Women's Directorate, Status of Women Canada, and Multiculturalism and Citizenship Canada. The kit has four sections: principles for working in community economic development with women and characteristics of successful initiatives; case studies demonstrating how the principles are applied; resources; and a training module. The case studies include a "violence-free zone" housing co-operative, a sewing collective, a travel agency, and a women's centre in Vancouver. The kit is intended to be used by women's community-based training programs, and any woman or community group looking for information on community economic development. ACTEW gratefully acknowledges the support and help of each of the sponsors.

ACTEW is a provincial Ontario umbrella group representing over 4,000 women across Ontario in pre-employment training programs. Our members are the agencies and organizations delivering training and employment services to women. ACTEW is mandated to take up the issues faced by member organizations and by the women who are learners in the programs. ACTEW distributes information regarding training and labour force development policy, advocates for women's quality training, consults with various levels of government, and networks among and between women's groups and training/education providers. ACTEW can be reached at 801 Eglinton Avenue West, Suite 301, Toronto, Ontario, M5N 1E3. Tel: (416) 783-3590. Fax: (416) 787-1500. Email: actew@web.net. Internet: http://www.web.net/~actew.

Principles for Successful Community Economic Development Initiatives

1. *Diversity and inclusivity*—acknowledging that there are differences in CED approaches, groups work in various ways, and it is important to appreciate the differences

as well as the similarities; learning how to work across diversities.

2. *Multiple bottom lines*—recognizing that members of a project each contribute to different degrees but all in equal value.

3. *Collective resources*—developing collective resources, such as pooling funds and community marketing, is an integral part of capacity building.

4. *Networking/support*—establishing support groups both business and social, identifying and learning about local and community resources.

5. *Sustainability and capacity building*—thinking in the long term; making sure that what is intitated can be maintained.

6. *Coping with the tension between competition and cooperation*—developing ways to address conflicting interests and different goals and recognizing the value of compromise.

7. *Redefining productivity*—valuing unpaid labour such as the work of caring for children, the elderly, and the home.

8. *Working for social justice*—recognizing that working for social justice is an integral part of this work although tensions between viability and social justice may arise.

9. *Fluidity*—allowing for differing levels of contribution to the CED group at different times; could depend on seasonal, or social reasons; recognizing that equity is not equality.

10. *Globalization/sense of shared destiny*—recognizing that individual and community destinies are interdependent; what happens locally affects what happens globally and vice-versa.

Characteristics of a Successful
Community Economic Development Initiative

•Policies of affirmative action/equity to ensure that women of colour and First Nations women join the co-operative, collective, or organization are embedded in the project.

•Altered definitions of productivity and bottom lines which are not only concerned with financial aspects of production but include social and environmental aspects as important considerations as well.

•There is provision made for profit sharing, equity, and/or equality within the organization or the project.

•There is an understanding to accomodate individual and diverse needs such as integrated child care programs, elder or dependent care, and flexible timing.

•Collective mutual trust and the pooling of resources such as sharing skills, child care, and transportation are crucial features.

Successful Case Studies

We have tried to focus on projects and initiatives that work with women facing multiple barriers. The following is a selection of case studies that illustrate the various experiences and unique traits of CED groups, each group having particular characteristics, geography, resources.

Fourteen Nations Circle Fund

Mandate

This is a micro-enterprise support fund which provides (primarily) Native women local entrepreneurs with loans to help create small businesses. Kim Hill, the resource manager, feels that this organization "is a stepping stone. Once the client becomes comfortable with this process we see them open up to new challenges and possibilities for their business." The goal of the fund is to provide small, affordable loans, allowing micro-enterprises to establish businesses, develop expertise, and to secure further funding through traditional lending institutions.

Origins

The Fund (based at Six Nations and New Credit Reserves, in Oshkweken, just outside of Burlington) began in 1990 when the communities of Six Nations and New Credit established lending circles for the purpose of starting up micro-enterprise. The first meeting was attended by ten people with small business ideas.

The seed money for the fund was provided by the two Band Councils, the First People's Fund (established by the Calmeadow Foundation), and the Royal Bank. By 1990, the combined Band Councils and the Royal Bank decided to assume a 50–50 split on financial underwriting.

In May of 1993, the Six Nations Council asked Community Futures to take over the administration of the fund to ensure a close connection with the community, efficient marketing, and access. There is a great demand for the loan, and the Community Futures office is busy with fundraising, loan administration, financial reporting, monitoring, and outreach to all loan members.

Program Delivery and Design

The loans are organized in a circle model. The criteria for participating in a "borrowers' circle" are that "borrower": be part of a separate housing unit; be a band member belonging to Six Nations or New Credit Bands; have an owner/operator type of business, or be willing to establish one (i.e., have a business plan or idea); be willing to discuss reasons for loan request and financial information pertaining to the business openly; attend and complete a "borrower's orientation session"; be 18 and over.

The circle formed for the loan is made up of four to seven small businesses. It is possible to join an existing circle, with approval of all members. The staff at Community Futures helps the interested person contact the group. Financing per business does not exceed $3,000 maximum. Loans are available for six to twelve month terms only, and interest is calculated monthly. Each business must attend an orientation session where details of the loan program and roles and responsibilities of the participants are explained. There is an application, approval, loan distribution, and loan repayment system.

A chairperson elected by the circle for a one-year term acts as a spokesperson, collects payments, and is the secretary at meetings. Monthly meetings are held to share information, make loan payments, and provide support to other members. Circle members are responsible for checking that loans are used for the requested purpose.

The distribution of the loan is bimonthly; for each circle, two members are eligible to receive loans in the first month, two more loans will be given two months later, and so on, according to the size of the group. New loans will not be approved if a member is in arrears.

Applications are simpler than one would find in a bank situation. Other advantages of the fund include shared risk (the fund approves loans for each business within the circle, but the risk of the loans is shared by the circle), a support system, and gaining the confidence to expand one's business.

Outcomes

In 1995, women comprised 68 per cent of the circle membership. A sample of the businesses currently operated by Native women include: Creative Native (traditional headdresses, crafts); Sue's Floral Shop (flowers and ballroom arrangements, gifts); Liz's Fast Food (sandwiches, pies); White Dove Tea Room (tea, crafts); Our Land (nutritional supplements, bath products).

Throughout the past four years of operation, the fund has assisted 26 businesses with a total of loans over $51,250. There has been a 100 per cent success rate in the repayment of loans attributed to the composition of the circles and the personal guarantee of each member to honour these loans. Sue's Floral Shop, White Dove Tea Room, and Creative Native have grown from homefront to storefront and are presently solidly established in the community. Some businesses have successfully acquired loans from other, more conventional lenders. There are many functioning circles: the First Nations Artistans, Painted Wooden Flowers, White Dove, Six Feathers and a Party of Five.

Future

The strong foundation of collective trust and confidence in each business in the circle is unique characteristic that supports the Fourteen Nation Circle Fund.

World Women Designers

Mandate

Their goal is to create clothing with fabric from different parts of the world, and to provide employment for skilled immigrant women. One of the three partners says "pooling of women's skills and resources in the spirit of trust, as ..." they "work towards the creation of a viable and profitable business" is part of it, but "working with interesting ethnic fabrics gives us opportunities to express our cultural heritage."

Origins

Three women seeking to express their cultures through their own clothing, collaborated efforts in the summer of 1995. They believe the present clothing market does not cater to women of different nationalities.

Participants and Service Delivery

The project operates out of the participants' homes, who are skilled immigrant seamstresses, designers, and marketers. The working model is constantly evolving as the direction of the co-op becomes clearer, and they become more aware of market demands. One member of the three-woman partnership believes that the secret of their success is the profit-sharing model utilized by all members of World Women Designers. They welcome immigrant women from North Bay and the surrounding area who are skilled seamstresses. On a small scale, they also train women who have basic sewing skills and want to improve. Grants or loans were not fundamental to this project. Personal savings were spent on fabric and the rented space for their debut selling day. Resources were pooled from all members. Sewing was done in the home.

They pride themselves on the wonderful fabrics they work with, imported from Jamaica, Brazil, and India. They have a quality measure for their products, insuring that all garments are carefully inspected before being sold. They have sold numerous pieces of clothing through direct sales at the summer Northern Heritage Festival as well as have clothes on consignment in Sudbury through connections made at the festival.

Impacts

World Women Designers has influenced the formation of other CED projects. They have become involved in the creation of the Sewing Workplace, located in one of the sewers' homes, where women have access to sewing machines as well as a central sewing Job Bank, located at a local school.

Future

The future looks bright for the World Women Designers group. They remain patient and focused on their vision of creating the World Women Designers' label.

Jackson Point Co-operative Homes Inc.

Mandate

Jackson Point is a co-op residence for families. The coordinator at the co-op says that "it is an excellent and safe environment for both children and independent parents."

Origins

The location is Jackson's Point Community in the town of Georgina, by Lake Simcoe. The co-op was developed by Lantana Non-Profit Homes and opened in 1989.

Participants and Delivery

The co-op consists of 41 townhouses and a community centre. Primarily families occupy the co-op, and 21 of their units are geared to income. Independent parents currently live in 22 of the units. Sports and recreation are an integral part of life at the co-op as Jackson Point is located within walking distance to the lake. In warm weather, swimming and water sports take place; in colder weather, snowmobiling, ice fishing, skating, and hockey are favourite pasttimes.

The co-op is a self-declared "domestic violence free zone." This declaration includes:

•the initiation of by-laws which will allow victims of domestic violence to petition the Board of Directors to terminate the membership of an abuser;

•the provision of a subsidy (if necessary) which will allow victims of domestic violence to remain in their home while they are seeking assistance;

•the provision of information on where to seek counselling and assistance;

•the development of a close working relationship with the local police force.

These terms are included in the occupancy agreement. The symbolism of the "domestic violence free zone" places the co-op and its members clearly in opposition to violence against women, and they were recently commended for their efforts by the Co-operative Housing Federation of Canada.

The members of the co-op are also environmentally aware and they make an effort to reduce garbage accumulation and pollution.

A volunteer Board of Directors and committees manage daily life at the co-op. The general members make decisions affecting the co-op, for example, approval of the annual budget and any housing charges increases.

Cooperation and concern for others is an advantage to co-op living. The support system aspect is especially beneficial for the independent parents.

Future

There is only one paid staff member. She works a 35-hour week, doing property management, financial management, and community development. The co-op is not planning on expansion in the near future but will work on their "existence as a co-op."

Community Economic Development Resource Guide

Books and Articles

1. *Making Communities Work: Women and CED*, by Lucy Alderson and Melanie Conn, in *Community Economic Development in Canada* by David J. A. Douglas.

2. *Bringing the Economy Home from the Market*, by Ross Dobson, defines CED as recreating local economies to ultimately bring back community living, advocates a feminine model, and stresses sustainability (continual productivity) in order to perpetuate cycles of life.

3. *Designing Housing for Women and Families*, by Marnie Tamaki, discusses the Entre Nous Femmes Housing Project.

4. *From the Bottom Up: The CED Approach, a Statement by the Economic Council of Canada*, Ministry of Supply and Services Canada, 1990, discusses Local Development Organizations, their barriers, and the confusion of jurisdiction between the three tiers of government, the need for public support, and the need for government programs to be aware of results. Includes a chart on federal and provincial support to business.

5. *No Place Like Home: Building Sustainable Communities*, by Marcia Nozick, discusses sustainable communities, economic self-reliance, community control over resources, ecological development. The book includes a number of case studies.

6. "Native Women and Micro-Enterprise," by Kelly M. O'Neill, in *Canadian Woman Studies*, Vol. 15, No. 1, Winter 1994 issue. The article discusses Native women's micro-enterprises and start-up grants for businesses in the Aboriginal community.

7. *Feminist Economics of Community Development*, by Dorothy Smith, discusses the emergence of 19 Community Development Corporations.

8. *Women and Sustainable Development, African Communities and their Challenges with CED*, by Ruth Meena, discusses the inability of women to influence policy-making, women are marginalized and are absorbing most of the poverty.

9. *Bread and Dignity*, by Shelia Rowthon, discusses women in the international community.

10. *Making Waves* is a quarterly publication which makes contact with the practitioners and policy-makers across Canada and abroad.

11. *Meeting Women's Training Needs: Case Studies in Women's Training, Phase II Report*, by Susan Wismer and Karen Lior, prepared for The Federal/Provincial/Territorial/Joint Working Group of Status of Women and Labour Market Officials on Education and Training, December 1994.

12. *Get a Life! A Green Cure for Canada's Economic Blues*, by Wayne Roberts (Get a Life Publishing House), Toronto, October 1994.

13. *Women Get Credit: An Introductory Kit on Alternative Financing*, by Lucy Alderson and Melanie Conn, WomenFutures CED Society, British Columbia, 1995. Contains up-to-date information on savings groups, lending circles, barter systems, loan guarantee funds, and guidelines for initiating CED projects in the community.

14. *Voices of Experience: CED Health Research Project*, Health Canada video distributed by Film Images, Canada, 1995 (43 minutes). The information contained in the video contributes to an evolving understanding of health and CED. Toronto CED business models such as non-profit and worker-owned, and the dynamics of business development with people who have experienced long-term unemployment are closely profiled.

15. *Counting Ourselves In: A Women's Community Economic Development Handbook*, by Lucy Alderson and Melanie Conn, Women Futures CED Society, and Social Planning and Research Council of British Columbia, July 1993 (82 pages). Designed to be a guide for women seeking to start a CED project, the handbook provides many examples and practical strategies.

16. *Community Economic Development Directory*, Metro Community Services,1992.

People and Organizations with Expertise in CED

1. Ontario Community Economic Development Alliance. Tel: (416) 703-5351.
2. The Canadian Women's Foundation. Tel: (416) 484-8268.
3. Ontario Worker Co-ops Foundation. Tel: (416) 462-9969.
4. Ontario CED Alliance. Tel: (416) 703-2097.
5. Self Employment Development Initiatives (SEDI). Tel: (416) 504-8730.
6. Our Local Economy (OLE), Erwin Jimenez 361-5814. Initiated in 1992, to be a project and organization.
7. CED projects in Metropolitan Toronto:

•Crafty Sisters, Sistering, 523 College Street, Toronto, Ontario, M6G 1A8. Tel: (416) 926-9762. Fax: (416) 926-1932.

•Inch By Inch Woodworking Collective, Dixon Hall Shelter, 30 St. Lawrence Street, Toronto, Ontario, M5A 3N1, c/o 58 Sumach Street, Toronto, Ontario, M5A 3J7.

•Parkdale Parents Primary Prevention Project, St. Joseph's Women's Health Centre, 30 The Queensway, Toronto, Ontario, M6R 1B5. Tel: (416) 530-6318.

•Ontario Coalition for Alternative Business (formerly Consumer/Survivor Business Council), 794 Broadview Avenue, Toronto, Ontario, M4K 2P7. Tel: (416) 465-8518.

•The Greeting Card Business, The Meeting Place, St. Christopher House, 201 Dufferin Street, Toronto, Ontario, M6K 3H9. Tel: (416) 533-7260.

•Toronto Women's CED Group, c/o 761 Queen Street West, 3rd Floor, Toronto, Ontario, M6J 1G1. Tel: (416) 363-6736.

Program Evaluations
Using Economic Analyses

by Olena Hankivsky

As the London Centre for Research on Violence Against Women's research established, there are numerous benefits to applying an economic analysis of violence against women. Calculating the estimated costs of violence against women in Canada can further substantiate the widespread impact of woman abuse. These costs can also help establish more clearly the economic burden borne by the state, survivors, and third parties of violence against women. Such costs can also be used to argue for continued and improved intervention and prevention financial support to reduce levels of violence against women in Canadian society.

Determining costs, however, is only one part of an economic analysis of violence against women in Canada. The other essential part of the process is evaluating program and service alternatives in terms of their comparative costs and consequences. Economic evaluations are not necessarily restricted to actual dollars spent, but also entail a consideration of whether resources could have been used for alternative purposes.

The potential benefits of economic analyses and evaluations, however, can also be used by organizations, groups, and individuals to make solid arguments regarding the importance of funding for prevention and intervention services affecting other significant social issues.

Economic Evaluation Models

Policy recommendations can be made by using a variety of economic evaluations. For the purposes of this study, cost-benefit, cost-effectiveness, and multiple regression analyses have been applied.

Cost-Benefit Analysis (CBA) is a technique used by analysts to consider systematically all financial consequences of a possible course of action. The bottom line of a CBA is a figure which represents the net benefit or cost of pursuing a given action. The bottom line indicates whether a monetary benefit to society would result from the implementation of a given policy, program, and/or service.

In some instances, however, it is difficult to attach a monetary value to an output of an action. Take, for example, a program which is directed at reducing violence against women and children. Such a program could have the potential to affect the woman's well-being, happiness, quality of life, satisfaction, self-esteem, amount of pain she experiences, and life expectancy. Such outputs do not lend themselves to easy economic evaluation. Some authors have used Cost-Effectiveness Analysis (CEA) as a way to avoid placing a monetary value on these non-financial outputs. For example, a program to combat violence against women could have a net cost of $1 million per year, but would reduce the number of women killed by their partners by ten. The net cost of this program could be $100,000 a year per life saved.

CBA and CEA have been used for decades by economists to choose between projects which compete for scarce resources. Such economic evaluations have become increasingly popular with those working within the health field. Because of rising health care expenditures, those working in the health care field (both economists and health care providers) have turned to CBA and CEA in an effort to understand and control costs. The need to undertake such evaluations was the focus of the October 1989 issue of the *Canadian Journal of Psychiatry* in which D. A. Wasylenki, Director of the Continuing Care Division, Clarke Institute of Psychiatry, wrote: "There is a natural disinclination to consider economics in relation to a human resource such as health care. Unfortunately, however, resources are finite and in the face of increasing pressures to provide more health and social services, attention invariably shifts to comparative costs and benefits" (631).

Accordingly, CBA/CEA have been both been used to assess the most cost-effective ways of treating many illnesses. A similar methodology has been used to estimate the cost of schizophrenia (Gunderson and Mosher), depression (Canadian Mental Health Association), and to estimate the health-related costs of violence against women (Day).

Moreover, in order to estimate the economic impact of sexual and physical abuse on survivors, it is important to estimate the impact of abuse on the individual's earnings. To do this, one can apply multiple regression analysis (MRA). Numerous economists and social scientists have relied upon MRA[1] to estimate the impact of sexual assault on health (see Hyman; Golding *et al.*; Barsky *et al.*; and Koss, Woodruff, and Koss), mental health (see Day; Golding; Barsky; Peters; Fox and Gilbert; Fromuth; Wind and Silvern; Rigg, Alario, and McHorney), educational attainment (Hyman), annual earnings (Hyman), use of alcohol and drugs (Miller), labour force participation, and occupational status (Hyman). In related work, MRA has been used to estimate the impact of health (see Bartel and Taubman; Chirikos and Nestle; and Benham), mental health (see Bartel and Taubman), self-esteem (Ellis and Taylor), and child poverty (Sherman) on earnings.

Bridges: A Case Study

An effective example of how an economic evaluation can be used to justify the efficacy of a program is demonstrated by a study undertaken in British Columbia by Bridges Employment Training Project. The program is sponsored by the B.C. Ministry of Skills, Training, and Labour. Its purpose is to provide unique employability training programs for abused women to assist them in making the transition to independence. Bridges has three intakes a year—in January, April, and September. About 15 women are admitted at each intake.

In May 1992, Bridges published the findings of a follow-up study on women who had graduated from the Bridges Project in the years 1988–1991. Among its findings, the evaluation showed that 62 per cent of those women who attended the program had removed themselves from welfare. According to the report, this represented a savings of $462,024 per year in support payments for the Ministry of Social Services and Housing in British Columbia (see Artz).

The cost of running the Bridges Employability Program for the year 1995–96 (as an example) was $393,000. Subtracted from the figure of $462,024, this represents a cost difference of $69,024. Therefore, Bridges was able to demonstrate considerable cost-benefits and cost-efficiencies of their program by undertaking an evaluation that included an economic analysis.

Conclusion

The government of Ontario is moving in the direction of re-evaluating their spending on existing programs because of financial constraints and cutbacks. It is within this public sector discourse framed in economic terms that existing programs must demonstrate their significance. While it is somewhat problematic to consider economic costs in relation to many essential and important services, any resistance to applying economic analyses should be weighed against the fact that fiscal concerns often determine the continuance of government funds for social programs.

It is also important to remember ethical issues surrounding such work. Economic costs of any important social issue should not be analyzed or applied without close attention to the human and social costs linked to such calculations. The costs of many social issues and problems, including violence against women, are enormous not only in monetary terms but in the personal costs to well-being, self-esteem, and safety. However, it is imperative that policies and programs be examined so that intervention and prevention make solid fiscal sense.

Olena Hankivsky is an assistant professor in the Department of Political Science and at the Centre for Women's Studies and Feminist Research at the University of Western Ontario. She is also current acting director at the Centre for Research on Violence Against Women and Children in London, Ontario. Her areas of interest also include feminist ethics, public policy development, and equality right interpretation under the Charter of Rights and Freedom.

[1]In regression analysis, one compares women who are alike in characteristics such as age, education, geographical location except for the amount of violence they have experienced. With this method, it can be determined whether violence has a significant effect on earnings and, if so, how much of an effect it has.

References

Artz, Sibylle. *Bridges Project Follow-Up Study: For the Years 1988–1991*. Victoria, BC: Bridge, 1992.

Barsky, Arthur, *et al.* "Histories of Childhood Trauma in Adult Hypochrondrical Patients." *American Journal of Psychiatry* (1994): 397–401.

Bartel, Ann, and Paul Taubman. "Health and Labour Market Success: The Role of Various Diseases." *Review of Economics and Statistics* 71 (1979): 1–8.

Benham, Lee, and Alexandra Benham. "Employment, Earnings, and Psychiatric Diagnoses." *Economic Aspects of Health*. Ed. Victor R. Fuchs. Chicago: University of Chicago Press, 1982.

Canadian Mental Health Association. *Depression: An Overview of the Literature*. Ottawa: Canadian Mental Health Association, 1995.

Chirikos, Thomas N., and Gilbert Nestle. "Further Evidence on the Economic Effects of Poor Health." *Review of Economics and Statistics* (1985): 61–69.

Day, Tanis. *The Health-Related Costs of Violence Against Women in Canada*. London: Centre for Research on Violence Against Women and Children, 1995.

Ellis, Rebecca A., and Susan M. Taylor. "Role of Self-Esteem Within the Job Search. *Journal of Applied Psychology* 68 (1983): 632–640.

Fox, Kathleen M., and Brenda O. Gilbert. "The Interpersonal and Psychological Functioning of Women Who Experienced Childhood Physical Abuse, Incest, and Parental Alcoholism." *Child Abuse and Neglect* (1994): 849–858.

Frank, Richard, and Paul Gertler. "An Assessment of Measurement Error Bias for Estimating the Effect of Mental Distress on Income." *Journal of Human Resources* 24 (1989): 154–164.

Fromuth, Mary Ellen. "The Relationship of Childhood Sexual Abuse with Later Psychological and Sexual Adjustment in a Sample of College Women." *Child Abuse and Neglect* (1986): 5–15.

Golding, Jacqueline M., *et al.* "Sexual Assault History and Use of Health and Mental Health Services." *American Journal of Community Psychology* (1988): 625–644.

Gunderson, John G., and Loren R. Mosher. "The Cost of Schizophrenia." *American Journal of Psychiatry* 132 (1975): 901–906.

Hyman, Batya. *Economic Consequences of Child Sexual Abuse in Women*. Waltham, MA: Brandeis University, Department of Philosophy, 1993.

Koss, Mary P., W. Joy Woodruff, and Paul Koss. "Relation of Criminal Victimization to Health Perceptions Among Women Medical Patients." *Journal of Consulting and Clinical Psychology* (1990): 147–152.

Miller, Brenda A., *et al.* "The Role of Childhood Sexual Abuse in the Development of Alcoholism in Women." *Violence and Victims* 2 (1987): 157–172.

Peters, Stephanie Doyle. "Child Sexual Abuse and Later Psychological Problems."

Lasting Effects of Child Sexual Abuse. Eds. Gail Elizabeth Wyatt and Gloria Johnson Powell. Newbury Park: Sage Publications: 1986.

Riggs, Suzanne, Anthony J. Alario, and Collen McHorney. "Health Risk Behaviours and Attempted Suicide in Adolescents Who Report Prior Maltreatment." *Journal of Pediatrics* 117 (1990): 815–821.

Sherman, Arloc. *Wasting America's Future: The Children's Defense Fund Report on the Costs of Child Poverty*. Boston: Beacon Press, 1994.

Wasylenki, D. A. "The Importance of Economic Evaluations." *Canadian Journal of Psychiatry* 34.7 (1989): 631–632.

Wind, Tiffany Weissmann, and Louise Silvern. "Parenting and Family Stress as Mediators of the Long-Term Effects of Child Abuse." *Child Abuse and Neglect* (1994): 439–453.

Stop Blaming the Poor!

Reprinted courtesy of Tony Biddle, Perfect World Productions.

Community Kitchens
"You Get a Bunch of People Cooking Together and You're Gabbing Away..."

by Valerie Tarasuk

In the early 1980s, communities across the country began to mobilize resources in response to reports of widespread and growing demand for charitable food assistance. The efforts culminated in the establishment of a massive ad hoc system of charitable food distribution. Although initially conceived as temporary crisis intervention, food banks have become a vital component of our welfare system as publicly-funded social programs continue to be eroded (Davis and Tarasuk; Riches). Nevertheless, it is widely acknowledged that food banks are "not the answer." Their capacity to address problems of food insecurity[1] which are rooted in severe and chronic poverty is clearly extremely limited (Tarasuk and Davis; Tarasuk and Maclean).

In the quest for more effective, participatory, community-based strategies, a variety of self-help and community development initiatives have recently emerged. These programs generally endeavour to alleviate food insecurity by providing resources and skills which will foster greater independence among participants (versus ongoing dependence on charity) and yield sustainable solutions (versus the "band-aid" solutions of food aid). One such strategy which has witnessed recent and rapid growth in popularity is community kitchens.

In 1995, a qualitative research project was initiated to examine the potential for community kitchens to alleviate the food insecurity of low-income families. This issue was explored from multiple perspectives, with data gathered from participant observations in ten kitchens in southern Ontario communities and from tape-recorded, in-depth interviews with a sample of 14 low-income participants and six community kitchen facilitators. The goal was not to evaluate the effectiveness of individual programs but to identify generic issues which might inform future thinking about community kitchens as a response to income-related food insecurity. The research was consequently restricted to kitchens which included low-income members and had an expressed focus on food security. Within these parameters, an effort was made to observe as wide a variety of community kitchens as possible. The focus on kitchens linked to community agencies (e.g. health units, community service agencies, food banks, etc.) enabled the exploration of community kitchens as intervention programs and community-based food security strategies, but readers are cautioned that this may limit the applicability of study findings to other kinds of community kitchens.

What is a Community Kitchen?

Community kitchen can loosely be defined as community-based cooking programs in which small groups of individuals (called "kitchens") meet to prepare one or more meals together. Within this framework, there is wide variation in models of operation.

The kitchens observed differed in terms of the relative emphasis they placed on quantity food preparation, cooking instruction, and communal dining—factors which helped shape the opportunities for social interaction within the kitchens and structured their potential to affect participants' food security. At the core of these differences lie three distinct models of participatory programming around food: collective kitchens, communal meal programs, and cooking classes.

Collective Kitchens

Most of the kitchens observed functioned as collective kitchens, characterized by the pooling of resources and labour to produce large quantities of food. The model has been well described in a number of locally-produced "how-to" manuals (see Desmeules *et al.*; Hubay, Jack, and Zwicker; London Good Food Project; MacGregor). Small groups of individuals usually meet twice a month, once to plan the menu and develop the shopping list, and then a second time to prepare four to five main-dish meals which are divided up and taken home for later consumption. The quantity of food prepared is determined not by the number of participants but by the sizes of their households so, for example, a group of four participants might be cooking five different dishes for 15 to 20 people. The volume of cooking means that collective kitchens tend to be small; those observed had one to four participants.

As a food security strategy, these kitchens are designed to help participants meet their families' food needs through the collectivization of food preparation and the economy of scale associated with large-volume food purchasing and preparation. Additionally, participants may acquire shopping and cooking skills which enhance their ability to manage independently, but this is generally not the primary focus of the kitchens.

Cooking Classes

In some community kitchens observed, groups gathered to watch demonstrations of the preparation of one or two dishes. Participation in these cooking sessions was limited to minor supportive roles (e.g., opening a can, chopping some onions) or structured experiences (e.g., filling an eggroll). The group members all sampled the featured dishes and usually took home a small amount of food.

However, the goal of the food preparation was not to produce food for group members and their families so much as to expose members to new foods and different methods of food preparation. This model works on the premise that enhanced food preparation skills will enable participans to use their food dollars more effectively and prepare more varied, nutritious, low cost meals at home.

Communal Meal Programs

The third kind of community kitchens are communal meal programs where participants gather periodically to prepare and consume a single meal together. The approach is exemplified in one kitchen observed which was part of a project to provide support to "high risk" mothers. The group gathered every two weeks for lunch. Pairs of participants took turns planning the menu and coordinating the meal preparation while others assumed supportive roles, helping to prepare vegetables, set the table, wash dishes, etc. Facilitation, child care, and food costs were covered by the project grant. The kitchen was a particularly popular program, with 12 women usually in attendance, each with at least one child in tow. Communal dining enabled participants to work together and socialize informally. Often kitchen participation led to involvement in other support services and groups available through the project. In community kitchens such as this, participants may gain some food-related skills and they may benefit from the occasional receipt of a free or reduced-cost meal, but the kitchen is primarily a mechanism for the provision of social recreation and support.

What do Community Kitchens do for People's Food Security?

Regardless of the specific model of operation, the cooperative nature of food preparation in community kitchens means that participation is fundamentally a social experience and one that provides participants with exposure to new foods and different ways of cooking. The atmosphere lends itself to the sharing of ideas and information. As Jen explained:

> *It's kind of like in the olden days ... a quilting bee. You know how women sit around and work together and make a quilt? The same kind of thing: you work together and make a meal, just sharing tidbits of information that come out of conversation.*

For some participants, involvement in a community kitchen was an opportunity to learn life skills and coping strategies to help them manage their limited resources.

In kitchens where the food is partially or completely subsidized, financial benefits accrue directly from participation since some of a household's food costs are offset by the receipt of free or reduced-cost food. For participants of collective kitchens, taking home four or five meals per family member after a cooking session meant having a supply of meals to draw upon during the latter part of the month when resources were commonly depleted.

> *It helps not to worry about where tomorrow's dinner is coming from, you know, for the next three days till the end of the month comes.*

In collective kitchens where participants covered most or all of the food costs, the assessment of cost benefits is more complicated. Participants in these programs contrasted the meals cooked collectively to meals they would prepare on their own. Some described collective kitchen meals in terms of improved food quality and the economy of scale arising from quantity food purchases. From Marianne's perspective,

The meals are better. Some of the things that we cook or eat I might not buy or whatever in my home. And some of the things that we cook maybe I couldn't afford if I had to pay the entire price, you know, to go to a grocery store and get all the ingredients.

The savings associated with collective food preparation for any one participant depend on the food costs being displaced by the community kitchen meals. This is a highly individual matter. In one collective kitchen which operates with only a partial subsidy for the purchase of staples, two long-term participants were interviewed. Jean claimed that her family spent less on food as a result of her participation, but Greta insisted that she could prepare meals as cheaply at home. As she put it, "*When it comes to making money stretch, I think I've got it down pat.*" A single mother of five, Greta came to the kitchen not for financial reasons but because it was a night out of the house with child care provided.

The subsidized aspects of some community kitchens and the economies of scale enjoyed by some participants of collective kitchens serve to ameliorate food insecurity which is rooted in financial constraints. These monetary benefits are limited, however, by the scope of operations. Most collective kitchens prepare only four to five meals a month; even if the food costs are completely subsidized, the amount of food any one participant would take home from such a program is likely to comprise less than five per cent of her family's food needs for the month.

Social Support: The Untapped Potential of Community Kitchens

Particularly for participants whose opportunities to socialize with other adults are limited by child care responsibilities and low incomes, community kitchens are valued social "outings." Elizabeth expressed this most clearly:

Out of the house, change of environment, new people, new experiences, ... [being a part of a community kitchen] was doing something that wasn't on my own. And it was companionship, and I was dying for that. I still basically am, so I come to the kitchen.

Some kitchens observed included both low- and middle-income participants, reflecting the coordinating groups' decisions not to restrict participation in ways which might segregate and stigmatize low-income participants. However, for women marginalized by extreme and chronic poverty and difficult life circumstances, kitchens comprised of individuals with shared struggles were invaluable in breaking down social isolation.

When you're a single mum on Family Benefits Allowance with no money, although you know there's other mums like that out there, because you hear about them, you're not really connected with them. I find that through the community kitchen you really get a sense [that] you're not alone. You're not alone with having no money for child care, no money for food, no money for entertainment.... Thinking other women are struggling with the same things I am, I don't have to feel so stupid or whatever.

Perhaps because food and cooking are typically seen as the core of community kitchen activities, the social aspects of these programs often appeared to be underdeveloped. In some kitchens, facilitators provided critical personal support to individual participants in crisis and those with special needs. In other kitchens, the facilitators' role was defined more narrowly as that of a nutrition educator or kitchen supervisor. While the social recreational component of community kitchens appears to be widely recognized, our observations suggest that these programs can be constructed so as to also help provide much-needed social and personal support to women whose lives are characterized by particularly difficult and isolating situations. The community kitchens which appeared most effective in this regard were geared towards participants with similar struggles, their cooking sessions were designed to include ample time for casual social interaction between participants and to foster an atmosphere of mutual support, and the kitchens had the benefit of a facilitator or coordinator with strong counselling and referral skills. Not surprisingly, these kitchens were also more likely to attract and sustain the participation of individuals with serious problems of food insecurity.

Financial Support—An Imperative

Costs are incurred directly or indirectly for food, child care, transportation, and the staffing costs associated with community kitchen facilitation or coordination. Approaches to and perspectives on the issue of financing varied dramatically between the kitchens observed. All had some form of financial support from project grants, agency funds, or local donations, although the amount and security of this funding varied. Perhaps because the kitchens observed had been initially construed as intervention programs, all of them operated with a paid facilitator or coordinator and most included some arrangement for child care. In most kitchens the food was partially or fully subsidized, and some made use of donated foods (usually from the local food bank). The amount of money participants were required to contribute ranged from nothing to one dollar per portion of food received.

The subsidization of food costs was a particularly important determinant of participation in collective kitchens. Kitchens requiring participants to contribute one dollar per portion were simply not accessible to very poor families. As one woman explained, *"I don't have 20 dollars to contribute. I only have 50 dollars left after I pay my rent!"* Two of the collective kitchens observed had begun with full subsidies from government start-up grants, but as the funding expired, organizers began seeking participant contributions for an increasing proportion of the food costs. The introduction of fees was regarded as a natural transition to self-sufficiency, but in fact it transformed the programs. In one kitchen, participants who perceived themselves unable to afford the new fees dropped out and were systematically replaced by higher income participants. In describing one woman's departure, another said, *"I heard her husband told her she couldn't come anymore 'cause it was too expensive."* Another participant explained, *"Our two new [members] feel that their husbands are making a good enough wage that they can participate properly."*

The issue of affordability also underpinned the sporadic attendance of members in some community kitchens. Another kitchen where the food subsidy had recently been withdrawn claimed ten members, but only two of these attended regularly. As one of these women explained,

Pat and I are always regulars … we always come, like every month. But everyone else, they change. Sometimes they come; it depends on their money…. Because like with Christmas coming up, a lot of people are just saving.

For these women, "saving" meant not attending the kitchen.

Concerns that costs would pose a barrier to participation for very low-income families prompted organizers in one community to develop a sponsorship structure for collective kitchens there. Most were "partnered" with community groups who donated up to $50 per month per kitchen for food. In some cases, the donor group also made cooking facilities available to the kitchen, but where this was not possible, a second "space partner" was also identified. The solicitation and coordination of donated facilities and funds was managed by a part-time staff person employed by the local health unit. In some kitchens, participants supplemented the subsidy with additional contributions (e.g. contributing one to two dollars per family member per cooking session), and three kitchens opted to reject the subsidy and finance themselves, but many worked with only the subsidy. Whereas many unsubsidized programs in other communities appear to have struggled to attract and maintain the involvement of low-income participants, the kitchens in this community were well attended—sometimes even with waiting lists. With five years of successful operation and 20 collective kitchens to their credit, this "community partner" model of funding was clearly viable and sustainable.

The ongoing provision of full subsidies raises questions about the potential for kitchen participation to be stigmatized in the same way that use of food banks and other charitable food assistance programs has been. Interestingly, kitchen participation did not appear to be a source of shame or embarrassment for members of subsidized programs. Several of the women interviewed had prior experience using food banks, and a few indicated still sometimes needing to seek such assistance. All were adamant that the experience of attending community kitchens was preferable. Not only was it "a lot less humiliating than going to the food bank," but the food was better.

The participatory aspect of community kitchens is a crucial difference between these and other food programs. In the community where most kitchens were supported by community partners, an examination of the promotional literature revealed that while the kitchens were clearly targeted at people experiencing income-related food insecurity (e.g. those "struggling to put food on the table"), the subsidies were not publicized. The programs were thus not cast in a charitable light, but instead portrayed more positively as participant-led programs and ways to collectivize cooking. This distinction was also particularly apparent in one of the communal meal programs observed which involved families with very severe financial constraints. One participant of that program described another woman's involvement like this:

She comes because she needs the food desperately, and I guess she needs some kind of social contact.... I know that she definitely comes right around when the lunch is going to be put on the table and eats quite healthfully.

Group participation in the planning and preparation of these meals and their location within the context of a broader parental support program importantly distinguished this kitchen from soup kitchens and other highly stigmatized, non-participatory forms of charitable food assistance which kitchen participants were more reluctant to use.

In conclusion, the results of this study suggest that community kitchens have limited potential to resolve food security issues which are rooted in severe and chronic poverty because they do not alter a household's economic circumstances in any substantial way. The savings to be accrued through strategies like collective food preparation cannot compensate for the depth of poverty experienced by many low-income households in Ontario today. Similarly, the financial benefits to be realized from the acquisition of enhanced food management skills are fairly limited for most poor families; their food costs are necessarily low to begin with and many of these families are already exceptionally resourceful. However, the participatory aspects of community kitchens make them potentially important sources of social interaction and support. If women marginalized by poverty and difficult life circumstances are to participate at all though, community kitchen programs must be subsidized. Where kitchens can be supported through sustainable community partnerships, the programs enable the transfer of resources within communities to occur without stigmatizing or demeaning recipients. This is perhaps the most important contribution community kitchens can make to participants' food security.

Valerie Tarasuk is an assistant professor in the Department of Nutritional Sciences at the University of Toronto. Her research focuses on the documentation of food and nutrition issues affecting low-income groups and on the examination of the social and economic context within which problems of hunger and food insecurity arise and are dealt with in Canada.

[1]Food insecurity refers to the inability to acquire sufficient, safe, nutritionally adequate, and personally acceptable foods in a manner that maintains human dignity, or the uncertaintly that one will be able to do so. The terms encompasses nutritional concerns as well as issues of social and psychological well-being related to food acquisition and consumption (Davis *et al.* 1991).

References

Davis, B., and V. Tarasuk. "Hunger in Canada." *Agriculture and Human Values* 11 (1994): 50–57.

Davis, B., S. Katamay, E. Desjardins, E. Sterken, and M. Pattillo. "Nutrition and Food Insecurity: A Role for the Canadian Dietetic Association." *Journal of the Canadian Dietetic Association* 52 (1991): 141–145.

Desmeules, C., S. Lynch, and V. Sanderson. *Community Kitchens.* Waterloo: Second Harvest, The Regional Municipality of Waterloo Nutrition Promotion Program and Foodshare, publishers. (no date)

Hubay, S., M. Jack, and C. Zwicker. *Collective Kitchen: Putting Food on the Table.* Peterborough: Peterborough Collective Kitchen Task Force, Vincent Press, Ltd., April, 1992.

London Good Food Project. *Collective Kitchen Manual.* London: London Good Food Project, 1992.

MacGregor, S. *Community Kitchens Volunteer Manual.* Kingston: North Kingston Community Health Centre, 1994.

Riches, G. "Hunger in Canada: Abandoning the Right to Food." *First World Hunger.* Ed. G. Riches. London: MacMillan Press Ltd., 1997.

Tarasuk, V., and B. Davis. "Responses to Food Insecurity in the Changing Canadian Welfare State." *Journal of Nutrition Education* 28 (1996): 71–75.

Tarasuk, V., and H. Maclean. "The Institutionalization of Food Banks in Canada: A Public Health Concern." *Canadian Journal of Public Health* 81 (1990): 331–332.

An Innovative Approach to Finding Jobs

by Rebecca Dupont

Job searching brings people, the private sector, and a community organization together in the City of York. Since 1978, the Learning Enrichment Foundation has provided community-based services in one of Metro Toronto's most disadvantaged areas. The non-profit organization offers employment supports and services to help people ease into the labour force.

To meet the child care needs of young families, often a major barrier to employment, the organization runs six child care centres. Its overall mandate is to provide economic and social benefits by using a community development approach.

A new marketing concept was tested two years ago. Local employers are contacted using an innovative community-based approach to job search. A year later, Action Centre for Employment (ACE), was established. ACE works to empower its participants and to develop relationships with local employers. For participants, the approach uncovers the hidden job market. Former ACE participant Patricia O'Toole says, "The self-marketing program teaches you to smile before you speak on the telephone, believe in yourself, maintain a positive attitude, and learn ways of searching for a job. I am now working!" For employers, this approach offers an opportunity to develop a relationship with a local organization and a source of skilled workers. By establishing contact, a future job opportunity may end up being advertised at the Foundation.

Here's how the program works. When job seekers feel ready, they join the ACE program. Program participants and employment counsellors work together to contact local employers. The one-to-one marketing strategy is the foundation of ACE's success. Rather than just finding a job for a worker, ACE builds a working relationship with the area's private sector employers.

A one-week self-marketing workshop helps participants concentrate on four areas:

•Learning the importance of target marketing and developing a network of contacts. The individual conducts research and lists 100 employer leads in the area of their interests and skills.

•Shifting perceptions. Developing a positive attitude in light of economic shifts is a crucial part of the training. We investigate labour trends and emphasize that jobs still exist but their form is changing.

•Redefining success and failure. We celebrate rejection. Job search is primarily a numbers game, so ACE clients learn to smile when they hear "sorry, we are not hiring now," because they know they are one step closer to success.

•Understanding the importance of communication skill development. We provide training and tools for effective presentation.

Former participant Effie Andicopoulos, now the self-marketing training coordinator, explains "The program encourages individuals to take charge of their lives and re-enter the workforce. I was a participant in the self-marketing program and now am involved in the day-to-day operations."

The next step is a move to the phone room. ACE participants spend three to four hours every day contacting employers on their target market list. A script is used to create a consistent approach. Employers are told about the Learning Enrichment Foundation and ACE, its free job search and matching service for people.

After the initial phone call, an information package is mailed to employers. Every three to four months, an employment counsellor does a follow-up call to update information and ask if they are hiring. Employers begin to understand the Foundation's role in helping people find work and eventually call us when they have a job vacancy.

"Having worked in the private sector for 25 years, I was amazed at the success rate the program is enjoying," says Peter Rapsey, customer service consultant. "The strategy is working. Employer contacts are being made and jobs found." Adds Clohe Williams, a former participant who now works for the Foundation: "It is really rewarding to see people leave ACE with a job."

Other services complement the program, including client and employer databases, personal development workshops, coaches and motivators, self-help work areas, employer recruitment, and direct marketing by staff to access the employer market.

"ACE has helped give hope and confidence to our clients, leading them to employment and a better future," says Ilene Taylor, an employment counsellor. Over 7,000 employers are listed in the database and at least 3,000 employers are donors, advisors, and sponsors of the Learning Enrichment Foundation community. Each relationship helps us further our goals of community, economic, and social development. ACE has been so successful as an employment model, that the Learning Enrichment Foundation has developed partnerships with seven other community organizations (COSTI, Humber College, Jewish Vocational Services, Skills for Change, Syme Wollner Family Centre, the Career Foundation, and Women Working Community Centre), whose clients are now accessing ACE.

The ACE phone room now consists of a multitude of phones and a network of computers for efficient employer outreach and database management. ACE is set for expansion into other communities outside Metro. It will be tailored to that community's unique needs.

This article has been reprinted with permission from the Spring 1996 issue of Community Economics, *2 Carlton St., Ste. 1001, Toronto, Ontario, M5B 1J3. Tel: (416) 351-0095, ext. 240. Fax: (416) 351-0107. Email: oceda@web.net. Rebecca Dupont is the marketing director of the Learning Enrichment Foundation. For more information please contact her at 116 Industry St., York, Ontario, M6M 4L8. Tel: (416) 760-2561.*

Mothers for Education
Working for Change in Thunder Bay

The total Ontario education budget was approximately $14 billion. Cuts to education for 1995/96 will total $400–$600 million Ontario wide. Proposed cuts call for another $1 billion for 1997/1998. Cuts of four per cent provincially, have translated into a much higher percentage locally. For example, Thunder Bay has experienced a 17–20 per cent reduction for its public school budget resulting in the loss of special education teachers and support personnel, a dramatic increase in class size, loss of librarians for 1997, the closing of schools and the amalgamation of small community schools into larger ones, reduced bussing service, elimination of extra curricular funds, tuition at Lakehead University increased by 20 per cent, and less money for adult education.

Let's look at how these are affecting women and children. It is now common practice to see Grade 7 and Grade 8 classes of 35–40 students; Grades 3 to 6 with 30–35 and junior kindergarten to Grade 2 with 25–30. A typical teacher in a junior division will most certainly have a split class—two grades in one classroom, say Grade 5/6. She is expected to use a multi-task approach to teaching—small group, large group, and individual, plus multi-testing techniques—observation, tests, self and peer evaluation. Add to this, reduced support from librarians and less special education support.

One positive result of the squeeze in education has been the solidarity of protests. A newly formed advocacy group in Thunder Bay, "Mothers For Education,", is making an impact. The founding members, Beverley Rizzi, Susan Gamble, and Pat Smith all have children in the public school system: each of them has one child with special needs.

The threesome drafted a letter to all media sources urging parents to write the provincial government about the cutbacks in education and their consequences on classroom learning. A national radio interview got the phone ringing off the hook. Parents from all over Ontario recounted tales of overcrowding and understaffing in their own schools.

Mothers for Education realize they have a big job ahead of them. Their first goal is to urge the public to inundate the government with letters, faxes, and phone calls protesting the cuts. Meanwhile you can call Beverley Rizzi at (807) 473-5264 or fax (807) 577-2463, and let her know you're with her on this one.

—Susanne Marquardt is a writer and education activist. She has two weekly columns with the *Thunder Bay Post* and voices commentaries for CBC Radio locally.

Ten Better Alternatives

by Duncan Cameron and Ed Finn

There are ways to restore the financial health of the Canadian economy. There are policies that will enrich Canadians, not continue to impoverish them. Here are ten better alternatives:

1.   The Bank of Canada should lower short-term interest rates.

It should aim to reduce rates below the rate of economic growth. Setting interest rates between one or two points above the level of inflation would be the ideal. In the light of the close integration of Canadian money markets and U.S. money markets, a policy of maintaining interest rates in a range of plus or minus one percentage point from short-term U.S. rate would be realistic.

Lower short-term rates would induce lenders to move funds into the longer-term end of the bond market. This would have the effect of lowering long-term rates, as well.

2.   The Bank of Canada should gradually acquire more Canadian government debt, provincial as well as federal.

It should replace private lending to governments at market interest rates with its own lending at zero interest.

In creating new money for the economy, more should be through Bank of Canada lending, less through chartered bank lending. This would substantially reduce the debt-servicing charges of the federal and provincial governments. In turn, the federal government could then—and should—restore its cash transfers to the provinces.

3.   Canada needs a public sector investment bank to make loans for new enterprises and to assist in restructuring existing industry.

Much of the Canadian economy is made up of one-industry towns. When the factory closes, or the mill shuts down, citizens lose not just their jobs, but also the value of their homes. The social infrastructure of hospitals, schools, parks, and roads is lost if the population is forced to leave.

In this type of situation, it makes sense to have an agency available in the public sector to work with investors, governments, and unions to create new industrial opportunities. The social costs of doing nothing far outweigh the costs of assisting new or restructured enterprises.

4.   Regulations governing the use of pension funds and other tax-supported financial instruments need substantial revision so that the interests of the beneficial owners of these funds— Canadian workers—are not being sold out in the vain pursuit of the highest gain.

Not only should the amount of pension funds that can be invested abroad (now 20 per cent) be reduced, or even eliminated, but additional control over these funds should also be vested by law in the hands of the employees who own them.

There is no excuse for allowing their pension money to be put into foreign investments (which often result in reducing jobs and job prospects in Canada)— especially when there is a shortage of capital for domestic purposes.

5.   Canada needs new legislation covering layoffs.

It is simply unacceptable that corporations which receive substantial tax advantages and are major beneficiaries of government spending should be able to treat employees like so much waste-paper whenever they want to impress stock speculators by improving short-term earnings.

Canada should adopt industrial relations practices harmonized on the European Community model, which requires considerable advance notice before corporate downsizing can take place.

6.   Canada needs to increase its social benefits for existing programs and create new programs.

Each dollar spent on pensions, welfare, and unemployment insurance is returned to the economy. At low levels of unemployment, much social spending is no longer needed. Benefits for those unable to work because of age, disability, or social circumstance should be generous. These payments are transfers financed by taxes from people who have a higher propensity to save to those who have a higher propensity to spend. All of us would benefit from the higher rate of economic growth produced by additional spending, rather than savings, that result from transfer payments.

7.   It is a disgrace that Canada does not have a universal child care system. One should be put into place immediately.

8.   Canada's unfair tax system encourages disrespect for needed public services. The principle of ability to pay should be used to make necessary reforms.

The CCPA/CHOICES Alternative Budget suggests a number of immediate reforms which would allow tax breaks for lower-income Canadians, no tax increases for middle-income Canadians, while still raising more tax revenue. Canada's corporate tax share should be set at the OECD average.

9.   Unequal access to hours of work is a significant concern.

While unemployment is high, many are working substantially more hours than they would voluntarily choose, because corporations prefer overtime to taking on new employees. The abuse of overtime should be severely curtailed.

Similarly, the abuse of part-time employees should be discouraged by law. The current practice of exploiting those who would prefer full-time work in order to avoid the responsibilities of taking on regular employees cannot be justified.

10.   Government spending on the arts, culture, and amateur sport should cease to be considered an expensive frill and valued for what it represents: the full expression of our humanity.

Major sums of money should be invested to encourage expression and appreciation of the best of our talents.

Excerpted from 10 Deficit Myths: The Truth About Government Debts and Why They Don't Justify Cutbacks, *by Duncan Cameron and Ed Finn (Ottawa: Canadian Centre for Policy Alternatives, 1996). Reprinted with permission.*

Coping with the Cuts
Some Useful Numbers

from Low Income Families Together (LIFT) and Foodshare, Metro Toronto

General Information and Referrals

Community Information Centre of Metropolitan Toronto, (416) 392-0505
425 Adelaide Street West, 2nd Floor, Toronto, Ontario, M5V 3C1.

This is the first number to try if you are looking for free or low-cost services that are not covered by the other numbers listed here. This 24-hour line can give you specific information about all the community services available in your neighbourhood.

Salvation Army Emergency Services, (416) 285-0080
304 Parliament Street, Toronto, Ontario, M5A 3A4

Referrals to food banks, shelters, sources of free clothing in your neighbourhood.

Financial Assistance

Social Services—Welfare, (416) 392-2956

Look up your local office in the telephone book or call this number to be referred to the closest office to you.

After-Hours Emergency Welfare Assistance, (416) 392-8600

Unemployment Insurance, (416) 730-1211

Food Assistance

Daily Bread Food Bank, (416) 203-0050, fax: (416) 203-0049, email: info@dailybread.ca
530 Lakeshore Boulevard West, Toronto, Ontario, M5V 1A5.

Largest food bank in Toronto, open seven days a week. Collects food from industry as well as public food drives and distributes it to over 200 local organizations. Offers direct food assistance, as well as referrals. Programs include advocacy work on behalf of food bank users, public education to increase awareness of hunger and its causes, and research to address the roots of food insecurity.

Hunger Hotline, (416) 392-6655

Provides information on the location of food banks, along with any restrictions or requirements and the hours of operation. Also provides information on other community services such as free meals. Can help with counselling for longer-term solutions to hunger.

North York Harvest, (416) 635-7771

Metro Toronto's second largest food bank. Collects and distributes food to a network of up to 40 food programs in North York, Etobicoke, Peel Region, and York Region.

Field to Table, (416) 363-6441, fax: (416) 363-0474

A non-profit fresh produce distribution system. Delivers boxes of fresh fruit and vegetables to drop-offs in neighbourhoods around Metro twice a month. Cost is $10–$20. Also has a catering company and "kitchen incubator" to help fledgling food businesses get started. Users have access to industrial food preparation equipment, a secure refrigerator, and dry goods storage. Technical and business assistance and the use of office equipment is also offered.

Global Pantry, (416) 465-6021

Riverdale Immigrant Women's Centre and Innstead Co-op sponsor this catering company which prepares a wide variety of food from many countries.

Origins, Foods from Around the World, (416) 923-9243

This catering company is run by residents of St. James Town.

Snack Shack, (416) 925-4363, ext. 137

The Snack Shack is a catering/snack bar business which operates in partnership with Central Neighbourhood House. It provides employment and training opportunities to young women from diverse ethno-racial and socio-economic communities.

St. Vincent de Paul, (416) 364-5577

Central number will refer you to emergency food services and clothing sources.

Salvation Army, (416) 285-0080

Will give referrals to Salvation Army food and clothing sources in your neighbourhood.

Trinity Square Enterprises, (416) 599-9315
Cawthra Square Cafe, 519 Church Street, Toronto
Trinity Square Cafe, 10 Trinity Square, Toronto

Trinity Square Enterprises operates two cafes providing low-cost, nutritious meals. Its mandate is to provide orientation, training, and employment opportunities for people with employment barriers.

World Bakery, (416) 863-0499

This group of women make and sell baked goods for sale through retail outlets or for community events. Participants include members of the Latin American, Jamaican, and African communities.

Free and Low-Cost Clothing

See numbers above for Saint Vincent de Paul and Salvation Army. The Community Information Centre (392-0505) or the Hunger Hotline (392-6655) can also refer you to sources of free clothing and furniture in your neighbourhood. For low-cost clothing and furniture, look in the phone book for the closest Goodwill or Salvation Army Thrift Store.

Housing

Below are some listings of emergency services for the homeless, as well as some registries that can help you find shared housing. Sharing a house or apartment with others is one way to cut costs. Another strategy to try: approach your landlord for a reduction in rent. He or she may find that it is less bother and expense to lower your rent than to find a new tenant.

Street Hotline, (416) 392-3777
Information line for the homeless. You can call collect from a pay phone.

Friendship Centre, (416) 368-8179
c/o All Saints Anglican Church, 323 Dundas Street East, Toronto, Ontario
Drop-in centre. Offers assistance with locating emergency housing, as well as meal services.

Open Door Centre and Rooms Registry, (416) 366-7124
315 Dundas Street East, Toronto, Ontario Room Registry, (416) 366-1482
Keeps a list of available rooms, flats, and some apartments. Also offers information and referral, typewriter, computer, and telephone use.

Housing Registry at Toronto Public Libraries, (416) 593-6918
Your local library keeps a listing of affordable housing—shared and self-contained.

COSTI Housing Help Centre, (416) 244-0724 (By appointment)
Offers information and assistance to immigrants with subsidized housing, emergency shelter, and operates a housing registry.

Operation Go Home, (416) 515-8608, fax: (416) 515-8944
95 Wellesley Street, Second Floor, Toronto, Ontario, M4Y 1H6
Referrals and counselling for youth on the street who either want to return home or go to an alternate safe environment.

Legal Services

Lawyer Referral Service, (416) 947-3330
Will assess your legal problem and refer you to a lawyer or legal service, where you can get a half-hour free consultation.

Legal Aid Information, (416) 598-0200

Arranges payment of lawyers through legal aid certificates. Will refer to independent legal clinics around city, where you can get free legal advice.

Bloor Information and Legal Service, (416) 531-4613

John Howard Society, (416) 925-4386

60 Wellesley Street West, Toronto, Ontario, M5S 2X3.

Assists offenders and ex-offenders with a range of issues, including information on legal system and service.

Community and Legal Aid Services Program, (416) 736-5029

Room 122, Osgoode Hall, York University, 4700 Keele Street, North York, Ontario, M3J 1P3

Free legal advice and representation provided by supervised law student volunteers.

Federation of Metro Tenants' Association, (416) 921-8583.

489 College Street, Suite 506, Toronto, Ontario, M6G 1A5. Tenant Hotline: (416) 921-9494.

The Federation of Metro Tenants' Association is an advocacy centre for tenant rights. It engages in law reform work as well as political lobbying to improve the legal protection of tenants. Its mandate is inform tenants of their legal rights and to help them organize tenants into self-help tenant associations.

Suicide Prevention and Counselling

Distress Centre, (416) 598-1121

Distress Centre, (416) 486-1456

Gerstein Centre Crisis Line, (416) 925-5200

Kids Help Phone, 1-800-668-6868

Assaulted Women's Helpline, (416) 863-0511

Reprinted with permission from Low Income Families Together (LIFT). LIFT began in response to Ontario's review of social assistance during 1986. Members have been involved in systemic advocacy, creating workshops on rights and solutions, consultation, policy development and gaining access to government, media, and non-government organizations. LIFT is committed to building a strong foundation in the community where the members gather, develop, and share resources to create sustainable people centred initiatives. LIFT can be reached at 238 Queen St. West, lower level, Toronto, Ontario, M5V 1Z7. Tel: (416) 597-9400. Fax: (416) 597-2128. Email: lift@centrenet.on.ca.

A Few of the Available Resources

Campaign 2000

c/o Family Service Association of Metropolitan Toronto, 355 Church Street, Toronto, Ontario, M5B 1Z8. Tel: (416) 595-9230. Fax: (416) 595-0242. Email: rpopham@ web.net. Internet: http://www.web.net/~rpopham/campaign2000/

Campaign 2000 is a non-partisan coalition of 18 national partners and a Canada wide network of 31 community partners committed to securing the implementation of the 1989 federal all-party House of Commons resolution "to seek to achieve the goal of eliminating poverty among Canadian children by the year 2000."

Canadian Centre for Policy Alternatives

251 Laurier Avenue West, Suite 804, Ottawa, Ontario, K1P 5J6. Tel: (613) 563-1341. Fax: (613) 233-1458. Email: ccpa@policyalternatives.ca. Internet: http:// www. policyalternatives.ca

The Canadian Centre for Policy Alternatives (CCPA) is a non-partisan research centre that promotes research on economic and social issues facing Canada. Produces many publications, notably The Alternative Federal Budget Papers 1997 *(recently released) and the CCPA* Monitor, *their monthly fact-filled newsletter.*

Co-Op Housing Federation of Canada-Ontario Region

2 Berkeley Street, Ste. 207, Toronto, Ontario, M5A 2W3. Tel: (416) 366-1711. Fax: (416) 366-3876. Email: ontreg@chfc.ca Internet: http://www.chfc.ca

The Co-operative Housing Federation of Canada is (CHF Canada) is the national voice of Canada's co-operative housing movement. Founded in 1968, it works actively for the growth, stability, and independence of the Canadian co-operative housing movement. CHF Canada offers its members a variety of services directly or through member organi-zations. More than 250,000 people in Canada live in nearly 89,000 co-operative homes in all provinces and territories of Canada.

National Action Committee on the Status of Women

234 Eglinton Avenue East, Suite 203, Toronto, Ontario, M4P 1K5. Tel: (416) 932-1718. Fax: (416) 932-0646. Email: nac@web.apc.org.

The National Action Committee on the Status of Women (NAC) is the largest feminist organization in Canada. A coalition of more than 50 member groups, NAC has been fighting for women's equality for 25 years. Women's groups involved with NAC are engaged in demonstrations, popular education work, direct action, letter-writing campaigns, lobbying before provincial and federal government committees, interna-tional solidarity work, conference organizing, and special events planning.

National Anti-Poverty Organization

440-325 Dalhousie St., Ottawa, Ontario, K1N 7G2. Tel: (613) 789-0096. Fax: (613) 789-0141. Email: napo@web.apc.org.

The National Anti-Poverty Organization (NAPO) was founded in 1971 at Canada's first nation-wide poor people's conference, to provide a voice for low-income Canadians on national issues and to assist local and regional organizations in bringing the voices of low-income Canadians to decision-making and policy-making processes in their communities. The goal of NAPO is the elimination of poverty in Canada.

Ontario Coalition for Better Child Care

500A Bloor Street West, 2nd Floor, Toronto, Ontario, M5S 1Y8. Tel: (416) 5389-0628. Fax: (416) 538-6737. Email: 76631,1004@compuserve.com. Internet: http://worldchat.com/public/tab/ocbcc/ocbcc.htm

The Ontario Coalition for Better Child Care was founded in 1981. Its membership includes representatives of women's, education, health care, labour, child welfare, injury prevention, rural, First Nations, Francophone, social policy, anti-poverty, professional and student organizations, in addition to community-based child care programs and 15 local coalitions across the province. The Coalition is a public awareness organization, bringing to the attention of the public and to policy makers the benefits of early childhood education and care programs.

Ontario Coalition for Social Justice

15 Gervais Drive, Don Mills, Ontario, M3C 1Y8. Tel: (416) 441-3714. Fax: (416) 441-4073.

The Ontario Coalition for Social Justice is a coalition of provincial and national organizations promoting social and economic justice. It is dedicated to expanding the quality, accessibility, and universality of health care, education, and social welfare programs; promoting anti-racism; advocating economic policies that lead to full employment; and working towards a fair tax system. The Ontario Coalition for Social Justice works with a network of approximately 30 local community coalitions across Ontario to bring organized labour and the community together for social justice.

Ontario Social Safety Network

c/o Social Planning Council, 2 Carleton Street, Suite 1001, Toronto, Ontario, M5B 1J3. Tel: (416) 351-0095. Fax: (416) 351-0107.

The Ontario Social Safety Network is a provincially-based coalition formed to fight attacks on social programs that make our "social safety net" and to support progressive social policy change. The network includes low-income individuals, anti-poverty groups, people with disabilities, labour groups, legal clinics, and others.

An Open Letter

by Cathy Crowe

I am a nurse and I like to believe I am a good nurse. I decided to become a nurse at the age of five. I love being a nurse and care about what I do. For the last 16 years I have worked in very poor areas of Toronto and I have seen it all. I have seen in real, human terms what makes people unhealthy: isolation, poverty, not enough food, inadequate housing. I am not weak in the stomach. I have seen scummy, rat-infested rooming houses, landlords sexually exploiting their tenants, the return of tuberculosis, frail old men surviving on cans of salmon and Ensure, children who go to school and can't concentrate because they are hungry, and their mothers who wait for their GST rebate to be able to buy extra food or that next size of running shoes.

I have come to realize that I can no longer nurse the way I need to. I now have to triage: Do I spend time with someone who has pneumonia, or spend time with someone who has frostbite and needs a shelter bed tonight? Nursing in Ontario means nursing in a war zone.

Every day I nurse people who are hungry, malnourished, who have sores on their body from malnutrition, who are forced to sleep outside or in shelters that are overcrowded and violent. I see men, women, and children who are decent people, forced to live in conditions that are undignified and harmful to them. And they are from area codes all around Ontario and other parts of Canada. Many have worked hard and paid their dues. Many have talents that I can only dream of having: music, art, writing … surviving.

The nursing that I and colleagues do is frequently damage control: bandaging stab wounds, scrounging up free medicines to give to people who cannot afford it, giving vitamins to people who never see fresh milk or fruit, trying to find a shelter bed for the night, and burying people.

And that brings me to the deaths. I am a community nurse, not a palliative care nurse, and although I should be used to my patients dying if they die of cancer or other terminal illness, I must tell you that I and other community nurses in this province are seeing too many deaths, and it is unacceptable. There are statistics to back this statement up.

But I want to tell you the human story. Men and women who have died, while homeless, in horribly sad ways. Freezing on the streets, bleeding to death while seeking warmth in a bus shelter, through violent trauma, from AIDS, and from an accumulation of wounds to their minds, bodies, and souls. All, while being homeless. No medicine cupboard, no one to make them chicken soup, no warm, safe place to call their own. I am in shock by what I see. I mourn what I see. I am angry about what I see.

During my 25 years of nursing, I always thought there was recourse to wrongful deaths and that there was a way to learn how to prevent them—the Coroners Act. I naively thought that Coroner's jury recommendations were to be acted upon. The beeping sounds that come from a truck backing up are a direct result of a coroner's verdict. Last year, for the first time in my career, I attended two inquests where I was a witness. Both were inquests into the deaths of homeless men. During the inquest into the freezing deaths of three homeless men we were not allowed to even speak about housing, yet a jury of decent people came up with incredibly powerful and useful recommendations that pertained to housing. Six months have passed and nothing has happened. I shouldn't say nothing has happened. We continue to bury people.

In 1987, a Toronto Councillor, in response to what he saw happening on the streets of Toronto moved a motion at city council to declare Toronto a disaster zone. Not surprisingly, this motion was not accepted as within the scope of reality by local politicians at the time. The reality, ten years later can only be described as nightmare. Tonight, I watched a television story on homelessness that showed a man living in a manhole, covered by cardboard. I scream inside. This even shocked me, but I am thankful I can still be shocked.

The simple truth is that bandaids and sleeping bags are not enough and policing the homeless by bringing back vagrancy laws will not make the problem go away. Volunteers can be kind but they cannot build housing or homes.

Yes, the solution is complex. But central to the solution is valuing human life and putting resources into efforts that value men, women, and children. Look to the coroner's jury recommendations. They spell it out.

Postscript: Between January 31 and September 1, 1997, there have been at least eight more homeless deaths.

Cathy Crowe is a nurse and anti-poverty activist. She currently provides health care to men, women, and youth who are homeless or underhoused.

Ad Hoc Committee for the Publication of
Confronting the Cuts: A Sourcebook for Women in Ontario

Sandy Birnie

Sandy Birnie is the director of the Community Programs Unit at St. Christopher House, a neighbourhood multi-service agency serving the communities located in the west end of Toronto. Core services include employment services, settlement services, adult education, community development, community economic development, youth programs, services to seniors, and services to the homeless and socially isolated. St. Christopher House provides a variety of services to a wide cross-section of people from diverse cultures through direct service, advocacy, and community development.

Lorraine Greaves

Lorraine Greaves is a sociologist, women's activist, writer, and educator, interested in issues of violence against women and women's health. She is the past director of the Centre for Research on Violence Against Women and Children in London, Ontario which is dedicated to doing feminist participatory action research.

Established in 1993, the Centre is one of five federally-funded research centres, and has three partner organizations: the University of Western Ontario, Fanshawe College, and the London Coordinating Committee to End Woman Abuse. The Centre for Research on Violence Against Women and Children has four major research areas: prevention, civil and criminal remedies, the evaulation of interventions, and education and training.

Karen Charnow Lior

Karen Charnow Lior is the Coordinator of Advocates for Community-Based Training and Education for Women (ACTEW), a provincial Ontario umbrella organization. ACTEW disseminates information regarding training and labour force development policy, advocates for women's quality training programs, consults with various levels of government, and networks between women's training and employment providers and the community.

Karen is the co-author of *Meeting Women's Training Needs: Case Studies in Women's Training*, which was prepared for the Federal/Provincial/Territorial Joint Working Group of Status of Women and Labour Market Officials on Education and Training and published in December 1994.

Elsie Nisonen

Elsie Nisonen is the executive assistant, Executive Office of the YWCA of Metropolitan Toronto. She handles all the communications material of the association and is the editor of *Y's Words*, an internal staff bi-weekly newsletter. Since 1873, the YWCA has demonstrated its commitment to women by providing superior programs in services in the areas of housing and shelters; life skills community programs, training and education programs, as well as active living and camping programs. The YWCA of Metropolitan Toronto is also part of a network of associations across the province and country.

Emily Scott

Emily Scott has worked as a social worker, a special education coordinator in Northern Manitoba, a resource teacher in Prince George, British Columbia, and as a service provider for students with disabilities at Lakehead University in Thunder Bay. She currently sits on the North Superior Training Board as the racial minorities director. She is public relations coordinator for the Board of Directors of the Caribbean-African Multicultural Organization of Canada. The organization collaborates with other community groups on antiracism initiatives, women's issues, and other social issues.

Lynne Slotek

Lynne Slotek is the past executive director of Sistering, a women's organization that offers practical and emotional support to women through programs which enable them to take greater control over their lives. Sistering works to change social conditions which endanger women's welfare. Sistering operates a drop-in centre and outreach program in Metropolitan Toronto for women who are marginalized, socially isolated, and living in poverty. Services provided include a hot meal program, day shelter, laundry facilities, advocacy/support, mental health crisis intervention and prevention counselling, information/referral, and social/recreational programming.

Rebecca Sugarman

Rebecca Sugarman has been involved in organizing and women's issues for the past 15 years. She has worked with the University of Guelph and Wilfrid Laurier University researching issues related to poor women and child care. She is the executive director for Opportunity for Advancement, an agency providing community based groups for women who are socially and economically disadvantaged. The groups, by providing support and information enable women to move from dependence, isolance, and stress to taking charge of their lives and making change.

June Larkin, Eimear O'Neill, Luciana Ricciutelli

June Larkin is the president, Eimear O'Neill is the past vice-president, and Luciana Ricciutelli is the editor/managing editor of Inanna Publications and Education Inc., a registered charitable, non-profit organization which for the past 20 years has been publishing a bilingual, feminist quarterly, *Canadian Woman Studies/les cahiers de la femme (CWS/cf)*. Inanna's mandate is to make current feminist research and writing on a wide variety of topics accessible to the largest possible community of women. *CWS/cf* provides an interdisciplinary forum in which activists, advocates, and academics can discuss ideas, analyses, and theory, and share their expertise, creativity, and personal experiences. By demystifying our communications with one another, we serve as a middle-ground between the scholarly and the popular, between theory and activism. We strive for different perspectives on gender, race, class and ethnicity issues. As we enlarge public awareness, we hope to promote the equality of women, particularly minority group women.

June Larkin teaches in the Women's Studies Program at the University of Toronto and gives workshops on sexual harassment across the country. Recently she has published a book, *Sexual Harassment: High School Girls Speak Out* (Second Story 1994, 1997). Eimear O'Neill is a feminist psychotherapist practising in Toronto. For over 20 years she has been an activist for community mental health and has recently published a chapter in *Canadian Families* (1995). Luciana Ricciutelli has been the editor and managing editor of *Canadian Woman Studies/les cahiers de la femme* for over six years.